Using GNU Fortran for GCC 6.1

A catalogue record for this book is available from the Hong Kong Public Libraries.

Published in Hong Kong by Samurai Media Limited.

Email: info@samuraimedia.org

ISBN 978-988-8406-44-9

i

Short Contents

Invoking GNU Fortran

Language Reference

Table of Contents

9   Intrinsic Procedures 85

1 Introduction

This manual documents the use of **gfortran**, the GNU Fortran compiler. You can find in this manual how to invoke **gfortran**, as well as its features and incompatibilities.

The GNU Fortran compiler front end was designed initially as a free replacement for, or alternative to, the Unix **f95** command; **gfortran** is the command you will use to invoke the compiler.

1.1 About GNU Fortran

The GNU Fortran compiler supports the Fortran 77, 90 and 95 standards completely, parts of the Fortran 2003 and Fortran 2008 standards, and several vendor extensions. The development goal is to provide the following features:

- Read a user's program, stored in a file and containing instructions written in Fortran 77, Fortran 90, Fortran 95, Fortran 2003 or Fortran 2008. This file contains *source code*.

- Translate the user's program into instructions a computer can carry out more quickly than it takes to translate the instructions in the first place. The result after compilation of a program is *machine code*, code designed to be efficiently translated and processed by a machine such as your computer. Humans usually are not as good writing machine code as they are at writing Fortran (or C++, Ada, or Java), because it is easy to make tiny mistakes writing machine code.

- Provide the user with information about the reasons why the compiler is unable to create a binary from the source code. Usually this will be the case if the source code is flawed. The Fortran 90 standard requires that the compiler can point out mistakes to the user. An incorrect usage of the language causes an *error message*.

  The compiler will also attempt to diagnose cases where the user's program contains a correct usage of the language, but instructs the computer to do something questionable. This kind of diagnostics message is called a *warning message*.

- Provide optional information about the translation passes from the source code to machine code. This can help a user of the compiler to find the cause of certain bugs which may not be obvious in the source code, but may be more easily found at a lower level compiler output. It also helps developers to find bugs in the compiler itself.

- Provide information in the generated machine code that can make it easier to find bugs in the program (using a debugging tool, called a *debugger*, such as the GNU Debugger **gdb**).

- Locate and gather machine code already generated to perform actions requested by statements in the user's program. This machine code is organized into *modules* and is located and *linked* to the user program.

The GNU Fortran compiler consists of several components:

- A version of the **gcc** command (which also might be installed as the system's **cc** command) that also understands and accepts Fortran source code. The **gcc** command is the *driver* program for all the languages in the GNU Compiler Collection (GCC); With **gcc**, you can compile the source code of any language for which a front end is available in GCC.

- The `gfortran` command itself, which also might be installed as the system's `f95` command. `gfortran` is just another driver program, but specifically for the Fortran compiler only. The difference with `gcc` is that `gfortran` will automatically link the correct libraries to your program.

- A collection of run-time libraries. These libraries contain the machine code needed to support capabilities of the Fortran language that are not directly provided by the machine code generated by the `gfortran` compilation phase, such as intrinsic functions and subroutines, and routines for interaction with files and the operating system.

- The Fortran compiler itself, (`f951`). This is the GNU Fortran parser and code generator, linked to and interfaced with the GCC backend library. `f951` "translates" the source code to assembler code. You would typically not use this program directly; instead, the `gcc` or `gfortran` driver programs will call it for you.

1.2 GNU Fortran and GCC

GNU Fortran is a part of GCC, the *GNU Compiler Collection*. GCC consists of a collection of front ends for various languages, which translate the source code into a language-independent form called *GENERIC*. This is then processed by a common middle end which provides optimization, and then passed to one of a collection of back ends which generate code for different computer architectures and operating systems.

Functionally, this is implemented with a driver program (`gcc`) which provides the command-line interface for the compiler. It calls the relevant compiler front-end program (e.g., `f951` for Fortran) for each file in the source code, and then calls the assembler and linker as appropriate to produce the compiled output. In a copy of GCC which has been compiled with Fortran language support enabled, `gcc` will recognize files with '.f', '.for', '.ftn', '.f90', '.f95', '.f03' and '.f08' extensions as Fortran source code, and compile it accordingly. A `gfortran` driver program is also provided, which is identical to `gcc` except that it automatically links the Fortran runtime libraries into the compiled program.

Source files with '.f', '.for', '.fpp', '.ftn', '.F', '.FOR', '.FPP', and '.FTN' extensions are treated as fixed form. Source files with '.f90', '.f95', '.f03', '.f08', '.F90', '.F95', '.F03' and '.F08' extensions are treated as free form. The capitalized versions of either form are run through preprocessing. Source files with the lower case '.fpp' extension are also run through preprocessing.

This manual specifically documents the Fortran front end, which handles the programming language's syntax and semantics. The aspects of GCC which relate to the optimization passes and the back-end code generation are documented in the GCC manual; see Section "Introduction" in *Using the GNU Compiler Collection (GCC)*. The two manuals together provide a complete reference for the GNU Fortran compiler.

1.3 Preprocessing and conditional compilation

Many Fortran compilers including GNU Fortran allow passing the source code through a C preprocessor (CPP; sometimes also called the Fortran preprocessor, FPP) to allow for conditional compilation. In the case of GNU Fortran, this is the GNU C Preprocessor in the traditional mode. On systems with case-preserving file names, the preprocessor is automatically invoked if the filename extension is '.F', '.FOR', '.FTN', '.fpp', '.FPP', '.F90',

'.F95', '.F03' or '.F08'. To manually invoke the preprocessor on any file, use '-cpp', to disable preprocessing on files where the preprocessor is run automatically, use '-nocpp'.

If a preprocessed file includes another file with the Fortran INCLUDE statement, the included file is not preprocessed. To preprocess included files, use the equivalent preprocessor statement #include.

If GNU Fortran invokes the preprocessor, __GFORTRAN__ is defined and __GNUC__, __GNUC_MINOR__ and __GNUC_PATCHLEVEL__ can be used to determine the version of the compiler. See Section "Overview" in *The C Preprocessor* for details.

While CPP is the de-facto standard for preprocessing Fortran code, Part 3 of the Fortran 95 standard (ISO/IEC 1539-3:1998) defines Conditional Compilation, which is not widely used and not directly supported by the GNU Fortran compiler. You can use the program coco to preprocess such files (http://www.daniellnagle.com/coco.html).

1.4 GNU Fortran and G77

The GNU Fortran compiler is the successor to g77, the Fortran 77 front end included in GCC prior to version 4. It is an entirely new program that has been designed to provide Fortran 95 support and extensibility for future Fortran language standards, as well as providing backwards compatibility for Fortran 77 and nearly all of the GNU language extensions supported by g77.

1.5 Project Status

> As soon as gfortran can parse all of the statements correctly, it will be in the "larva" state. When we generate code, the "puppa" state. When gfortran is done, we'll see if it will be a beautiful butterfly, or just a big bug....

–Andy Vaught, April 2000

The start of the GNU Fortran 95 project was announced on the GCC homepage in March 18, 2000 (even though Andy had already been working on it for a while, of course).

The GNU Fortran compiler is able to compile nearly all standard-compliant Fortran 95, Fortran 90, and Fortran 77 programs, including a number of standard and non-standard extensions, and can be used on real-world programs. In particular, the supported extensions include OpenMP, Cray-style pointers, and several Fortran 2003 and Fortran 2008 features, including TR 15581. However, it is still under development and has a few remaining rough edges. There also is initial support for OpenACC. Note that this is an experimental feature, incomplete, and subject to change in future versions of GCC. See https://gcc.gnu.org/wiki/OpenACC for more information.

At present, the GNU Fortran compiler passes the NIST Fortran 77 Test Suite, and produces acceptable results on the LAPACK Test Suite. It also provides respectable performance on the Polyhedron Fortran compiler benchmarks and the Livermore Fortran Kernels test. It has been used to compile a number of large real-world programs, including the HARMONIE and HIRLAM weather forecasting code and the Tonto quantum chemistry package; see https://gcc.gnu.org/wiki/GfortranApps for an extended list.

Among other things, the GNU Fortran compiler is intended as a replacement for G77. At this point, nearly all programs that could be compiled with G77 can be compiled with GNU Fortran, although there are a few minor known regressions.

The primary work remaining to be done on GNU Fortran falls into three categories: bug fixing (primarily regarding the treatment of invalid code and providing useful error messages), improving the compiler optimizations and the performance of compiled code, and extending the compiler to support future standards—in particular, Fortran 2003 and Fortran 2008.

1.6 Standards

The GNU Fortran compiler implements ISO/IEC 1539:1997 (Fortran 95). As such, it can also compile essentially all standard-compliant Fortran 90 and Fortran 77 programs. It also supports the ISO/IEC TR-15581 enhancements to allocatable arrays.

GNU Fortran also have a partial support for ISO/IEC 1539-1:2004 (Fortran 2003), ISO/IEC 1539-1:2010 (Fortran 2008), the Technical Specification `Further Interoperability of Fortran with C` (ISO/IEC TS 29113:2012). Full support of those standards and future Fortran standards is planned. The current status of the support is can be found in the Section 4.1 [Fortran 2003 status], page 35, Section 4.2 [Fortran 2008 status], page 36, Section 4.3 [TS 29113 status], page 38 and Section 4.4 [TS 18508 status], page 38 sections of the documentation.

Additionally, the GNU Fortran compilers supports the OpenMP specification (version 4.0, `http://openmp.org/wp/openmp-specifications/`). There also is initial support for the OpenACC specification (targeting version 2.0, `http://www.openacc.org/`). Note that this is an experimental feature, incomplete, and subject to change in future versions of GCC. See `https://gcc.gnu.org/wiki/OpenACC` for more information.

1.6.1 Varying Length Character Strings

The Fortran 95 standard specifies in Part 2 (ISO/IEC 1539-2:2000) varying length character strings. While GNU Fortran currently does not support such strings directly, there exist two Fortran implementations for them, which work with GNU Fortran. They can be found at `http://www.fortran.com/iso_varying_string.f95` and at `ftp://ftp.nag.co.uk/sc22wg5/ISO_VARYING_STRING/`.

Deferred-length character strings of Fortran 2003 supports part of the features of `ISO_VARYING_STRING` and should be considered as replacement. (Namely, allocatable or pointers of the type `character(len=:)`.)

Part I: Invoking GNU Fortran

2 GNU Fortran Command Options

The `gfortran` command supports all the options supported by the `gcc` command. Only options specific to GNU Fortran are documented here.

See Section "GCC Command Options" in *Using the GNU Compiler Collection (GCC)*, for information on the non-Fortran-specific aspects of the `gcc` command (and, therefore, the `gfortran` command).

All GCC and GNU Fortran options are accepted both by `gfortran` and by `gcc` (as well as any other drivers built at the same time, such as `g++`), since adding GNU Fortran to the GCC distribution enables acceptance of GNU Fortran options by all of the relevant drivers.

In some cases, options have positive and negative forms; the negative form of '`-ffoo`' would be '`-fno-foo`'. This manual documents only one of these two forms, whichever one is not the default.

2.1 Option summary

Here is a summary of all the options specific to GNU Fortran, grouped by type. Explanations are in the following sections.

Fortran Language Options
> See Section 2.2 [Options controlling Fortran dialect], page 8.
>
> > ```
> > -fall-intrinsics -fbackslash -fcray-pointer -fd-lines-as-code
> > -fd-lines-as-comments -fdefault-double-8 -fdefault-integer-8
> > -fdefault-real-8 -fdollar-ok -ffixed-line-length-n
> > -ffixed-line-length-none -ffree-form -ffree-line-length-n
> > -ffree-line-length-none -fimplicit-none -finteger-4-integer-8
> > -fmax-identifier-length -fmodule-private -ffixed-form -fno-range-check
> > -fopenacc -fopenmp -freal-4-real-10 -freal-4-real-16 -freal-4-real-8
> > -freal-8-real-10 -freal-8-real-16 -freal-8-real-4 -std=std
> > ```

Preprocessing Options
> See Section 2.3 [Enable and customize preprocessing], page 11.
>
> > ```
> > -A-question[=answer] -Aquestion=answer -C -CC -Dmacro[=defn] -H -P
> > -Umacro -cpp -dD -dI -dM -dN -dU -fworking-directory -imultilib dir
> > -iprefix file -iquote -isysroot dir -isystem dir -nocpp -nostdinc
> > -undef
> > ```

Error and Warning Options
> See Section 2.4 [Options to request or suppress errors and warnings], page 14.
>
> > ```
> > -Waliasing -Wall -Wampersand -Warray-bounds -Wc-binding-type -Wcharacter-
> > truncation
> > -Wconversion -Wfunction-elimination -Wimplicit-interface
> > -Wimplicit-procedure -Wintrinsic-shadow -Wuse-without-only -Wintrinsics-std
> > -Wline-truncation -Wno-align-commons -Wno-tabs -Wreal-q-constant
> > -Wsurprising -Wunderflow -Wunused-parameter -Wrealloc-lhs -Wrealloc-lhs-all
> > -Wtarget-lifetime -fmax-errors=n -fsyntax-only -pedantic -pedantic-errors
> > ```

Debugging Options
> See Section 2.5 [Options for debugging your program or GNU Fortran], page 18.
>
> > ```
> > -fbacktrace -fdump-fortran-optimized -fdump-fortran-original
> > -fdump-parse-tree -ffpe-trap=list -ffpe-summary=list
> > ```

Directory Options

> See Section 2.6 [Options for directory search], page 19.
>
> > `-Idir -Jdir -fintrinsic-modules-path dir`

Link Options

> See Section 2.7 [Options for influencing the linking step], page 20.
>
> > `-static-libgfortran`

Runtime Options

> See Section 2.8 [Options for influencing runtime behavior], page 20.
>
> > `-fconvert=conversion -fmax-subrecord-length=length`
> > `-frecord-marker=length -fsign-zero`

Code Generation Options

> See Section 2.9 [Options for code generation conventions], page 21.
>
> > `-faggressive-function-elimination -fblas-matmul-limit=n`
> > `-fbounds-check -fcheck-array-temporaries`
> > `-fcheck=<all|array-temps|bounds|do|mem|pointer|recursion>`
> > `-fcoarray=<none|single|lib> -fexternal-blas -ff2c -ffrontend-optimize`
> > `-finit-character=n -finit-integer=n -finit-local-zero`
> > `-finit-logical=<true|false> -finit-real=<zero|inf|-inf|nan|snan>`
> > `-finline-matmul-limit=n`
> > `-fmax-array-constructor=n -fmax-stack-var-size=n -fno-align-commons`
> > `-fno-automatic -fno-protect-parens -fno-underscoring`
> > `-fsecond-underscore -fpack-derived -frealloc-lhs -frecursive`
> > `-frepack-arrays -fshort-enums -fstack-arrays`

2.2 Options controlling Fortran dialect

The following options control the details of the Fortran dialect accepted by the compiler:

`-ffree-form`
`-ffixed-form`

> Specify the layout used by the source file. The free form layout was introduced in Fortran 90. Fixed form was traditionally used in older Fortran programs. When neither option is specified, the source form is determined by the file extension.

`-fall-intrinsics`

> This option causes all intrinsic procedures (including the GNU-specific extensions) to be accepted. This can be useful with '-std=f95' to force standard-compliance but get access to the full range of intrinsics available with gfortran. As a consequence, '-Wintrinsics-std' will be ignored and no user-defined procedure with the same name as any intrinsic will be called except when it is explicitly declared EXTERNAL.

`-fd-lines-as-code`
`-fd-lines-as-comments`

> Enable special treatment for lines beginning with d or D in fixed form sources. If the '-fd-lines-as-code' option is given they are treated as if the first column contained a blank. If the '-fd-lines-as-comments' option is given, they are treated as comment lines.

`-fdollar-ok`

> Allow '$' as a valid non-first character in a symbol name. Symbols that start with '$' are rejected since it is unclear which rules to apply to implicit typing as different vendors implement different rules. Using '$' in IMPLICIT statements is also rejected.

`-fbackslash`

> Change the interpretation of backslashes in string literals from a single back-slash character to "C-style" escape characters. The following combinations are expanded \a, \b, \f, \n, \r, \t, \v, \\, and \0 to the ASCII characters alert, backspace, form feed, newline, carriage return, horizontal tab, vertical tab, backslash, and NUL, respectively. Additionally, \x*nn*, \u*nnnn* and \U*nnnnnnnn* (where each *n* is a hexadecimal digit) are translated into the Unicode characters corresponding to the specified code points. All other combinations of a character preceded by \ are unexpanded.

`-fmodule-private`

> Set the default accessibility of module entities to PRIVATE. Use-associated entities will not be accessible unless they are explicitly declared as PUBLIC.

`-ffixed-line-length-`*n*

> Set column after which characters are ignored in typical fixed-form lines in the source file, and through which spaces are assumed (as if padded to that length) after the ends of short fixed-form lines.
>
> Popular values for *n* include 72 (the standard and the default), 80 (card image), and 132 (corresponding to "extended-source" options in some popular compilers). *n* may also be 'none', meaning that the entire line is meaningful and that continued character constants never have implicit spaces appended to them to fill out the line. '-ffixed-line-length-0' means the same thing as '-ffixed-line-length-none'.

`-ffree-line-length-`*n*

> Set column after which characters are ignored in typical free-form lines in the source file. The default value is 132. *n* may be 'none', meaning that the entire line is meaningful. '-ffree-line-length-0' means the same thing as '-ffree-line-length-none'.

`-fmax-identifier-length=`*n*

> Specify the maximum allowed identifier length. Typical values are 31 (Fortran 95) and 63 (Fortran 2003 and Fortran 2008).

`-fimplicit-none`

> Specify that no implicit typing is allowed, unless overridden by explicit IMPLICIT statements. This is the equivalent of adding implicit none to the start of every procedure.

`-fcray-pointer`

> Enable the Cray pointer extension, which provides C-like pointer functionality.

`-fopenacc`

> Enable the OpenACC extensions. This includes OpenACC !$acc directives in free form and c$acc, *$acc and !$acc directives in fixed form, !$ conditional

compilation sentinels in free form and c$, *$ and !$ sentinels in fixed form, and when linking arranges for the OpenACC runtime library to be linked in.

Note that this is an experimental feature, incomplete, and subject to change in future versions of GCC. See `https://gcc.gnu.org/wiki/OpenACC` for more information.

-fopenmp Enable the OpenMP extensions. This includes OpenMP `!$omp` directives in free form and `c$omp`, `*$omp` and `!$omp` directives in fixed form, `!$` conditional compilation sentinels in free form and `c$`, `*$` and `!$` sentinels in fixed form, and when linking arranges for the OpenMP runtime library to be linked in. The option '-fopenmp' implies '-frecursive'.

-fno-range-check

Disable range checking on results of simplification of constant expressions during compilation. For example, GNU Fortran will give an error at compile time when simplifying a = 1. / 0. With this option, no error will be given and a will be assigned the value +Infinity. If an expression evaluates to a value outside of the relevant range of [-HUGE():HUGE()], then the expression will be replaced by -Inf or +Inf as appropriate. Similarly, DATA i/Z'FFFFFFFF'/ will result in an integer overflow on most systems, but with '-fno-range-check' the value will "wrap around" and i will be initialized to −1 instead.

-fdefault-integer-8

Set the default integer and logical types to an 8 byte wide type. This option also affects the kind of integer constants like 42. Unlike '-finteger-4-integer-8', it does not promote variables with explicit kind declaration.

-fdefault-real-8

Set the default real type to an 8 byte wide type. This option also affects the kind of non-double real constants like 1.0, and does promote the default width of DOUBLE PRECISION to 16 bytes if possible, unless -fdefault-double-8 is given, too. Unlike '-freal-4-real-8', it does not promote variables with explicit kind declaration.

-fdefault-double-8

Set the DOUBLE PRECISION type to an 8 byte wide type. Do nothing if this is already the default. If '-fdefault-real-8' is given, DOUBLE PRECISION would instead be promoted to 16 bytes if possible, and '-fdefault-double-8' can be used to prevent this. The kind of real constants like 1.d0 will not be changed by '-fdefault-real-8' though, so also '-fdefault-double-8' does not affect it.

-finteger-4-integer-8

Promote all INTEGER(KIND=4) entities to an INTEGER(KIND=8) entities. If KIND=8 is unavailable, then an error will be issued. This option should be used with care and may not be suitable for your codes. Areas of possible concern include calls to external procedures, alignment in EQUIVALENCE and/or COMMON, generic interfaces, BOZ literal constant conversion, and I/O. Inspection of the intermediate representation of the translated Fortran code, produced by '-fdump-tree-original', is suggested.

```
-freal-4-real-8
-freal-4-real-10
-freal-4-real-16
-freal-8-real-4
-freal-8-real-10
-freal-8-real-16
```

Promote all `REAL(KIND=M)` entities to `REAL(KIND=N)` entities. If `REAL(KIND=N)` is unavailable, then an error will be issued. All other real kind types are unaffected by this option. These options should be used with care and may not be suitable for your codes. Areas of possible concern include calls to external procedures, alignment in `EQUIVALENCE` and/or `COMMON`, generic interfaces, BOZ literal constant conversion, and I/O. Inspection of the intermediate representation of the translated Fortran code, produced by '`-fdump-tree-original`', is suggested.

`-std=std`   Specify the standard to which the program is expected to conform, which may be one of '`f95`', '`f2003`', '`f2008`', '`gnu`', or '`legacy`'. The default value for *std* is '`gnu`', which specifies a superset of the Fortran 95 standard that includes all of the extensions supported by GNU Fortran, although warnings will be given for obsolete extensions not recommended for use in new code. The '`legacy`' value is equivalent but without the warnings for obsolete extensions, and may be useful for old non-standard programs. The '`f95`', '`f2003`' and '`f2008`' values specify strict conformance to the Fortran 95, Fortran 2003 and Fortran 2008 standards, respectively; errors are given for all extensions beyond the relevant language standard, and warnings are given for the Fortran 77 features that are permitted but obsolescent in later standards. '`-std=f2008ts`' allows the Fortran 2008 standard including the additions of the Technical Specification (TS) 29113 on Further Interoperability of Fortran with C and TS 18508 on Additional Parallel Features in Fortran.

2.3 Enable and customize preprocessing

Preprocessor related options. See section Section 1.3 [Preprocessing and conditional compilation], page 2 for more detailed information on preprocessing in `gfortran`.

`-cpp`
`-nocpp`   Enable preprocessing. The preprocessor is automatically invoked if the file extension is '`.fpp`', '`.FPP`', '`.F`', '`.FOR`', '`.FTN`', '`.F90`', '`.F95`', '`.F03`' or '`.F08`'. Use this option to manually enable preprocessing of any kind of Fortran file.

To disable preprocessing of files with any of the above listed extensions, use the negative form: '`-nocpp`'.

The preprocessor is run in traditional mode. Any restrictions of the file-format, especially the limits on line length, apply for preprocessed output as well, so it might be advisable to use the '`-ffree-line-length-none`' or '`-ffixed-line-length-none`' options.

`-dM`   Instead of the normal output, generate a list of '`#define`' directives for all the macros defined during the execution of the preprocessor, including predefined

macros. This gives you a way of finding out what is predefined in your version
of the preprocessor. Assuming you have no file 'foo.f90', the command

```
touch foo.f90; gfortran -cpp -E -dM foo.f90
```

will show all the predefined macros.

-dD   Like '-dM' except in two respects: it does not include the predefined macros, and
            it outputs both the #define directives and the result of preprocessing. Both
            kinds of output go to the standard output file.

-dN   Like '-dD', but emit only the macro names, not their expansions.

-dU   Like 'dD' except that only macros that are expanded, or whose definedness is
            tested in preprocessor directives, are output; the output is delayed until the use
            or test of the macro; and '#undef' directives are also output for macros tested
            but undefined at the time.

-dI   Output '#include' directives in addition to the result of preprocessing.

-fworking-directory
            Enable generation of linemarkers in the preprocessor output that will let the
            compiler know the current working directory at the time of preprocessing.
            When this option is enabled, the preprocessor will emit, after the initial line-
            marker, a second linemarker with the current working directory followed by
            two slashes. GCC will use this directory, when it is present in the prepro-
            cessed input, as the directory emitted as the current working directory in some
            debugging information formats. This option is implicitly enabled if debug-
            ging information is enabled, but this can be inhibited with the negated form
            '-fno-working-directory'. If the '-P' flag is present in the command line,
            this option has no effect, since no #line directives are emitted whatsoever.

-idirafter dir
            Search dir for include files, but do it after all directories specified with '-I'
            and the standard system directories have been exhausted. dir is treated as a
            system include directory. If dir begins with =, then the = will be replaced by
            the sysroot prefix; see '--sysroot' and '-isysroot'.

-imultilib dir
            Use dir as a subdirectory of the directory containing target-specific C++ headers.

-iprefix prefix
            Specify prefix as the prefix for subsequent '-iwithprefix' options. If the prefix
            represents a directory, you should include the final '/'.

-isysroot dir
            This option is like the '--sysroot' option, but applies only to header files. See
            the '--sysroot' option for more information.

-iquote dir
            Search dir only for header files requested with #include "file"; they are not
            searched for #include <file>, before all directories specified by '-I' and before
            the standard system directories. If dir begins with =, then the = will be replaced
            by the sysroot prefix; see '--sysroot' and '-isysroot'.

`-isystem` *dir*

> Search *dir* for header files, after all directories specified by '`-I`' but before the standard system directories. Mark it as a system directory, so that it gets the same special treatment as is applied to the standard system directories. If *dir* begins with =, then the = will be replaced by the sysroot prefix; see '`--sysroot`' and '`-isysroot`'.

`-nostdinc`

> Do not search the standard system directories for header files. Only the directories you have specified with '`-I`' options (and the directory of the current file, if appropriate) are searched.

`-undef`   Do not predefine any system-specific or GCC-specific macros. The standard predefined macros remain defined.

`-A`*predicate*`=`*answer*

> Make an assertion with the predicate *predicate* and answer *answer*. This form is preferred to the older form -A predicate(answer), which is still supported, because it does not use shell special characters.

`-A-`*predicate*`=`*answer*

> Cancel an assertion with the predicate *predicate* and answer *answer*.

`-C`   Do not discard comments. All comments are passed through to the output file, except for comments in processed directives, which are deleted along with the directive.

> You should be prepared for side effects when using '`-C`'; it causes the preprocessor to treat comments as tokens in their own right. For example, comments appearing at the start of what would be a directive line have the effect of turning that line into an ordinary source line, since the first token on the line is no longer a '#'.

> Warning: this currently handles C-Style comments only. The preprocessor does not yet recognize Fortran-style comments.

`-CC`   Do not discard comments, including during macro expansion. This is like '`-C`', except that comments contained within macros are also passed through to the output file where the macro is expanded.

> In addition to the side-effects of the '`-C`' option, the '`-CC`' option causes all C++-style comments inside a macro to be converted to C-style comments. This is to prevent later use of that macro from inadvertently commenting out the remainder of the source line. The '`-CC`' option is generally used to support lint comments.

> Warning: this currently handles C- and C++-Style comments only. The preprocessor does not yet recognize Fortran-style comments.

`-D`*name*   Predefine name as a macro, with definition 1.

`-D`*name*`=`*definition*

> The contents of *definition* are tokenized and processed as if they appeared during translation phase three in a '#define' directive. In particular, the definition will be truncated by embedded newline characters.

If you are invoking the preprocessor from a shell or shell-like program you may need to use the shell's quoting syntax to protect characters such as spaces that have a meaning in the shell syntax.

If you wish to define a function-like macro on the command line, write its argument list with surrounding parentheses before the equals sign (if any). Parentheses are meaningful to most shells, so you will need to quote the option. With sh and csh, `-D'name(args...)=definition'` works.

'-D' and '-U' options are processed in the order they are given on the command line. All -imacros file and -include file options are processed after all -D and -U options.

-H   Print the name of each header file used, in addition to other normal activities. Each name is indented to show how deep in the '#include' stack it is.

-P   Inhibit generation of linemarkers in the output from the preprocessor. This might be useful when running the preprocessor on something that is not C code, and will be sent to a program which might be confused by the linemarkers.

-Uname   Cancel any previous definition of *name*, either built in or provided with a '-D' option.

2.4 Options to request or suppress errors and warnings

Errors are diagnostic messages that report that the GNU Fortran compiler cannot compile the relevant piece of source code. The compiler will continue to process the program in an attempt to report further errors to aid in debugging, but will not produce any compiled output.

Warnings are diagnostic messages that report constructions which are not inherently erroneous but which are risky or suggest there is likely to be a bug in the program. Unless '-Werror' is specified, they do not prevent compilation of the program.

You can request many specific warnings with options beginning '-W', for example '-Wimplicit' to request warnings on implicit declarations. Each of these specific warning options also has a negative form beginning '-Wno-' to turn off warnings; for example, '-Wno-implicit'. This manual lists only one of the two forms, whichever is not the default.

These options control the amount and kinds of errors and warnings produced by GNU Fortran:

-fmax-errors=n
            Limits the maximum number of error messages to *n*, at which point GNU Fortran bails out rather than attempting to continue processing the source code. If *n* is 0, there is no limit on the number of error messages produced.

-fsyntax-only
            Check the code for syntax errors, but do not actually compile it. This will generate module files for each module present in the code, but no other output file.

`-pedantic`

Issue warnings for uses of extensions to Fortran 95. '`-pedantic`' also applies to C-language constructs where they occur in GNU Fortran source files, such as use of '\e' in a character constant within a directive like `#include`.

Valid Fortran 95 programs should compile properly with or without this option. However, without this option, certain GNU extensions and traditional Fortran features are supported as well. With this option, many of them are rejected.

Some users try to use '`-pedantic`' to check programs for conformance. They soon find that it does not quite what they want—it finds some nonstandard practices, but not all. However, improvements to GNU Fortran in this area are welcome.

This should be used in conjunction with '`-std=f95`', '`-std=f2003`' or '`-std=f2008`'.

`-pedantic-errors`

Like '`-pedantic`', except that errors are produced rather than warnings.

`-Wall`   Enables commonly used warning options pertaining to usage that we recommend avoiding and that we believe are easy to avoid. This currently includes '`-Waliasing`', '`-Wampersand`', '`-Wconversion`', '`-Wsurprising`', '`-Wc-binding-type`', '`-Wintrinsics-std`', '`-Wtabs`', '`-Wintrinsic-shadow`', '`-Wline-truncation`', '`-Wtarget-lifetime`', '`-Winteger-division`', '`-Wreal-q-constant`' and '`-Wunused`'.

`-Waliasing`

Warn about possible aliasing of dummy arguments. Specifically, it warns if the same actual argument is associated with a dummy argument with `INTENT(IN)` and a dummy argument with `INTENT(OUT)` in a call with an explicit interface.

The following example will trigger the warning.

```
interface
  subroutine bar(a,b)
    integer, intent(in) :: a
    integer, intent(out) :: b
  end subroutine
end interface
integer :: a

call bar(a,a)
```

`-Wampersand`

Warn about missing ampersand in continued character constants. The warning is given with '`-Wampersand`', '`-pedantic`', '`-std=f95`', '`-std=f2003`' and '`-std=f2008`'. Note: With no ampersand given in a continued character constant, GNU Fortran assumes continuation at the first non-comment, non-whitespace character after the ampersand that initiated the continuation.

`-Warray-temporaries`

Warn about array temporaries generated by the compiler. The information generated by this warning is sometimes useful in optimization, in order to avoid such temporaries.

-Wc-binding-type
> Warn if the a variable might not be C interoperable. In particular, warn if the variable has been declared using an intrinsic type with default kind instead of using a kind parameter defined for C interoperability in the intrinsic `ISO_C_Binding` module. This option is implied by '`-Wall`'.

-Wcharacter-truncation
> Warn when a character assignment will truncate the assigned string.

-Wline-truncation
> Warn when a source code line will be truncated. This option is implied by '`-Wall`'. For free-form source code, the default is '`-Werror=line-truncation`' such that truncations are reported as error.

-Wconversion
> Warn about implicit conversions that are likely to change the value of the expression after conversion. Implied by '`-Wall`'.

-Wconversion-extra
> Warn about implicit conversions between different types and kinds. This option does *not* imply '`-Wconversion`'.

-Wextra
> Enables some warning options for usages of language features which may be problematic. This currently includes '`-Wcompare-reals`' and '`-Wunused-parameter`'.

-Wimplicit-interface
> Warn if a procedure is called without an explicit interface. Note this only checks that an explicit interface is present. It does not check that the declared interfaces are consistent across program units.

-Wimplicit-procedure
> Warn if a procedure is called that has neither an explicit interface nor has been declared as `EXTERNAL`.

-Winteger-division
> Warn if a constant integer division truncates it result. As an example, 3/5 evaluates to 0.

-Wintrinsics-std
> Warn if **gfortran** finds a procedure named like an intrinsic not available in the currently selected standard (with '`-std`') and treats it as `EXTERNAL` procedure because of this. '`-fall-intrinsics`' can be used to never trigger this behavior and always link to the intrinsic regardless of the selected standard.

-Wreal-q-constant
> Produce a warning if a real-literal-constant contains a `q` exponent-letter.

-Wsurprising
> Produce a warning when "suspicious" code constructs are encountered. While technically legal these usually indicate that an error has been made.
>
> This currently produces a warning under the following circumstances:

- An INTEGER SELECT construct has a CASE that can never be matched as its lower value is greater than its upper value.
- A LOGICAL SELECT construct has three CASE statements.
- A TRANSFER specifies a source that is shorter than the destination.
- The type of a function result is declared more than once with the same type. If '-pedantic' or standard-conforming mode is enabled, this is an error.
- A CHARACTER variable is declared with negative length.

-Wtabs   By default, tabs are accepted as whitespace, but tabs are not members of the Fortran Character Set. For continuation lines, a tab followed by a digit between 1 and 9 is supported. '-Wtabs' will cause a warning to be issued if a tab is encountered. Note, '-Wtabs' is active for '-pedantic', '-std=f95', '-std=f2003', '-std=f2008', '-std=f2008ts' and '-Wall'.

-Wunderflow
              Produce a warning when numerical constant expressions are encountered, which yield an UNDERFLOW during compilation. Enabled by default.

-Wintrinsic-shadow
              Warn if a user-defined procedure or module procedure has the same name as an intrinsic; in this case, an explicit interface or EXTERNAL or INTRINSIC declaration might be needed to get calls later resolved to the desired intrinsic/procedure. This option is implied by '-Wall'.

-Wuse-without-only
              Warn if a USE statement has no ONLY qualifier and thus implicitly imports all public entities of the used module.

-Wunused-dummy-argument
              Warn about unused dummy arguments. This option is implied by '-Wall'.

-Wunused-parameter
              Contrary to gcc's meaning of '-Wunused-parameter', gfortran's implementation of this option does not warn about unused dummy arguments (see '-Wunused-dummy-argument'), but about unused PARAMETER values. '-Wunused-parameter' is implied by '-Wextra' if also '-Wunused' or '-Wall' is used.

-Walign-commons
              By default, gfortran warns about any occasion of variables being padded for proper alignment inside a COMMON block. This warning can be turned off via '-Wno-align-commons'. See also '-falign-commons'.

-Wfunction-elimination
              Warn if any calls to functions are eliminated by the optimizations enabled by the '-ffrontend-optimize' option.

-Wrealloc-lhs
              Warn when the compiler might insert code to for allocation or reallocation of an allocatable array variable of intrinsic type in intrinsic assignments. In hot

loops, the Fortran 2003 reallocation feature may reduce the performance. If the array is already allocated with the correct shape, consider using a whole-array array-spec (e.g. `(:,:,:)`) for the variable on the left-hand side to prevent the reallocation check. Note that in some cases the warning is shown, even if the compiler will optimize reallocation checks away. For instance, when the right-hand side contains the same variable multiplied by a scalar. See also '-frealloc-lhs'.

-Wrealloc-lhs-all
   Warn when the compiler inserts code to for allocation or reallocation of an allocatable variable; this includes scalars and derived types.

-Wcompare-reals
   Warn when comparing real or complex types for equality or inequality. This option is implied by '-Wextra'.

-Wtarget-lifetime
   Warn if the pointer in a pointer assignment might be longer than the its target. This option is implied by '-Wall'.

-Wzerotrip
   Warn if a DO loop is known to execute zero times at compile time. This option is implied by '-Wall'.

-Werror   Turns all warnings into errors.

See Section "Options to Request or Suppress Errors and Warnings" in *Using the GNU Compiler Collection (GCC)*, for information on more options offered by the GBE shared by gfortran, gcc and other GNU compilers.

Some of these have no effect when compiling programs written in Fortran.

2.5 Options for debugging your program or GNU Fortran

GNU Fortran has various special options that are used for debugging either your program or the GNU Fortran compiler.

-fdump-fortran-original
   Output the internal parse tree after translating the source program into internal representation. Only really useful for debugging the GNU Fortran compiler itself.

-fdump-fortran-optimized
   Output the parse tree after front-end optimization. Only really useful for debugging the GNU Fortran compiler itself.

-fdump-parse-tree
   Output the internal parse tree after translating the source program into internal representation. Only really useful for debugging the GNU Fortran compiler itself. This option is deprecated; use -fdump-fortran-original instead.

-ffpe-trap=*list*
   Specify a list of floating point exception traps to enable. On most systems, if a floating point exception occurs and the trap for that exception is enabled, a

SIGFPE signal will be sent and the program being aborted, producing a core file useful for debugging. *list* is a (possibly empty) comma-separated list of the following exceptions: 'invalid' (invalid floating point operation, such as SQRT(-1.0)), 'zero' (division by zero), 'overflow' (overflow in a floating point operation), 'underflow' (underflow in a floating point operation), 'inexact' (loss of precision during operation), and 'denormal' (operation performed on a denormal value). The first five exceptions correspond to the five IEEE 754 exceptions, whereas the last one ('denormal') is not part of the IEEE 754 standard but is available on some common architectures such as x86.

The first three exceptions ('invalid', 'zero', and 'overflow') often indicate serious errors, and unless the program has provisions for dealing with these exceptions, enabling traps for these three exceptions is probably a good idea.

Many, if not most, floating point operations incur loss of precision due to rounding, and hence the ffpe-trap=inexact is likely to be uninteresting in practice.

By default no exception traps are enabled.

-ffpe-summary=*list*

Specify a list of floating-point exceptions, whose flag status is printed to ERROR_UNIT when invoking STOP and ERROR STOP. *list* can be either 'none', 'all' or a comma-separated list of the following exceptions: 'invalid', 'zero', 'overflow', 'underflow', 'inexact' and 'denormal'. (See '-ffpe-trap' for a description of the exceptions.)

By default, a summary for all exceptions but 'inexact' is shown.

-fno-backtrace

When a serious runtime error is encountered or a deadly signal is emitted (segmentation fault, illegal instruction, bus error, floating-point exception, and the other POSIX signals that have the action 'core'), the Fortran runtime library tries to output a backtrace of the error. -fno-backtrace disables the backtrace generation. This option only has influence for compilation of the Fortran main program.

See Section "Options for Debugging Your Program or GCC" in *Using the GNU Compiler Collection (GCC)*, for more information on debugging options.

2.6 Options for directory search

These options affect how GNU Fortran searches for files specified by the INCLUDE directive and where it searches for previously compiled modules.

It also affects the search paths used by cpp when used to preprocess Fortran source.

-I*dir*   These affect interpretation of the INCLUDE directive (as well as of the #include directive of the cpp preprocessor).

Also note that the general behavior of '-I' and INCLUDE is pretty much the same as of '-I' with #include in the cpp preprocessor, with regard to looking for 'header.gcc' files and other such things.

This path is also used to search for '.mod' files when previously compiled modules are required by a USE statement.

See Section "Options for Directory Search" in *Using the GNU Compiler Collection (GCC)*, for information on the '-I' option.

-J*dir*   This option specifies where to put '.mod' files for compiled modules. It is also added to the list of directories to searched by an USE statement.

The default is the current directory.

-fintrinsic-modules-path *dir*

This option specifies the location of pre-compiled intrinsic modules, if they are not in the default location expected by the compiler.

2.7 Influencing the linking step

These options come into play when the compiler links object files into an executable output file. They are meaningless if the compiler is not doing a link step.

-static-libgfortran

On systems that provide 'libgfortran' as a shared and a static library, this option forces the use of the static version. If no shared version of 'libgfortran' was built when the compiler was configured, this option has no effect.

2.8 Influencing runtime behavior

These options affect the runtime behavior of programs compiled with GNU Fortran.

-fconvert=*conversion*

Specify the representation of data for unformatted files. Valid values for conversion are: 'native', the default; 'swap', swap between big- and little-endian; 'big-endian', use big-endian representation for unformatted files; 'little-endian', use little-endian representation for unformatted files.

This option has an effect only when used in the main program. The CONVERT *specifier and the GFORTRAN_CONVERT_UNIT environment variable override the default specified by '-fconvert'.*

-frecord-marker=*length*

Specify the length of record markers for unformatted files. Valid values for *length* are 4 and 8. Default is 4. *This is different from previous versions of* gfortran, *which specified a default record marker length of 8 on most systems. If you want to read or write files compatible with earlier versions of* gfortran, *use '-frecord-marker=8'.*

-fmax-subrecord-length=*length*

Specify the maximum length for a subrecord. The maximum permitted value for length is 2147483639, which is also the default. Only really useful for use by the gfortran testsuite.

-fsign-zero

When enabled, floating point numbers of value zero with the sign bit set are written as negative number in formatted output and treated as negative in the SIGN intrinsic. '-fno-sign-zero' does not print the negative sign of zero values (or values rounded to zero for I/O) and regards zero as positive number in the SIGN intrinsic for compatibility with Fortran 77. The default is '-fsign-zero'.

2.9 Options for code generation conventions

These machine-independent options control the interface conventions used in code generation.

Most of them have both positive and negative forms; the negative form of '-ffoo' would be '-fno-foo'. In the table below, only one of the forms is listed—the one which is not the default. You can figure out the other form by either removing 'no-' or adding it.

-fno-automatic

Treat each program unit (except those marked as RECURSIVE) as if the SAVE statement were specified for every local variable and array referenced in it. Does not affect common blocks. (Some Fortran compilers provide this option under the name '-static' or '-save'.) The default, which is '-fautomatic', uses the stack for local variables smaller than the value given by '-fmax-stack-var-size'. Use the option '-frecursive' to use no static memory.

-ff2c   Generate code designed to be compatible with code generated by g77 and f2c.

The calling conventions used by g77 (originally implemented in f2c) require functions that return type default REAL to actually return the C type double, and functions that return type COMPLEX to return the values via an extra argument in the calling sequence that points to where to store the return value. Under the default GNU calling conventions, such functions simply return their results as they would in GNU C—default REAL functions return the C type float, and COMPLEX functions return the GNU C type complex. Additionally, this option implies the '-fsecond-underscore' option, unless '-fno-second-underscore' is explicitly requested.

This does not affect the generation of code that interfaces with the libgfortran library.

Caution: It is not a good idea to mix Fortran code compiled with '-ff2c' with code compiled with the default '-fno-f2c' calling conventions as, calling COMPLEX or default REAL functions between program parts which were compiled with different calling conventions will break at execution time.

Caution: This will break code which passes intrinsic functions of type default REAL or COMPLEX as actual arguments, as the library implementations use the '-fno-f2c' calling conventions.

-fno-underscoring

Do not transform names of entities specified in the Fortran source file by appending underscores to them.

With '-funderscoring' in effect, GNU Fortran appends one underscore to external names with no underscores. This is done to ensure compatibility with code produced by many UNIX Fortran compilers.

Caution: The default behavior of GNU Fortran is incompatible with f2c and g77, please use the '-ff2c' option if you want object files compiled with GNU Fortran to be compatible with object code created with these tools.

Use of '-fno-underscoring' is not recommended unless you are experimenting with issues such as integration of GNU Fortran into existing system environments (vis-à-vis existing libraries, tools, and so on).

For example, with '-funderscoring', and assuming that j() and max_count() are external functions while my_var and lvar are local variables, a statement like

        I = J() + MAX_COUNT (MY_VAR, LVAR)

is implemented as something akin to:

        i = j_() + max_count__(&my_var__, &lvar);

With '-fno-underscoring', the same statement is implemented as:

        i = j() + max_count(&my_var, &lvar);

Use of '-fno-underscoring' allows direct specification of user-defined names while debugging and when interfacing GNU Fortran code with other languages.

Note that just because the names match does *not* mean that the interface implemented by GNU Fortran for an external name matches the interface implemented by some other language for that same name. That is, getting code produced by GNU Fortran to link to code produced by some other compiler using this or any other method can be only a small part of the overall solution—getting the code generated by both compilers to agree on issues other than naming can require significant effort, and, unlike naming disagreements, linkers normally cannot detect disagreements in these other areas.

Also, note that with '-fno-underscoring', the lack of appended underscores introduces the very real possibility that a user-defined external name will conflict with a name in a system library, which could make finding unresolved-reference bugs quite difficult in some cases—they might occur at program run time, and show up only as buggy behavior at run time.

In future versions of GNU Fortran we hope to improve naming and linking issues so that debugging always involves using the names as they appear in the source, even if the names as seen by the linker are mangled to prevent accidental linking between procedures with incompatible interfaces.

-fsecond-underscore

By default, GNU Fortran appends an underscore to external names. If this option is used GNU Fortran appends two underscores to names with underscores and one underscore to external names with no underscores. GNU Fortran also appends two underscores to internal names with underscores to avoid naming collisions with external names.

This option has no effect if '-fno-underscoring' is in effect. It is implied by the '-ff2c' option.

Otherwise, with this option, an external name such as MAX_COUNT is implemented as a reference to the link-time external symbol max_count__, instead of max_count_. This is required for compatibility with g77 and f2c, and is implied by use of the '-ff2c' option.

-fcoarray=<keyword>

'none'   Disable coarray support; using coarray declarations and image-control statements will produce a compile-time error. (Default) 'single'   Single-image mode, i.e. **num_images()** is always one.

'lib'   Library-based coarray parallelization; a suitable GNU Fortran coarray library needs to be linked.

-fcheck=<keyword>

Enable the generation of run-time checks; the argument shall be a comma-delimited list of the following keywords. Prefixing a check with 'no-' disables it if it was activated by a previous specification.

'all'   Enable all run-time test of '-fcheck'.

'array-temps'

Warns at run time when for passing an actual argument a temporary array had to be generated. The information generated by this warning is sometimes useful in optimization, in order to avoid such temporaries.

Note: The warning is only printed once per location.

'bounds'   Enable generation of run-time checks for array subscripts and against the declared minimum and maximum values. It also checks array indices for assumed and deferred shape arrays against the actual allocated bounds and ensures that all string lengths are equal for character array constructors without an explicit typespec.

Some checks require that '-fcheck=bounds' is set for the compilation of the main program.

Note: In the future this may also include other forms of checking, e.g., checking substring references.

'do'   Enable generation of run-time checks for invalid modification of loop iteration variables.

'mem'   Enable generation of run-time checks for memory allocation. Note: This option does not affect explicit allocations using the **ALLOCATE** statement, which will be always checked.

'pointer'   Enable generation of run-time checks for pointers and allocatables.

'recursion'

Enable generation of run-time checks for recursively called subroutines and functions which are not marked as recursive. See also '-frecursive'. Note: This check does not work for OpenMP programs and is disabled if used together with '-frecursive' and '-fopenmp'.

Example: Assuming you have a file 'foo.f90', the command

        gfortran -fcheck=all,no-array-temps foo.f90

will compile the file with all checks enabled as specified above except warnings for generated array temporaries.

-fbounds-check

Deprecated alias for '-fcheck=bounds'.

-fcheck-array-temporaries
          Deprecated alias for '-fcheck=array-temps'.

-fmax-array-constructor=n
          This option can be used to increase the upper limit permitted in array con-
          structors. The code below requires this option to expand the array at compile
          time.

```
program test
implicit none
integer j
integer, parameter :: n = 100000
integer, parameter :: i(n) = (/ (2*j, j = 1, n) /)
print '(10(I0,1X))', i
end program test
```

          *Caution: This option can lead to long compile times and excessively large object
          files.*

          The default value for *n* is 65535.

-fmax-stack-var-size=n
          This option specifies the size in bytes of the largest array that will be put on
          the stack; if the size is exceeded static memory is used (except in procedures
          marked as RECURSIVE). Use the option '-frecursive' to allow for recursive
          procedures which do not have a RECURSIVE attribute or for parallel programs.
          Use '-fno-automatic' to never use the stack.

          This option currently only affects local arrays declared with constant bounds,
          and may not apply to all character variables. Future versions of GNU Fortran
          may improve this behavior.

          The default value for *n* is 32768.

-fstack-arrays
          Adding this option will make the Fortran compiler put all local arrays, even
          those of unknown size onto stack memory. If your program uses very large
          local arrays it is possible that you will have to extend your runtime limits for
          stack memory on some operating systems. This flag is enabled by default at
          optimization level '-Ofast'.

-fpack-derived
          This option tells GNU Fortran to pack derived type members as closely as
          possible. Code compiled with this option is likely to be incompatible with code
          compiled without this option, and may execute slower.

-frepack-arrays
          In some circumstances GNU Fortran may pass assumed shape array sections
          via a descriptor describing a noncontiguous area of memory. This option adds
          code to the function prologue to repack the data into a contiguous block at
          runtime.

          This should result in faster accesses to the array. However it can introduce
          significant overhead to the function call, especially when the passed data is
          noncontiguous.

-fshort-enums

>This option is provided for interoperability with C code that was compiled with the '-fshort-enums' option. It will make GNU Fortran choose the smallest INTEGER kind a given enumerator set will fit in, and give all its enumerators this kind.

-fexternal-blas

>This option will make gfortran generate calls to BLAS functions for some matrix operations like MATMUL, instead of using our own algorithms, if the size of the matrices involved is larger than a given limit (see '-fblas-matmul-limit'). This may be profitable if an optimized vendor BLAS library is available. The BLAS library will have to be specified at link time.

-fblas-matmul-limit=n

>Only significant when '-fexternal-blas' is in effect. Matrix multiplication of matrices with size larger than (or equal to) n will be performed by calls to BLAS functions, while others will be handled by gfortran internal algorithms. If the matrices involved are not square, the size comparison is performed using the geometric mean of the dimensions of the argument and result matrices.

>The default value for n is 30.

-finline-matmul-limit=n

>When front-end optimiztion is active, some calls to the MATMUL intrinsic function will be inlined. This may result in code size increase if the size of the matrix cannot be determined at compile time, as code for both cases is generated. Setting -finline-matmul-limit=0 will disable inlining in all cases. Setting this option with a value of n will produce inline code for matrices with size up to n. If the matrices involved are not square, the size comparison is performed using the geometric mean of the dimensions of the argument and result matrices.

>The default value for n is the value specified for -fblas-matmul-limit if this option is specified, or unlimitited otherwise.

-frecursive

>Allow indirect recursion by forcing all local arrays to be allocated on the stack. This flag cannot be used together with '-fmax-stack-var-size=' or '-fno-automatic'.

-finit-local-zero
-finit-integer=n
-finit-real=<zero|inf|-inf|nan|snan>
-finit-logical=<true|false>
-finit-character=n

>The '-finit-local-zero' option instructs the compiler to initialize local INTEGER, REAL, and COMPLEX variables to zero, LOGICAL variables to false, and CHARACTER variables to a string of null bytes. Finer-grained initialization options are provided by the '-finit-integer=n', '-finit-real=<zero|inf|-inf|nan|snan>' (which also initializes the real and imaginary parts of local COMPLEX variables), '-finit-logical=<true|false>', and '-finit-character=n' (where n is an ASCII character value) options. These options do not initialize

- allocatable arrays
- components of derived type variables
- variables that appear in an `EQUIVALENCE` statement.

(These limitations may be removed in future releases).

Note that the '`-finit-real=nan`' option initializes `REAL` and `COMPLEX` variables with a quiet NaN. For a signalling NaN use '`-finit-real=snan`'; note, however, that compile-time optimizations may convert them into quiet NaN and that trapping needs to be enabled (e.g. via '`-ffpe-trap`').

Finally, note that enabling any of the '`-finit-*`' options will silence warnings that would have been emitted by '`-Wuninitialized`' for the affected local variables.

`-falign-commons`

By default, **gfortran** enforces proper alignment of all variables in a `COMMON` block by padding them as needed. On certain platforms this is mandatory, on others it increases performance. If a `COMMON` block is not declared with consistent data types everywhere, this padding can cause trouble, and '`-fno-align-commons`' can be used to disable automatic alignment. The same form of this option should be used for all files that share a `COMMON` block. To avoid potential alignment issues in `COMMON` blocks, it is recommended to order objects from largest to smallest.

`-fno-protect-parens`

By default the parentheses in expression are honored for all optimization levels such that the compiler does not do any re-association. Using '`-fno-protect-parens`' allows the compiler to reorder `REAL` and `COMPLEX` expressions to produce faster code. Note that for the re-association optimization '`-fno-signed-zeros`' and '`-fno-trapping-math`' need to be in effect. The parentheses protection is enabled by default, unless '`-Ofast`' is given.

`-frealloc-lhs`

An allocatable left-hand side of an intrinsic assignment is automatically (re)allocated if it is either unallocated or has a different shape. The option is enabled by default except when '`-std=f95`' is given. See also '`-Wrealloc-lhs`'.

`-faggressive-function-elimination`

Functions with identical argument lists are eliminated within statements, regardless of whether these functions are marked `PURE` or not. For example, in

```
a = f(b,c) + f(b,c)
```

there will only be a single call to `f`. This option only works if '`-ffrontend-optimize`' is in effect.

`-ffrontend-optimize`

This option performs front-end optimization, based on manipulating parts the Fortran parse tree. Enabled by default by any '`-O`' option. Optimizations enabled by this option include inlining calls to `MATMUL`, elimination of identical function calls within expressions, removing unnecessary calls to TRIM in comparisons and assignments and replacing TRIM(a) with a(1:LEN_TRIM(a)). It can be deselected by specifying '-fno-frontend-optimize'.

See Section "Options for Code Generation Conventions" in *Using the GNU Compiler Collection (GCC)*, for information on more options offered by the GBE shared by gfortran, gcc, and other GNU compilers.

2.10 Environment variables affecting gfortran

The gfortran compiler currently does not make use of any environment variables to control its operation above and beyond those that affect the operation of gcc.

See Section "Environment Variables Affecting GCC" in *Using the GNU Compiler Collection (GCC)*, for information on environment variables.

See Chapter 3 [Runtime], page 29, for environment variables that affect the run-time behavior of programs compiled with GNU Fortran.

3 Runtime: Influencing runtime behavior with environment variables

The behavior of the `gfortran` can be influenced by environment variables.

Malformed environment variables are silently ignored.

3.1 TMPDIR—Directory for scratch files

When opening a file with `STATUS='SCRATCH'`, GNU Fortran tries to create the file in one of the potential directories by testing each directory in the order below.

1. The environment variable `TMPDIR`, if it exists.
2. On the MinGW target, the directory returned by the `GetTempPath` function. Alternatively, on the Cygwin target, the `TMP` and `TEMP` environment variables, if they exist, in that order.
3. The `P_tmpdir` macro if it is defined, otherwise the directory '`/tmp`'.

3.2 GFORTRAN_STDIN_UNIT—Unit number for standard input

This environment variable can be used to select the unit number preconnected to standard input. This must be a positive integer. The default value is 5.

3.3 GFORTRAN_STDOUT_UNIT—Unit number for standard output

This environment variable can be used to select the unit number preconnected to standard output. This must be a positive integer. The default value is 6.

3.4 GFORTRAN_STDERR_UNIT—Unit number for standard error

This environment variable can be used to select the unit number preconnected to standard error. This must be a positive integer. The default value is 0.

3.5 GFORTRAN_UNBUFFERED_ALL—Do not buffer I/O on all units

This environment variable controls whether all I/O is unbuffered. If the first letter is 'y', 'Y' or '1', all I/O is unbuffered. This will slow down small sequential reads and writes. If the first letter is 'n', 'N' or '0', I/O is buffered. This is the default.

3.6 GFORTRAN_UNBUFFERED_PRECONNECTED—Do not buffer I/O on preconnected units

The environment variable named `GFORTRAN_UNBUFFERED_PRECONNECTED` controls whether I/O on a preconnected unit (i.e. STDOUT or STDERR) is unbuffered. If the first letter is 'y', 'Y' or '1', I/O is unbuffered. This will slow down small sequential reads and writes. If the first letter is 'n', 'N' or '0', I/O is buffered. This is the default.

3.7 GFORTRAN_SHOW_LOCUS—Show location for runtime errors

If the first letter is 'y', 'Y' or '1', filename and line numbers for runtime errors are printed. If the first letter is 'n', 'N' or '0', do not print filename and line numbers for runtime errors. The default is to print the location.

3.8 GFORTRAN_OPTIONAL_PLUS—Print leading + where permitted

If the first letter is 'y', 'Y' or '1', a plus sign is printed where permitted by the Fortran standard. If the first letter is 'n', 'N' or '0', a plus sign is not printed in most cases. Default is not to print plus signs.

3.9 GFORTRAN_DEFAULT_RECL—Default record length for new files

This environment variable specifies the default record length, in bytes, for files which are opened without a RECL tag in the OPEN statement. This must be a positive integer. The default value is 1073741824 bytes (1 GB).

3.10 GFORTRAN_LIST_SEPARATOR—Separator for list output

This environment variable specifies the separator when writing list-directed output. It may contain any number of spaces and at most one comma. If you specify this on the command line, be sure to quote spaces, as in

```
$ GFORTRAN_LIST_SEPARATOR='  ,  ' ./a.out
```

when a.out is the compiled Fortran program that you want to run. Default is a single space.

3.11 GFORTRAN_CONVERT_UNIT—Set endianness for unformatted I/O

By setting the GFORTRAN_CONVERT_UNIT variable, it is possible to change the representation of data for unformatted files. The syntax for the GFORTRAN_CONVERT_UNIT variable is:

```
GFORTRAN_CONVERT_UNIT: mode | mode ';' exception | exception ;
mode: 'native' | 'swap' | 'big_endian' | 'little_endian' ;
exception: mode ':' unit_list | unit_list ;
unit_list: unit_spec | unit_list unit_spec ;
unit_spec: INTEGER | INTEGER '-' INTEGER ;
```

The variable consists of an optional default mode, followed by a list of optional exceptions, which are separated by semicolons from the preceding default and each other. Each exception consists of a format and a comma-separated list of units. Valid values for the modes are the same as for the CONVERT specifier:

NATIVE Use the native format. This is the default.

SWAP Swap between little- and big-endian.

LITTLE_ENDIAN Use the little-endian format for unformatted files.

BIG_ENDIAN Use the big-endian format for unformatted files.

A missing mode for an exception is taken to mean BIG_ENDIAN. Examples of values for GFORTRAN_CONVERT_UNIT are:

'big_endian' Do all unformatted I/O in big-endian mode.

'little_endian;native:10-20,25' Do all unformatted I/O in little-endian mode, except for units 10 to 20 and 25, which are in native format.

'10-20' Units 10 to 20 are big-endian, the rest is native.

Setting the environment variables should be done on the command line or via the `export` command for `sh`-compatible shells and via `setenv` for `csh`-compatible shells.

Example for `sh`:

```
$ gfortran foo.f90
$ GFORTRAN_CONVERT_UNIT='big_endian;native:10-20' ./a.out
```

Example code for `csh`:

```
% gfortran foo.f90
% setenv GFORTRAN_CONVERT_UNIT 'big_endian;native:10-20'
% ./a.out
```

Using anything but the native representation for unformatted data carries a significant speed overhead. If speed in this area matters to you, it is best if you use this only for data that needs to be portable.

See Section 6.1.15 [CONVERT specifier], page 49, for an alternative way to specify the data representation for unformatted files. See Section 2.8 [Runtime Options], page 20, for setting a default data representation for the whole program. The `CONVERT` specifier overrides the '`-fconvert`' compile options.

Note that the values specified via the GFORTRAN_CONVERT_UNIT environment variable will override the CONVERT specifier in the open statement. This is to give control over data formats to users who do not have the source code of their program available.

3.12 `GFORTRAN_ERROR_BACKTRACE`—Show backtrace on run-time errors

If the `GFORTRAN_ERROR_BACKTRACE` variable is set to 'y', 'Y' or '1' (only the first letter is relevant) then a backtrace is printed when a serious run-time error occurs. To disable the backtracing, set the variable to 'n', 'N', '0'. Default is to print a backtrace unless the '`-fno-backtrace`' compile option was used.

Part II: Language Reference

4 Fortran 2003 and 2008 Status

4.1 Fortran 2003 status

GNU Fortran supports several Fortran 2003 features; an incomplete list can be found below. See also the wiki page about Fortran 2003.

- Procedure pointers including procedure-pointer components with `PASS` attribute.

- Procedures which are bound to a derived type (type-bound procedures) including `PASS`, `PROCEDURE` and `GENERIC`, and operators bound to a type.

- Abstract interfaces and type extension with the possibility to override type-bound procedures or to have deferred binding.

- Polymorphic entities ("`CLASS`") for derived types and unlimited polymorphism ("`CLASS(*)`") – including `SAME_TYPE_AS`, `EXTENDS_TYPE_OF` and `SELECT TYPE` for scalars and arrays and finalization.

- Generic interface names, which have the same name as derived types, are now supported. This allows one to write constructor functions. Note that Fortran does not support static constructor functions. For static variables, only default initialization or structure-constructor initialization are available.

- The `ASSOCIATE` construct.

- Interoperability with C including enumerations,

- In structure constructors the components with default values may be omitted.

- Extensions to the `ALLOCATE` statement, allowing for a type-specification with type parameter and for allocation and initialization from a `SOURCE=` expression; `ALLOCATE` and `DEALLOCATE` optionally return an error message string via `ERRMSG=`.

- Reallocation on assignment: If an intrinsic assignment is used, an allocatable variable on the left-hand side is automatically allocated (if unallocated) or reallocated (if the shape is different). Currently, scalar deferred character length left-hand sides are correctly handled but arrays are not yet fully implemented.

- Deferred-length character variables and scalar deferred-length character components of derived types are supported. (Note that array-valued compoents are not yet implemented.)

- Transferring of allocations via `MOVE_ALLOC`.

- The `PRIVATE` and `PUBLIC` attributes may be given individually to derived-type components.

- In pointer assignments, the lower bound may be specified and the remapping of elements is supported.

- For pointers an `INTENT` may be specified which affect the association status not the value of the pointer target.

- Intrinsics `command_argument_count`, `get_command`, `get_command_argument`, and `get_environment_variable`.

- Support for Unicode characters (ISO 10646) and UTF-8, including the `SELECTED_CHAR_KIND` and `NEW_LINE` intrinsic functions.

- Support for binary, octal and hexadecimal (BOZ) constants in the intrinsic functions INT, REAL, CMPLX and DBLE.

- Support for namelist variables with allocatable and pointer attribute and nonconstant length type parameter.

- Array constructors using square brackets. That is, [...] rather than (/.../). Type-specification for array constructors like (/ some-type :: ... /).

- Extensions to the specification and initialization expressions, including the support for intrinsics with real and complex arguments.

- Support for the asynchronous input/output syntax; however, the data transfer is currently always synchronously performed.

- FLUSH statement.

- IOMSG= specifier for I/O statements.

- Support for the declaration of enumeration constants via the ENUM and ENUMERATOR statements. Interoperability with gcc is guaranteed also for the case where the -fshort-enums command line option is given.

- TR 15581:

  - ALLOCATABLE dummy arguments.

  - ALLOCATABLE function results

  - ALLOCATABLE components of derived types

- The OPEN statement supports the ACCESS='STREAM' specifier, allowing I/O without any record structure.

- Namelist input/output for internal files.

- Minor I/O features: Rounding during formatted output, using of a decimal comma instead of a decimal point, setting whether a plus sign should appear for positive numbers. On systems where strtod honours the rounding mode, the rounding mode is also supported for input.

- The PROTECTED statement and attribute.

- The VALUE statement and attribute.

- The VOLATILE statement and attribute.

- The IMPORT statement, allowing to import host-associated derived types.

- The intrinsic modules ISO_FORTRAN_ENVIRONMENT is supported, which contains parameters of the I/O units, storage sizes. Additionally, procedures for C interoperability are available in the ISO_C_BINDING module.

- USE statement with INTRINSIC and NON_INTRINSIC attribute; supported intrinsic modules: ISO_FORTRAN_ENV, ISO_C_BINDING, OMP_LIB and OMP_LIB_KINDS, and OPENACC.

- Renaming of operators in the USE statement.

4.2 Fortran 2008 status

The latest version of the Fortran standard is ISO/IEC 1539-1:2010, informally known as Fortran 2008. The official version is available from International Organization for Standardization (ISO) or its national member organizations. The the final draft (FDIS) can be downloaded free of charge from http://www.nag.co.uk/sc22wg5/links.html. Fortran is developed by the Working Group 5 of Sub-Committee 22 of the Joint Technical Committee 1 of the International Organization for Standardization and the International Electrotechnical Commission (IEC). This group is known as WG5.

The GNU Fortran compiler supports several of the new features of Fortran 2008; the wiki has some information about the current Fortran 2008 implementation status. In particular, the following is implemented.

- The '-std=f2008' option and support for the file extensions '.f08' and '.F08'.

- The OPEN statement now supports the NEWUNIT= option, which returns a unique file unit, thus preventing inadvertent use of the same unit in different parts of the program.

- The g0 format descriptor and unlimited format items.

- The mathematical intrinsics ASINH, ACOSH, ATANH, ERF, ERFC, GAMMA, LOG_GAMMA, BESSEL_J0, BESSEL_J1, BESSEL_JN, BESSEL_Y0, BESSEL_Y1, BESSEL_YN, HYPOT, NORM2, and ERFC_SCALED.

- Using complex arguments with TAN, SINH, COSH, TANH, ASIN, ACOS, and ATAN is now possible; ATAN(Y,X) is now an alias for ATAN2(Y,X).

- Support of the PARITY intrinsic functions.

- The following bit intrinsics: LEADZ and TRAILZ for counting the number of leading and trailing zero bits, POPCNT and POPPAR for counting the number of one bits and returning the parity; BGE, BGT, BLE, and BLT for bitwise comparisons; DSHIFTL and DSHIFTR for combined left and right shifts, MASKL and MASKR for simple left and right justified masks, MERGE_BITS for a bitwise merge using a mask, SHIFTA, SHIFTL and SHIFTR for shift operations, and the transformational bit intrinsics IALL, IANY and IPARITY.

- Support of the EXECUTE_COMMAND_LINE intrinsic subroutine.

- Support for the STORAGE_SIZE intrinsic inquiry function.

- The INT{8,16,32} and REAL{32,64,128} kind type parameters and the array-valued named constants INTEGER_KINDS, LOGICAL_KINDS, REAL_KINDS and CHARACTER_KINDS of the intrinsic module ISO_FORTRAN_ENV.

- The module procedures C_SIZEOF of the intrinsic module ISO_C_BINDINGS and COMPILER_VERSION and COMPILER_OPTIONS of ISO_FORTRAN_ENV.

- Coarray support for serial programs with '-fcoarray=single' flag and experimental support for multiple images with the '-fcoarray=lib' flag.

- Submodules are supported. It should noted that MODULEs do not produce the smod file needed by the descendent SUBMODULEs unless they contain at least one MODULE PROCEDURE interface. The reason for this is that SUBMODULEs are useless without MODULE PROCEDUREs. See http://j3-fortran.org/doc/meeting/207/15-209.txt for a discussion and a draft interpretation. Adopting this interpretation has the advantage that code that does not use submodules does not generate smod files.

- The DO CONCURRENT construct is supported.

- The BLOCK construct is supported.

- The STOP and the new ERROR STOP statements now support all constant expressions. Both show the signals which were signaling at termination.

- Support for the CONTIGUOUS attribute.

- Support for `ALLOCATE` with `MOLD`.
- Support for the `IMPURE` attribute for procedures, which allows for `ELEMENTAL` procedures without the restrictions of `PURE`.
- Null pointers (including `NULL()`) and not-allocated variables can be used as actual argument to optional non-pointer, non-allocatable dummy arguments, denoting an absent argument.
- Non-pointer variables with `TARGET` attribute can be used as actual argument to `POINTER` dummies with `INTENT(IN)`.
- Pointers including procedure pointers and those in a derived type (pointer components) can now be initialized by a target instead of only by `NULL`.
- The `EXIT` statement (with construct-name) can be now be used to leave not only the `DO` but also the `ASSOCIATE`, `BLOCK`, `IF`, `SELECT CASE` and `SELECT TYPE` constructs.
- Internal procedures can now be used as actual argument.
- Minor features: obsolesce diagnostics for `ENTRY` with '`-std=f2008`'; a line may start with a semicolon; for internal and module procedures `END` can be used instead of `END SUBROUTINE` and `END FUNCTION`; `SELECTED_REAL_KIND` now also takes a `RADIX` argument; intrinsic types are supported for `TYPE`(*intrinsic-type-spec*); multiple type-bound procedures can be declared in a single `PROCEDURE` statement; implied-shape arrays are supported for named constants (`PARAMETER`).

4.3 Technical Specification 29113 Status

GNU Fortran supports some of the new features of the Technical Specification (TS) 29113 on Further Interoperability of Fortran with C. The wiki has some information about the current TS 29113 implementation status. In particular, the following is implemented.

See also Section 7.1.6 [Further Interoperability of Fortran with C], page 60.

- The '`-std=f2008ts`' option.
- The `OPTIONAL` attribute is allowed for dummy arguments of `BIND(C) procedures`.
- The `RANK` intrinsic is supported.
- GNU Fortran's implementation for variables with `ASYNCHRONOUS` attribute is compatible with TS 29113.
- Assumed types (`TYPE(*)`).
- Assumed-rank (`DIMENSION(..)`). However, the array descriptor of the TS is not yet supported.

4.4 Technical Specification 18508 Status

GNU Fortran supports the following new features of the Technical Specification 18508 on Additional Parallel Features in Fortran:

- The new atomic ADD, CAS, FETCH and ADD/OR/XOR, OR and XOR intrinsics.
- The `CO_MIN` and `CO_MAX` and `SUM` reduction intrinsics. And the `CO_BROADCAST` and `CO_REDUCE` intrinsic, except that those do not support polymorphic types or types with allocatable, pointer or polymorphic components.
- Events (`EVENT POST`, `EVENT WAIT`, `EVENT_QUERY`)

5 Compiler Characteristics

This chapter describes certain characteristics of the GNU Fortran compiler, that are not specified by the Fortran standard, but which might in some way or another become visible to the programmer.

5.1 KIND Type Parameters

The KIND type parameters supported by GNU Fortran for the primitive data types are:

INTEGER   1, 2, 4, 8*, 16*, default: 4**

LOGICAL   1, 2, 4, 8*, 16*, default: 4**

REAL   4, 8, 10*, 16*, default: 4***

COMPLEX   4, 8, 10*, 16*, default: 4***

DOUBLE PRECISION
     4, 8, 10*, 16*, default: 8***

CHARACTER
     1, 4, default: 1

* not available on all systems
** unless '-fdefault-integer-8' is used
*** unless '-fdefault-real-8' is used (see Section 2.2 [Fortran Dialect Options], page 8)

The KIND value matches the storage size in bytes, except for COMPLEX where the storage size is twice as much (or both real and imaginary part are a real value of the given size). It is recommended to use the Section 9.230 [SELECTED_CHAR_KIND], page 222, Section 9.231 [SELECTED_INT_KIND], page 223 and Section 9.232 [SELECTED_REAL_KIND], page 223 intrinsics or the INT8, INT16, INT32, INT64, REAL32, REAL64, and REAL128 parameters of the ISO_FORTRAN_ENV module instead of the concrete values. The available kind parameters can be found in the constant arrays CHARACTER_KINDS, INTEGER_KINDS, LOGICAL_KINDS and REAL_KINDS in the Section 10.1 [ISO_FORTRAN_ENV], page 249 module. For C interoperability, the kind parameters of the Section 10.2 [ISO_C_BINDING], page 251 module should be used.

5.2 Internal representation of LOGICAL variables

The Fortran standard does not specify how variables of LOGICAL type are represented, beyond requiring that LOGICAL variables of default kind have the same storage size as default INTEGER and REAL variables. The GNU Fortran internal representation is as follows.

A LOGICAL(KIND=N) variable is represented as an INTEGER(KIND=N) variable, however, with only two permissible values: 1 for .TRUE. and 0 for .FALSE.. Any other integer value results in undefined behavior.

See also Section 7.4.2 [Argument passing conventions], page 66 and Section 7.1 [Interoperability with C], page 55.

5.3 Thread-safety of the runtime library

GNU Fortran can be used in programs with multiple threads, e.g. by using OpenMP, by calling OS thread handling functions via the `ISO_C_BINDING` facility, or by GNU Fortran compiled library code being called from a multi-threaded program.

The GNU Fortran runtime library, (`libgfortran`), supports being called concurrently from multiple threads with the following exceptions.

During library initialization, the C `getenv` function is used, which need not be thread-safe. Similarly, the `getenv` function is used to implement the `GET_ENVIRONMENT_VARIABLE` and `GETENV` intrinsics. It is the responsibility of the user to ensure that the environment is not being updated concurrently when any of these actions are taking place.

The `EXECUTE_COMMAND_LINE` and `SYSTEM` intrinsics are implemented with the `system` function, which need not be thread-safe. It is the responsibility of the user to ensure that `system` is not called concurrently.

For platforms not supporting thread-safe POSIX functions, further functionality might not be thread-safe. For details, please consult the documentation for your operating system.

The GNU Fortran runtime library uses various C library functions that depend on the locale, such as `strtod` and `snprintf`. In order to work correctly in locale-aware programs that set the locale using `setlocale`, the locale is reset to the default "C" locale while executing a formatted `READ` or `WRITE` statement. On targets supporting the POSIX 2008 per-thread locale functions (e.g. `newlocale`, `uselocale`, `freelocale`), these are used and thus the global locale set using `setlocale` or the per-thread locales in other threads are not affected. However, on targets lacking this functionality, the global LC_NUMERIC locale is set to "C" during the formatted I/O. Thus, on such targets it's not safe to call `setlocale` concurrently from another thread while a Fortran formatted I/O operation is in progress. Also, other threads doing something dependent on the LC_NUMERIC locale might not work correctly if a formatted I/O operation is in progress in another thread.

5.4 Data consistency and durability

This section contains a brief overview of data and metadata consistency and durability issues when doing I/O.

With respect to durability, GNU Fortran makes no effort to ensure that data is committed to stable storage. If this is required, the GNU Fortran programmer can use the intrinsic `FNUM` to retrieve the low level file descriptor corresponding to an open Fortran unit. Then, using e.g. the `ISO_C_BINDING` feature, one can call the underlying system call to flush dirty data to stable storage, such as `fsync` on POSIX, `_commit` on MingW, or `fcntl(fd, F_FULLSYNC, 0)` on Mac OS X. The following example shows how to call fsync:

```
! Declare the interface for POSIX fsync function
interface
  function fsync (fd) bind(c,name="fsync")
  use iso_c_binding, only: c_int
    integer(c_int), value :: fd
    integer(c_int) :: fsync
  end function fsync
end interface

! Variable declaration
```

```
integer :: ret

! Opening unit 10
open (10,file="foo")

! ...
! Perform I/O on unit 10
! ...

! Flush and sync
flush(10)
ret = fsync(fnum(10))

! Handle possible error
if (ret /= 0) stop "Error calling FSYNC"
```

With respect to consistency, for regular files GNU Fortran uses buffered I/O in order to improve performance. This buffer is flushed automatically when full and in some other situations, e.g. when closing a unit. It can also be explicitly flushed with the FLUSH statement. Also, the buffering can be turned off with the GFORTRAN_UNBUFFERED_ALL and GFORTRAN_UNBUFFERED_PRECONNECTED environment variables. Special files, such as terminals and pipes, are always unbuffered. Sometimes, however, further things may need to be done in order to allow other processes to see data that GNU Fortran has written, as follows.

The Windows platform supports a relaxed metadata consistency model, where file metadata is written to the directory lazily. This means that, for instance, the dir command can show a stale size for a file. One can force a directory metadata update by closing the unit, or by calling _commit on the file descriptor. Note, though, that _commit will force all dirty data to stable storage, which is often a very slow operation.

The Network File System (NFS) implements a relaxed consistency model called open-to-close consistency. Closing a file forces dirty data and metadata to be flushed to the server, and opening a file forces the client to contact the server in order to revalidate cached data. fsync will also force a flush of dirty data and metadata to the server. Similar to open and close, acquiring and releasing fcntl file locks, if the server supports them, will also force cache validation and flushing dirty data and metadata.

5.5 Files opened without an explicit ACTION= specifier

The Fortran standard says that if an OPEN statement is executed without an explicit ACTION= specifier, the default value is processor dependent. GNU Fortran behaves as follows:

1. Attempt to open the file with ACTION='READWRITE'
2. If that fails, try to open with ACTION='READ'
3. If that fails, try to open with ACTION='WRITE'
4. If that fails, generate an error

5.6 File operations on symbolic links

This section documents the behavior of GNU Fortran for file operations on symbolic links, on systems that support them.

- Results of INQUIRE statements of the "inquire by file" form will relate to the target of the symbolic link. For example, INQUIRE(FILE="foo",EXIST=ex) will set ex to

.*true.* if *foo* is a symbolic link pointing to an existing file, and .*false.* if *foo* points to an non-existing file ("dangling" symbolic link).

- Using the `OPEN` statement with a `STATUS="NEW"` specifier on a symbolic link will result in an error condition, whether the symbolic link points to an existing target or is dangling.
- If a symbolic link was connected, using the `CLOSE` statement with a `STATUS="DELETE"` specifier will cause the symbolic link itself to be deleted, not its target.

6 Extensions

The two sections below detail the extensions to standard Fortran that are implemented in GNU Fortran, as well as some of the popular or historically important extensions that are not (or not yet) implemented. For the latter case, we explain the alternatives available to GNU Fortran users, including replacement by standard-conforming code or GNU extensions.

6.1 Extensions implemented in GNU Fortran

GNU Fortran implements a number of extensions over standard Fortran. This chapter contains information on their syntax and meaning. There are currently two categories of GNU Fortran extensions, those that provide functionality beyond that provided by any standard, and those that are supported by GNU Fortran purely for backward compatibility with legacy compilers. By default, '-std=gnu' allows the compiler to accept both types of extensions, but to warn about the use of the latter. Specifying either '-std=f95', '-std=f2003' or '-std=f2008' disables both types of extensions, and '-std=legacy' allows both without warning.

6.1.1 Old-style kind specifications

GNU Fortran allows old-style kind specifications in declarations. These look like:

```
TYPESPEC*size x,y,z
```

where `TYPESPEC` is a basic type (`INTEGER`, `REAL`, etc.), and where `size` is a byte count corresponding to the storage size of a valid kind for that type. (For `COMPLEX` variables, `size` is the total size of the real and imaginary parts.) The statement then declares x, y and z to be of type `TYPESPEC` with the appropriate kind. This is equivalent to the standard-conforming declaration

```
TYPESPEC(k) x,y,z
```

where `k` is the kind parameter suitable for the intended precision. As kind parameters are implementation-dependent, use the `KIND`, `SELECTED_INT_KIND` and `SELECTED_REAL_KIND` intrinsics to retrieve the correct value, for instance `REAL*8 x` can be replaced by:

```
INTEGER, PARAMETER :: dbl = KIND(1.0d0)
REAL(KIND=dbl) :: x
```

6.1.2 Old-style variable initialization

GNU Fortran allows old-style initialization of variables of the form:

```
INTEGER i/1/,j/2/
REAL x(2,2) /3*0.,1./
```

The syntax for the initializers is as for the `DATA` statement, but unlike in a `DATA` statement, an initializer only applies to the variable immediately preceding the initialization. In other words, something like `INTEGER I,J/2,3/` is not valid. This style of initialization is only allowed in declarations without double colons (`::`); the double colons were introduced in Fortran 90, which also introduced a standard syntax for initializing variables in type declarations.

Examples of standard-conforming code equivalent to the above example are:

```
! Fortran 90
    INTEGER :: i = 1, j = 2
    REAL :: x(2,2) = RESHAPE((/0.,0.,0.,1./),SHAPE(x))
```

```
! Fortran 77
      INTEGER i, j
      REAL x(2,2)
      DATA i/1/, j/2/, x/3*0.,1./
```

Note that variables which are explicitly initialized in declarations or in `DATA` statements automatically acquire the `SAVE` attribute.

6.1.3 Extensions to namelist

GNU Fortran fully supports the Fortran 95 standard for namelist I/O including array qualifiers, substrings and fully qualified derived types. The output from a namelist write is compatible with namelist read. The output has all names in upper case and indentation to column 1 after the namelist name. Two extensions are permitted:

Old-style use of '`$`' instead of '`&`'

```
$MYNML
 X(:)%Y(2) = 1.0 2.0 3.0
 CH(1:4) = "abcd"
$END
```

It should be noted that the default terminator is '`/`' rather than '`&END`'.

Querying of the namelist when inputting from stdin. After at least one space, entering '`?`' sends to stdout the namelist name and the names of the variables in the namelist:

```
?

&mynml
 x
 x%y
 ch
&end
```

Entering '`=?`' outputs the namelist to stdout, as if `WRITE(*,NML = mynml)` had been called:

```
=?

&MYNML
 X(1)%Y=  0.000000    , 1.000000    , 0.000000    ,
 X(2)%Y=  0.000000    , 2.000000    , 0.000000    ,
 X(3)%Y=  0.000000    , 3.000000    , 0.000000    ,
 CH=abcd,  /
```

To aid this dialog, when input is from stdin, errors send their messages to stderr and execution continues, even if `IOSTAT` is set.

`PRINT` namelist is permitted. This causes an error if '`-std=f95`' is used.

```
PROGRAM test_print
  REAL, dimension (4)  ::  x = (/1.0, 2.0, 3.0, 4.0/)
  NAMELIST /mynml/ x
  PRINT mynml
END PROGRAM test_print
```

Expanded namelist reads are permitted. This causes an error if '`-std=f95`' is used. In the following example, the first element of the array will be given the value 0.00 and the two succeeding elements will be given the values 1.00 and 2.00.

```
&MYNML
 X(1,1) = 0.00 , 1.00 , 2.00
 /
```

When writing a namelist, if no `DELIM=` is specified, by default a double quote is used to delimit character strings. If -std=F95, F2003, or F2008, etc, the delim status is set to 'none'. Defaulting to quotes ensures that namelists with character strings can be subsequently read back in accurately.

6.1.4 X format descriptor without count field

To support legacy codes, GNU Fortran permits the count field of the `X` edit descriptor in `FORMAT` statements to be omitted. When omitted, the count is implicitly assumed to be one.

```
        PRINT 10, 2, 3
   10   FORMAT (I1, X, I1)
```

6.1.5 Commas in `FORMAT` specifications

To support legacy codes, GNU Fortran allows the comma separator to be omitted immediately before and after character string edit descriptors in `FORMAT` statements.

```
        PRINT 10, 2, 3
   10   FORMAT ('FOO='I1' BAR='I2)
```

6.1.6 Missing period in `FORMAT` specifications

To support legacy codes, GNU Fortran allows missing periods in format specifications if and only if '-std=legacy' is given on the command line. This is considered non-conforming code and is discouraged.

```
        REAL :: value
        READ(*,10) value
   10   FORMAT ('F4')
```

6.1.7 I/O item lists

To support legacy codes, GNU Fortran allows the input item list of the `READ` statement, and the output item lists of the `WRITE` and `PRINT` statements, to start with a comma.

6.1.8 Q exponent-letter

GNU Fortran accepts real literal constants with an exponent-letter of `Q`, for example, `1.23Q45`. The constant is interpreted as a `REAL(16)` entity on targets that support this type. If the target does not support `REAL(16)` but has a `REAL(10)` type, then the real-literal-constant will be interpreted as a `REAL(10)` entity. In the absence of `REAL(16)` and `REAL(10)`, an error will occur.

6.1.9 BOZ literal constants

Besides decimal constants, Fortran also supports binary (`b`), octal (`o`) and hexadecimal (`z`) integer constants. The syntax is: '`prefix quote digits quote`', were the prefix is either `b`, `o` or `z`, quote is either ' or " and the digits are for binary 0 or 1, for octal between 0 and 7, and for hexadecimal between 0 and `F`. (Example: `b'01011101'`.)

Up to Fortran 95, BOZ literals were only allowed to initialize integer variables in DATA statements. Since Fortran 2003 BOZ literals are also allowed as argument of `REAL`, `DBLE`, `INT` and `CMPLX`; the result is the same as if the integer BOZ literal had been converted by `TRANSFER` to, respectively, `real`, `double precision`, `integer` or `complex`. As GNU Fortran extension the intrinsic procedures `FLOAT`, `DFLOAT`, `COMPLEX` and `DCMPLX` are treated alike.

As an extension, GNU Fortran allows hexadecimal BOZ literal constants to be specified using the X prefix, in addition to the standard Z prefix. The BOZ literal can also be specified by adding a suffix to the string, for example, Z'ABC' and 'ABC'Z are equivalent.

Furthermore, GNU Fortran allows using BOZ literal constants outside DATA statements and the four intrinsic functions allowed by Fortran 2003. In DATA statements, in direct assignments, where the right-hand side only contains a BOZ literal constant, and for old-style initializers of the form integer i /o'0173'/, the constant is transferred as if TRANSFER had been used; for COMPLEX numbers, only the real part is initialized unless CMPLX is used. In all other cases, the BOZ literal constant is converted to an INTEGER value with the largest decimal representation. This value is then converted numerically to the type and kind of the variable in question. (For instance, real :: r = b'0000001' + 1 initializes r with 2.0.) As different compilers implement the extension differently, one should be careful when doing bitwise initialization of non-integer variables.

Note that initializing an INTEGER variable with a statement such as DATA i/Z'FFFFFFFF'/ will give an integer overflow error rather than the desired result of −1 when i is a 32-bit integer on a system that supports 64-bit integers. The '-fno-range-check' option can be used as a workaround for legacy code that initializes integers in this manner.

6.1.10 Real array indices

As an extension, GNU Fortran allows the use of REAL expressions or variables as array indices.

6.1.11 Unary operators

As an extension, GNU Fortran allows unary plus and unary minus operators to appear as the second operand of binary arithmetic operators without the need for parenthesis.

```
X = Y * -Z
```

6.1.12 Implicitly convert LOGICAL and INTEGER values

As an extension for backwards compatibility with other compilers, GNU Fortran allows the implicit conversion of LOGICAL values to INTEGER values and vice versa. When converting from a LOGICAL to an INTEGER, .FALSE. is interpreted as zero, and .TRUE. is interpreted as one. When converting from INTEGER to LOGICAL, the value zero is interpreted as .FALSE. and any nonzero value is interpreted as .TRUE..

```
LOGICAL :: l
l = 1
INTEGER :: i
i = .TRUE.
```

However, there is no implicit conversion of INTEGER values in if-statements, nor of LOGICAL or INTEGER values in I/O operations.

6.1.13 Hollerith constants support

GNU Fortran supports Hollerith constants in assignments, function arguments, and DATA and ASSIGN statements. A Hollerith constant is written as a string of characters preceded by an integer constant indicating the character count, and the letter H or h, and stored in bytewise fashion in a numeric (INTEGER, REAL, or complex) or LOGICAL variable. The constant will be padded or truncated to fit the size of the variable in which it is stored.

Examples of valid uses of Hollerith constants:

```
complex*16 x(2)
data x /16Habcdefghijklmnop, 16Hqrstuvwxyz012345/
x(1) = 16HABCDEFGHIJKLMNOP
call foo (4h abc)
```

Invalid Hollerith constants examples:

```
integer*4 a
a = 8H12345678 ! Valid, but the Hollerith constant will be truncated.
a = 0H         ! At least one character is needed.
```

In general, Hollerith constants were used to provide a rudimentary facility for handling character strings in early Fortran compilers, prior to the introduction of CHARACTER variables in Fortran 77; in those cases, the standard-compliant equivalent is to convert the program to use proper character strings. On occasion, there may be a case where the intent is specifically to initialize a numeric variable with a given byte sequence. In these cases, the same result can be obtained by using the TRANSFER statement, as in this example.

```
INTEGER(KIND=4) :: a
a = TRANSFER ("abcd", a)      ! equivalent to: a = 4Habcd
```

6.1.14 Cray pointers

Cray pointers are part of a non-standard extension that provides a C-like pointer in Fortran. This is accomplished through a pair of variables: an integer "pointer" that holds a memory address, and a "pointee" that is used to dereference the pointer.

Pointer/pointee pairs are declared in statements of the form:

```
pointer ( <pointer> , <pointee> )
```

or,

```
pointer ( <pointer1> , <pointee1> ), ( <pointer2> , <pointee2> ), ...
```

The pointer is an integer that is intended to hold a memory address. The pointee may be an array or scalar. A pointee can be an assumed size array—that is, the last dimension may be left unspecified by using a * in place of a value—but a pointee cannot be an assumed shape array. No space is allocated for the pointee.

The pointee may have its type declared before or after the pointer statement, and its array specification (if any) may be declared before, during, or after the pointer statement. The pointer may be declared as an integer prior to the pointer statement. However, some machines have default integer sizes that are different than the size of a pointer, and so the following code is not portable:

```
integer ipt
pointer (ipt, iarr)
```

If a pointer is declared with a kind that is too small, the compiler will issue a warning; the resulting binary will probably not work correctly, because the memory addresses stored in the pointers may be truncated. It is safer to omit the first line of the above example; if explicit declaration of ipt's type is omitted, then the compiler will ensure that ipt is an integer variable large enough to hold a pointer.

Pointer arithmetic is valid with Cray pointers, but it is not the same as C pointer arithmetic. Cray pointers are just ordinary integers, so the user is responsible for determining how many bytes to add to a pointer in order to increment it. Consider the following example:

```
real target(10)
real pointee(10)
pointer (ipt, pointee)
ipt = loc (target)
ipt = ipt + 1
```

The last statement does not set `ipt` to the address of `target(1)`, as it would in C pointer arithmetic. Adding 1 to `ipt` just adds one byte to the address stored in `ipt`.

Any expression involving the pointee will be translated to use the value stored in the pointer as the base address.

To get the address of elements, this extension provides an intrinsic function `LOC()`. The `LOC()` function is equivalent to the `&` operator in C, except the address is cast to an integer type:

```
real ar(10)
pointer(ipt, arpte(10))
real arpte
ipt = loc(ar)  ! Makes arpte is an alias for ar
arpte(1) = 1.0 ! Sets ar(1) to 1.0
```

The pointer can also be set by a call to the `MALLOC` intrinsic (see Section 9.176 [MALLOC], page 192).

Cray pointees often are used to alias an existing variable. For example:

```
integer target(10)
integer iarr(10)
pointer (ipt, iarr)
ipt = loc(target)
```

As long as `ipt` remains unchanged, `iarr` is now an alias for `target`. The optimizer, however, will not detect this aliasing, so it is unsafe to use `iarr` and `target` simultaneously. Using a pointee in any way that violates the Fortran aliasing rules or assumptions is illegal. It is the user's responsibility to avoid doing this; the compiler works under the assumption that no such aliasing occurs.

Cray pointers will work correctly when there is no aliasing (i.e., when they are used to access a dynamically allocated block of memory), and also in any routine where a pointee is used, but any variable with which it shares storage is not used. Code that violates these rules may not run as the user intends. This is not a bug in the optimizer; any code that violates the aliasing rules is illegal. (Note that this is not unique to GNU Fortran; any Fortran compiler that supports Cray pointers will "incorrectly" optimize code with illegal aliasing.)

There are a number of restrictions on the attributes that can be applied to Cray pointers and pointees. Pointees may not have the `ALLOCATABLE`, `INTENT`, `OPTIONAL`, `DUMMY`, `TARGET`, `INTRINSIC`, or `POINTER` attributes. Pointers may not have the `DIMENSION`, `POINTER`, `TARGET`, `ALLOCATABLE`, `EXTERNAL`, or `INTRINSIC` attributes, nor may they be function results. Pointees may not occur in more than one pointer statement. A pointee cannot be a pointer. Pointees cannot occur in equivalence, common, or data statements.

A Cray pointer may also point to a function or a subroutine. For example, the following excerpt is valid:

```
implicit none
external sub
pointer (subptr,subpte)
external subpte
```

```
subptr = loc(sub)
call subpte()
[...]
subroutine sub
[...]
end subroutine sub
```

A pointer may be modified during the course of a program, and this will change the location to which the pointee refers. However, when pointees are passed as arguments, they are treated as ordinary variables in the invoked function. Subsequent changes to the pointer will not change the base address of the array that was passed.

6.1.15 CONVERT specifier

GNU Fortran allows the conversion of unformatted data between little- and big-endian representation to facilitate moving of data between different systems. The conversion can be indicated with the CONVERT specifier on the OPEN statement. See Section 3.11 [GFOR-TRAN_CONVERT_UNIT], page 30, for an alternative way of specifying the data format via an environment variable.

Valid values for CONVERT are:

CONVERT='NATIVE' Use the native format. This is the default.

CONVERT='SWAP' Swap between little- and big-endian.

CONVERT='LITTLE_ENDIAN' Use the little-endian representation for unformatted files.

CONVERT='BIG_ENDIAN' Use the big-endian representation for unformatted files.

Using the option could look like this:

```
open(file='big.dat',form='unformatted',access='sequential', &
     convert='big_endian')
```

The value of the conversion can be queried by using INQUIRE(CONVERT=ch). The values returned are 'BIG_ENDIAN' and 'LITTLE_ENDIAN'.

CONVERT works between big- and little-endian for INTEGER values of all supported kinds and for REAL on IEEE systems of kinds 4 and 8. Conversion between different "extended double" types on different architectures such as m68k and x86_64, which GNU Fortran supports as REAL(KIND=10) and REAL(KIND=16), will probably not work.

Note that the values specified via the GFORTRAN_CONVERT_UNIT environment variable will override the CONVERT specifier in the open statement. This is to give control over data formats to users who do not have the source code of their program available.

Using anything but the native representation for unformatted data carries a significant speed overhead. If speed in this area matters to you, it is best if you use this only for data that needs to be portable.

6.1.16 OpenMP

OpenMP (Open Multi-Processing) is an application programming interface (API) that supports multi-platform shared memory multiprocessing programming in C/C++ and Fortran on many architectures, including Unix and Microsoft Windows platforms. It consists of a set of compiler directives, library routines, and environment variables that influence run-time behavior.

GNU Fortran strives to be compatible to the OpenMP Application Program Interface v4.0.

To enable the processing of the OpenMP directive `!$omp` in free-form source code; the `c$omp`, `*$omp` and `!$omp` directives in fixed form; the `!$` conditional compilation sentinels in free form; and the `c$`, `*$` and `!$` sentinels in fixed form, gfortran needs to be invoked with the '-fopenmp'. This also arranges for automatic linking of the GNU Offloading and Multi Processing Runtime Library Section "libgomp" in *GNU Offloading and Multi Processing Runtime Library*.

The OpenMP Fortran runtime library routines are provided both in a form of a Fortran 90 module named `omp_lib` and in a form of a Fortran `include` file named 'omp_lib.h'.

An example of a parallelized loop taken from Appendix A.1 of the OpenMP Application Program Interface v2.5:

```
SUBROUTINE A1(N, A, B)
  INTEGER I, N
  REAL B(N), A(N)
!$OMP PARALLEL DO !I is private by default
  DO I=2,N
    B(I) = (A(I) + A(I-1)) / 2.0
  ENDDO
!$OMP END PARALLEL DO
END SUBROUTINE A1
```

Please note:

- '-fopenmp' implies '-frecursive', i.e., all local arrays will be allocated on the stack. When porting existing code to OpenMP, this may lead to surprising results, especially to segmentation faults if the stacksize is limited.

- On glibc-based systems, OpenMP enabled applications cannot be statically linked due to limitations of the underlying pthreads-implementation. It might be possible to get a working solution if `-Wl,--whole-archive -lpthread -Wl,--no-whole-archive` is added to the command line. However, this is not supported by gcc and thus not recommended.

6.1.17 OpenACC

OpenACC is an application programming interface (API) that supports offloading of code to accelerator devices. It consists of a set of compiler directives, library routines, and environment variables that influence run-time behavior.

GNU Fortran strives to be compatible to the OpenACC Application Programming Interface v2.0.

To enable the processing of the OpenACC directive `!$acc` in free-form source code; the `c$acc`, `*$acc` and `!$acc` directives in fixed form; the `!$` conditional compilation sentinels in free form; and the `c$`, `*$` and `!$` sentinels in fixed form, gfortran needs to be invoked with the '-fopenacc'. This also arranges for automatic linking of the GNU Offloading and Multi Processing Runtime Library Section "libgomp" in *GNU Offloading and Multi Processing Runtime Library*.

The OpenACC Fortran runtime library routines are provided both in a form of a Fortran 90 module named `openacc` and in a form of a Fortran `include` file named 'openacc_lib.h'.

Note that this is an experimental feature, incomplete, and subject to change in future versions of GCC. See https://gcc.gnu.org/wiki/OpenACC for more information.

6.1.18 Argument list functions %VAL, %REF and %LOC

GNU Fortran supports argument list functions %VAL, %REF and %LOC statements, for backward compatibility with g77. It is recommended that these should be used only for code that is accessing facilities outside of GNU Fortran, such as operating system or windowing facilities. It is best to constrain such uses to isolated portions of a program–portions that deal specifically and exclusively with low-level, system-dependent facilities. Such portions might well provide a portable interface for use by the program as a whole, but are themselves not portable, and should be thoroughly tested each time they are rebuilt using a new compiler or version of a compiler.

%VAL passes a scalar argument by value, %REF passes it by reference and %LOC passes its memory location. Since gfortran already passes scalar arguments by reference, %REF is in effect a do-nothing. %LOC has the same effect as a Fortran pointer.

An example of passing an argument by value to a C subroutine foo.:

```
C
C prototype      void foo_ (float x);
C
      external foo
      real*4 x
      x = 3.14159
      call foo (%VAL (x))
      end
```

For details refer to the g77 manual https://gcc.gnu.org/onlinedocs/gcc-3.4.6/g77/index.html#Top.

Also, c_by_val.f and its partner c_by_val.c of the GNU Fortran testsuite are worth a look.

6.1.19 Read/Write after EOF marker

Some legacy codes rely on allowing READ or WRITE after the EOF file marker in order to find the end of a file. GNU Fortran normally rejects these codes with a run-time error message and suggests the user consider BACKSPACE or REWIND to properly position the file before the EOF marker. As an extension, the run-time error may be disabled using -std=legacy.

6.2 Extensions not implemented in GNU Fortran

The long history of the Fortran language, its wide use and broad userbase, the large number of different compiler vendors and the lack of some features crucial to users in the first standards have lead to the existence of a number of important extensions to the language. While some of the most useful or popular extensions are supported by the GNU Fortran compiler, not all existing extensions are supported. This section aims at listing these extensions and offering advice on how best make code that uses them running with the GNU Fortran compiler.

6.2.1 STRUCTURE and RECORD

Record structures are a pre-Fortran-90 vendor extension to create user-defined aggregate data types. GNU Fortran does not support record structures, only Fortran 90's "derived types", which have a different syntax.

In many cases, record structures can easily be converted to derived types. To convert, replace STRUCTURE /*structure-name*/ by TYPE *type-name*. Additionally, replace RECORD /*structure-name*/ by TYPE(*type-name*). Finally, in the component access, replace the period (.) by the percent sign (%).

Here is an example of code using the non portable record structure syntax:

```
! Declaring a structure named ''item'' and containing three fields:
! an integer ID, an description string and a floating-point price.
STRUCTURE /item/
  INTEGER id
  CHARACTER(LEN=200) description
  REAL price
END STRUCTURE

! Define two variables, an single record of type ''item''
! named ''pear'', and an array of items named ''store_catalog''
RECORD /item/ pear, store_catalog(100)

! We can directly access the fields of both variables
pear.id = 92316
pear.description = "juicy D'Anjou pear"
pear.price = 0.15
store_catalog(7).id = 7831
store_catalog(7).description = "milk bottle"
store_catalog(7).price = 1.2

! We can also manipulate the whole structure
store_catalog(12) = pear
print *, store_catalog(12)
```

This code can easily be rewritten in the Fortran 90 syntax as following:

```
! ''STRUCTURE /name/ ... END STRUCTURE'' becomes
! ''TYPE name ... END TYPE''
TYPE item
  INTEGER id
  CHARACTER(LEN=200) description
  REAL price
END TYPE

! ''RECORD /name/ variable'' becomes ''TYPE(name) variable''
TYPE(item) pear, store_catalog(100)

! Instead of using a dot (.) to access fields of a record, the
! standard syntax uses a percent sign (%)
pear%id = 92316
pear%description = "juicy D'Anjou pear"
pear%price = 0.15
store_catalog(7)%id = 7831
```

```
      store_catalog(7)%description = "milk bottle"
      store_catalog(7)%price = 1.2

      ! Assignments of a whole variable do not change
      store_catalog(12) = pear
      print *, store_catalog(12)
```

6.2.2 ENCODE and DECODE statements

GNU Fortran does not support the ENCODE and DECODE statements. These statements are best replaced by READ and WRITE statements involving internal files (CHARACTER variables and arrays), which have been part of the Fortran standard since Fortran 77. For example, replace a code fragment like

```
          INTEGER*1 LINE(80)
          REAL A, B, C
   c      ... Code that sets LINE
          DECODE (80, 9000, LINE) A, B, C
   9000 FORMAT (1X, 3(F10.5))
```

with the following:

```
          CHARACTER(LEN=80) LINE
          REAL A, B, C
   c      ... Code that sets LINE
          READ (UNIT=LINE, FMT=9000) A, B, C
   9000 FORMAT (1X, 3(F10.5))
```

Similarly, replace a code fragment like

```
          INTEGER*1 LINE(80)
          REAL A, B, C
   c      ... Code that sets A, B and C
          ENCODE (80, 9000, LINE) A, B, C
   9000 FORMAT (1X, 'OUTPUT IS ', 3(F10.5))
```

with the following:

```
          CHARACTER(LEN=80) LINE
          REAL A, B, C
   c      ... Code that sets A, B and C
          WRITE (UNIT=LINE, FMT=9000) A, B, C
   9000 FORMAT (1X, 'OUTPUT IS ', 3(F10.5))
```

6.2.3 Variable FORMAT expressions

A variable FORMAT expression is format statement which includes angle brackets enclosing a Fortran expression: FORMAT(I<N>). GNU Fortran does not support this legacy extension. The effect of variable format expressions can be reproduced by using the more powerful (and standard) combination of internal output and string formats. For example, replace a code fragment like this:

```
          WRITE(6,20) INT1
   20     FORMAT(I<N+1>)
```

with the following:

```
   c      Variable declaration
          CHARACTER(LEN=20) FMT
   c
   c      Other code here...
   c
```

```
      WRITE(FMT,'("(I", I0, ")")') N+1
      WRITE(6,FMT) INT1
```

or with:

```
c     Variable declaration
      CHARACTER(LEN=20) FMT
c
c     Other code here...
c
      WRITE(FMT,*) N+1
      WRITE(6,"(I" // ADJUSTL(FMT) // ")") INT1
```

6.2.4 Alternate complex function syntax

Some Fortran compilers, including g77, let the user declare complex functions with the syntax COMPLEX FUNCTION name*16(), as well as COMPLEX*16 FUNCTION name(). Both are non-standard, legacy extensions. gfortran accepts the latter form, which is more common, but not the former.

6.2.5 Volatile COMMON blocks

Some Fortran compilers, including g77, let the user declare COMMON with the VOLATILE attribute. This is invalid standard Fortran syntax and is not supported by gfortran. Note that gfortran accepts VOLATILE variables in COMMON blocks since revision 4.3.

6.2.6 OPEN(... NAME=)

Some Fortran compilers, including g77, let the user declare OPEN(... NAME=). This is invalid standard Fortran syntax and is not supported by gfortran. OPEN(... NAME=) should be replaced with OPEN(... FILE=).

7 Mixed-Language Programming

This chapter is about mixed-language interoperability, but also applies if one links Fortran code compiled by different compilers. In most cases, use of the C Binding features of the Fortran 2003 standard is sufficient, and their use is highly recommended.

7.1 Interoperability with C

Since Fortran 2003 (ISO/IEC 1539-1:2004(E)) there is a standardized way to generate procedure and derived-type declarations and global variables which are interoperable with C (ISO/IEC 9899:1999). The `bind(C)` attribute has been added to inform the compiler that a symbol shall be interoperable with C; also, some constraints are added. Note, however, that not all C features have a Fortran equivalent or vice versa. For instance, neither C's unsigned integers nor C's functions with variable number of arguments have an equivalent in Fortran.

Note that array dimensions are reversely ordered in C and that arrays in C always start with index 0 while in Fortran they start by default with 1. Thus, an array declaration `A(n,m)` in Fortran matches `A[m][n]` in C and accessing the element `A(i,j)` matches `A[j-1][i-1]`. The element following `A(i,j)` (C: `A[j-1][i-1]`; assuming $i < n$) in memory is `A(i+1,j)` (C: `A[j-1][i]`).

7.1.1 Intrinsic Types

In order to ensure that exactly the same variable type and kind is used in C and Fortran, the named constants shall be used which are defined in the `ISO_C_BINDING` intrinsic module. That module contains named constants for kind parameters and character named constants for the escape sequences in C. For a list of the constants, see Section 10.2 [ISO_C_BINDING], page 251.

For logical types, please note that the Fortran standard only guarantees interoperability between C99's `_Bool` and Fortran's `C_Bool`-kind logicals and C99 defines that `true` has the value 1 and `false` the value 0. Using any other integer value with GNU Fortran's `LOGICAL` (with any kind parameter) gives an undefined result. (Passing other integer values than 0 and 1 to GCC's `_Bool` is also undefined, unless the integer is explicitly or implicitly casted to `_Bool`.)

7.1.2 Derived Types and struct

For compatibility of derived types with `struct`, one needs to use the `BIND(C)` attribute in the type declaration. For instance, the following type declaration

```
USE ISO_C_BINDING
TYPE, BIND(C) :: myType
  INTEGER(C_INT) :: i1, i2
  INTEGER(C_SIGNED_CHAR) :: i3
  REAL(C_DOUBLE) :: d1
  COMPLEX(C_FLOAT_COMPLEX) :: c1
  CHARACTER(KIND=C_CHAR) :: str(5)
END TYPE
```

matches the following `struct` declaration in C

```
struct {
  int i1, i2;
```

```
        /* Note: "char" might be signed or unsigned.  */
        signed char i3;
        double d1;
        float _Complex c1;
        char str[5];
    } myType;
```

Derived types with the C binding attribute shall not have the **sequence** attribute, type parameters, the **extends** attribute, nor type-bound procedures. Every component must be of interoperable type and kind and may not have the **pointer** or **allocatable** attribute. The names of the components are irrelevant for interoperability.

As there exist no direct Fortran equivalents, neither unions nor structs with bit field or variable-length array members are interoperable.

7.1.3 Interoperable Global Variables

Variables can be made accessible from C using the C binding attribute, optionally together with specifying a binding name. Those variables have to be declared in the declaration part of a MODULE, be of interoperable type, and have neither the **pointer** nor the **allocatable** attribute.

```
        MODULE m
          USE myType_module
          USE ISO_C_BINDING
          integer(C_INT), bind(C, name="_MyProject_flags") :: global_flag
          type(myType), bind(C) :: tp
        END MODULE
```

Here, **_MyProject_flags** is the case-sensitive name of the variable as seen from C programs while **global_flag** is the case-insensitive name as seen from Fortran. If no binding name is specified, as for *tp*, the C binding name is the (lowercase) Fortran binding name. If a binding name is specified, only a single variable may be after the double colon. Note of warning: You cannot use a global variable to access *errno* of the C library as the C standard allows it to be a macro. Use the **IERRNO** intrinsic (GNU extension) instead.

7.1.4 Interoperable Subroutines and Functions

Subroutines and functions have to have the BIND(C) attribute to be compatible with C. The dummy argument declaration is relatively straightforward. However, one needs to be careful because C uses call-by-value by default while Fortran behaves usually similar to call-by-reference. Furthermore, strings and pointers are handled differently. Note that in Fortran 2003 and 2008 only explicit size and assumed-size arrays are supported but not assumed-shape or deferred-shape (i.e. allocatable or pointer) arrays. However, those are allowed since the Technical Specification 29113, see Section 7.1.6 [Further Interoperability of Fortran with C], page 60

To pass a variable by value, use the **VALUE** attribute. Thus, the following C prototype

```
    int func(int i, int *j)
```

matches the Fortran declaration

```
        integer(c_int) function func(i,j)
          use iso_c_binding, only: c_int
          integer(c_int), VALUE :: i
          integer(c_int) :: j
```

Note that pointer arguments also frequently need the `VALUE` attribute, see Section 7.1.5 [Working with Pointers], page 58.

Strings are handled quite differently in C and Fortran. In C a string is a `NUL`-terminated array of characters while in Fortran each string has a length associated with it and is thus not terminated (by e.g. `NUL`). For example, if one wants to use the following C function,

```
#include <stdio.h>
void print_C(char *string) /* equivalent: char string[]  */
{
    printf("%s\n", string);
}
```

to print "Hello World" from Fortran, one can call it using

```
use iso_c_binding, only: C_CHAR, C_NULL_CHAR
interface
  subroutine print_c(string) bind(C, name="print_C")
    use iso_c_binding, only: c_char
    character(kind=c_char) :: string(*)
  end subroutine print_c
end interface
call print_c(C_CHAR_"Hello World"//C_NULL_CHAR)
```

As the example shows, one needs to ensure that the string is `NUL` terminated. Additionally, the dummy argument *string* of `print_C` is a length-one assumed-size array; using `character(len=*)` is not allowed. The example above uses `c_char_"Hello World"` to ensure the string literal has the right type; typically the default character kind and `c_char` are the same and thus `"Hello World"` is equivalent. However, the standard does not guarantee this.

The use of strings is now further illustrated using the C library function `strncpy`, whose prototype is

```
char *strncpy(char *restrict s1, const char *restrict s2, size_t n);
```

The function `strncpy` copies at most *n* characters from string *s2* to *s1* and returns *s1*. In the following example, we ignore the return value:

```
use iso_c_binding
implicit none
character(len=30) :: str,str2
interface
  ! Ignore the return value of strncpy -> subroutine
  ! "restrict" is always assumed if we do not pass a pointer
  subroutine strncpy(dest, src, n) bind(C)
    import
    character(kind=c_char),  intent(out) :: dest(*)
    character(kind=c_char),  intent(in)  :: src(*)
    integer(c_size_t), value, intent(in) :: n
  end subroutine strncpy
end interface
str = repeat('X',30) ! Initialize whole string with 'X'
call strncpy(str, c_char_"Hello World"//C_NULL_CHAR, &
             len(c_char_"Hello World",kind=c_size_t))
print '(a)', str ! prints: "Hello WorldXXXXXXXXXXXXXXXXXXX"
end
```

The intrinsic procedures are described in Chapter 9 [Intrinsic Procedures], page 85.

7.1.5 Working with Pointers

C pointers are represented in Fortran via the special opaque derived type `type(c_ptr)` (with private components). Thus one needs to use intrinsic conversion procedures to convert from or to C pointers.

For some applications, using an assumed type (`TYPE(*)`) can be an alternative to a C pointer; see Section 7.1.6 [Further Interoperability of Fortran with C], page 60.

For example,

```
use iso_c_binding
type(c_ptr) :: cptr1, cptr2
integer, target :: array(7), scalar
integer, pointer :: pa(:), ps
cptr1 = c_loc(array(1)) ! The programmer needs to ensure that the
                        ! array is contiguous if required by the C
                        ! procedure
cptr2 = c_loc(scalar)
call c_f_pointer(cptr2, ps)
call c_f_pointer(cptr2, pa, shape=[7])
```

When converting C to Fortran arrays, the one-dimensional `SHAPE` argument has to be passed.

If a pointer is a dummy-argument of an interoperable procedure, it usually has to be declared using the `VALUE` attribute. `void*` matches `TYPE(C_PTR)`, `VALUE`, while `TYPE(C_PTR)` alone matches `void**`.

Procedure pointers are handled analogously to pointers; the C type is `TYPE(C_FUNPTR)` and the intrinsic conversion procedures are `C_F_PROCPOINTER` and `C_FUNLOC`.

Let us consider two examples of actually passing a procedure pointer from C to Fortran and vice versa. Note that these examples are also very similar to passing ordinary pointers between both languages. First, consider this code in C:

```
/* Procedure implemented in Fortran.  */
void get_values (void (*)(double));

/* Call-back routine we want called from Fortran.  */
void
print_it (double x)
{
  printf ("Number is %f.\n", x);
}

/* Call Fortran routine and pass call-back to it.  */
void
foobar ()
{
  get_values (&print_it);
}
```

A matching implementation for `get_values` in Fortran, that correctly receives the procedure pointer from C and is able to call it, is given in the following `MODULE`:

```
MODULE m
  IMPLICIT NONE

  ! Define interface of call-back routine.
  ABSTRACT INTERFACE
    SUBROUTINE callback (x)
```

```
      USE, INTRINSIC :: ISO_C_BINDING
      REAL(KIND=C_DOUBLE), INTENT(IN), VALUE :: x
    END SUBROUTINE callback
  END INTERFACE

CONTAINS

  ! Define C-bound procedure.
  SUBROUTINE get_values (cproc) BIND(C)
    USE, INTRINSIC :: ISO_C_BINDING
    TYPE(C_FUNPTR), INTENT(IN), VALUE :: cproc

    PROCEDURE(callback), POINTER :: proc

    ! Convert C to Fortran procedure pointer.
    CALL C_F_PROCPOINTER (cproc, proc)

    ! Call it.
    CALL proc (1.0_C_DOUBLE)
    CALL proc (-42.0_C_DOUBLE)
    CALL proc (18.12_C_DOUBLE)
  END SUBROUTINE get_values

END MODULE m
```

Next, we want to call a C routine that expects a procedure pointer argument and pass it a Fortran procedure (which clearly must be interoperable!). Again, the C function may be:

```
int
call_it (int (*func)(int), int arg)
{
  return func (arg);
}
```

It can be used as in the following Fortran code:

```
MODULE m
  USE, INTRINSIC :: ISO_C_BINDING
  IMPLICIT NONE

  ! Define interface of C function.
  INTERFACE
    INTEGER(KIND=C_INT) FUNCTION call_it (func, arg) BIND(C)
      USE, INTRINSIC :: ISO_C_BINDING
      TYPE(C_FUNPTR), INTENT(IN), VALUE :: func
      INTEGER(KIND=C_INT), INTENT(IN), VALUE :: arg
    END FUNCTION call_it
  END INTERFACE

CONTAINS

  ! Define procedure passed to C function.
  ! It must be interoperable!
  INTEGER(KIND=C_INT) FUNCTION double_it (arg) BIND(C)
    INTEGER(KIND=C_INT), INTENT(IN), VALUE :: arg
    double_it = arg + arg
  END FUNCTION double_it

  ! Call C function.
```

```
SUBROUTINE foobar ()
  TYPE(C_FUNPTR) :: cproc
  INTEGER(KIND=C_INT) :: i

  ! Get C procedure pointer.
  cproc = C_FUNLOC (double_it)

  ! Use it.
  DO i = 1_C_INT, 10_C_INT
    PRINT *, call_it (cproc, i)
  END DO
END SUBROUTINE foobar

END MODULE m
```

7.1.6 Further Interoperability of Fortran with C

The Technical Specification ISO/IEC TS 29113:2012 on further interoperability of Fortran with C extends the interoperability support of Fortran 2003 and Fortran 2008. Besides removing some restrictions and constraints, it adds assumed-type (TYPE(*)) and assumed-rank (dimension) variables and allows for interoperability of assumed-shape, assumed-rank and deferred-shape arrays, including allocatables and pointers.

Note: Currently, GNU Fortran does not support the array descriptor (dope vector) as specified in the Technical Specification, but uses an array descriptor with different fields. The Chasm Language Interoperability Tools, http://chasm-interop.sourceforge.net/ , provide an interface to GNU Fortran's array descriptor.

The Technical Specification adds the following new features, which are supported by GNU Fortran:

- The ASYNCHRONOUS attribute has been clarified and extended to allow its use with asynchronous communication in user-provided libraries such as in implementations of the Message Passing Interface specification.

- Many constraints have been relaxed, in particular for the C_LOC and C_F_POINTER intrinsics.

- The OPTIONAL attribute is now allowed for dummy arguments; an absent argument matches a NULL pointer.

- Assumed types (TYPE(*)) have been added, which may only be used for dummy arguments. They are unlimited polymorphic but contrary to CLASS(*) they do not contain any type information, similar to C's void * pointers. Expressions of any type and kind can be passed; thus, it can be used as replacement for TYPE(C_PTR), avoiding the use of C_LOC in the caller.

  Note, however, that TYPE(*) only accepts scalar arguments, unless the DIMENSION is explicitly specified. As DIMENSION(*) only supports array (including array elements) but no scalars, it is not a full replacement for C_LOC. On the other hand, assumed-type assumed-rank dummy arguments (TYPE(*), DIMENSION(..)) allow for both scalars and arrays, but require special code on the callee side to handle the array descriptor.

- Assumed-rank arrays (DIMENSION(..)) as dummy argument allow that scalars and arrays of any rank can be passed as actual argument. As the Technical Specification does not provide for direct means to operate with them, they have to be used either from the C side or be converted using `C_LOC` and `C_F_POINTER` to scalars or arrays of a specific rank. The rank can be determined using the `RANK` intrinisic.

Currently unimplemented:

- GNU Fortran always uses an array descriptor, which does not match the one of the Technical Specification. The `ISO_Fortran_binding.h` header file and the C functions it specifies are not available.

- Using assumed-shape, assumed-rank and deferred-shape arrays in `BIND(C)` procedures is not fully supported. In particular, C interoperable strings of other length than one are not supported as this requires the new array descriptor.

7.2 GNU Fortran Compiler Directives

The Fortran standard describes how a conforming program shall behave; however, the exact implementation is not standardized. In order to allow the user to choose specific implementation details, compiler directives can be used to set attributes of variables and procedures which are not part of the standard. Whether a given attribute is supported and its exact effects depend on both the operating system and on the processor; see Section "C Extensions" in *Using the GNU Compiler Collection (GCC)* for details.

For procedures and procedure pointers, the following attributes can be used to change the calling convention:

- `CDECL` – standard C calling convention

- `STDCALL` – convention where the called procedure pops the stack

- `FASTCALL` – part of the arguments are passed via registers instead using the stack

Besides changing the calling convention, the attributes also influence the decoration of the symbol name, e.g., by a leading underscore or by a trailing at-sign followed by the number of bytes on the stack. When assigning a procedure to a procedure pointer, both should use the same calling convention.

On some systems, procedures and global variables (module variables and `COMMON` blocks) need special handling to be accessible when they are in a shared library. The following attributes are available:

- `DLLEXPORT` – provide a global pointer to a pointer in the DLL

- `DLLIMPORT` – reference the function or variable using a global pointer

For dummy arguments, the `NO_ARG_CHECK` attribute can be used; in other compilers, it is also known as `IGNORE_TKR`. For dummy arguments with this attribute actual arguments of any type and kind (similar to `TYPE(*)`), scalars and arrays of any rank (no equivalent in Fortran standard) are accepted. As with `TYPE(*)`, the argument is unlimited polymorphic and no type information is available. Additionally, the argument may only be passed to dummy arguments with the `NO_ARG_CHECK` attribute and as argument to the `PRESENT` intrinsic function and to `C_LOC` of the `ISO_C_BINDING` module.

Variables with `NO_ARG_CHECK` attribute shall be of assumed-type (`TYPE(*)`; recommended) or of type `INTEGER`, `LOGICAL`, `REAL` or `COMPLEX`. They shall not have the `ALLOCATE`, `CODIMENSION`, `INTENT(OUT)`, `POINTER` or `VALUE` attribute; furthermore, they shall be either scalar or of assumed-size (`dimension(*)`). As `TYPE(*)`, the `NO_ARG_CHECK` attribute requires an explicit interface.

- `NO_ARG_CHECK` – disable the type, kind and rank checking

The attributes are specified using the syntax

`!GCC$ ATTRIBUTES` *attribute-list* `::` *variable-list*

where in free-form source code only whitespace is allowed before `!GCC$` and in fixed-form source code `!GCC$`, `cGCC$` or `*GCC$` shall start in the first column.

For procedures, the compiler directives shall be placed into the body of the procedure; for variables and procedure pointers, they shall be in the same declaration part as the variable or procedure pointer.

7.3 Non-Fortran Main Program

Even if you are doing mixed-language programming, it is very likely that you do not need to know or use the information in this section. Since it is about the internal structure of GNU Fortran, it may also change in GCC minor releases.

When you compile a `PROGRAM` with GNU Fortran, a function with the name `main` (in the symbol table of the object file) is generated, which initializes the libgfortran library and then calls the actual program which uses the name `MAIN__`, for historic reasons. If you link GNU Fortran compiled procedures to, e.g., a C or C++ program or to a Fortran program compiled by a different compiler, the libgfortran library is not initialized and thus a few intrinsic procedures do not work properly, e.g. those for obtaining the command-line arguments.

Therefore, if your `PROGRAM` is not compiled with GNU Fortran and the GNU Fortran compiled procedures require intrinsics relying on the library initialization, you need to initialize the library yourself. Using the default options, gfortran calls `_gfortran_set_args` and `_gfortran_set_options`. The initialization of the former is needed if the called procedures access the command line (and for backtracing); the latter sets some flags based on the standard chosen or to enable backtracing. In typical programs, it is not necessary to call any initialization function.

If your `PROGRAM` is compiled with GNU Fortran, you shall not call any of the following functions. The libgfortran initialization functions are shown in C syntax but using C bindings they are also accessible from Fortran.

7.3.1 `_gfortran_set_args` — Save command-line arguments

Description:

> `_gfortran_set_args` saves the command-line arguments; this initialization is required if any of the command-line intrinsics is called. Additionally, it shall be called if backtracing is enabled (see `_gfortran_set_options`).

Syntax: `void _gfortran_set_args (int argc, char *argv[])`

Arguments:

> argc   number of command line argument strings
>
> argv   the command-line argument strings; argv[0] is the pathname of the executable itself.

Example:

```
int main (int argc, char *argv[])
{
  /* Initialize libgfortran.  */
  _gfortran_set_args (argc, argv);
  return 0;
}
```

7.3.2 _gfortran_set_options — Set library option flags

Description:

       _gfortran_set_options sets several flags related to the Fortran standard to be used, whether backtracing should be enabled and whether range checks should be performed. The syntax allows for upward compatibility since the number of passed flags is specified; for non-passed flags, the default value is used. See also see Section 2.9 [Code Gen Options], page 21. Please note that not all flags are actually used.

Syntax: void _gfortran_set_options (int num, int options[])

Arguments:

num	number of options passed
argv	The list of flag values

option flag list:

option[0]	Allowed standard; can give run-time errors if e.g. an input-output edit descriptor is invalid in a given standard. Possible values are (bitwise or-ed) GFC_STD_F77 (1), GFC_STD_F95_OBS (2), GFC_STD_F95_DEL (4), GFC_STD_F95 (8), GFC_STD_F2003 (16), GFC_STD_GNU (32), GFC_STD_LEGACY (64), GFC_STD_F2008 (128), GFC_STD_F2008_OBS (256) and GFC_STD_F2008_TS (512). Default: GFC_STD_F95_OBS | GFC_STD_F95_DEL | GFC_STD_F95 | GFC_STD_F2003 | GFC_STD_F2008 | GFC_STD_F2008_TS | GFC_STD_F2008_OBS | GFC_STD_F77 | GFC_STD_GNU | GFC_STD_LEGACY.
option[1]	Standard-warning flag; prints a warning to standard error. Default: GFC_STD_F95_DEL | GFC_STD_LEGACY.
option[2]	If non zero, enable pedantic checking. Default: off.
option[3]	Unused.
option[4]	If non zero, enable backtracing on run-time errors. Default: off. (Default in the compiler: on.) Note: Installs a signal handler and requires command-line initialization using _gfortran_set_args.
option[5]	If non zero, supports signed zeros. Default: enabled.
option[6]	Enables run-time checking. Possible values are (bitwise or-ed): GFC_RTCHECK_BOUNDS (1), GFC_RTCHECK_ARRAY_TEMPS (2), GFC_RTCHECK_RECURSION (4), GFC_RTCHECK_DO (16), GFC_RTCHECK_POINTER (32). Default: disabled.
option[7]	Unused.

option[8] Show a warning when invoking `STOP` and `ERROR STOP` if a floating-point exception occurred. Possible values are (bitwise or-ed) `GFC_FPE_INVALID` (1), `GFC_FPE_DENORMAL` (2), `GFC_FPE_ZERO` (4), `GFC_FPE_OVERFLOW` (8), `GFC_FPE_UNDERFLOW` (16), `GFC_FPE_INEXACT` (32). Default: None (0). (Default in the compiler: `GFC_FPE_INVALID | GFC_FPE_DENORMAL | GFC_FPE_ZERO | GFC_FPE_OVERFLOW | GFC_FPE_UNDERFLOW`.)

Example:

```
/* Use gfortran 4.9 default options.  */
static int options[] = {68, 511, 0, 0, 1, 1, 0, 0, 31};
_gfortran_set_options (9, &options);
```

7.3.3 `_gfortran_set_convert` — Set endian conversion

Description:

`_gfortran_set_convert` set the representation of data for unformatted files.

Syntax: `void _gfortran_set_convert (int conv)`

Arguments:

conv Endian conversion, possible values: GFC_CONVERT_NATIVE (0, default), GFC_CONVERT_SWAP (1), GFC_CONVERT_BIG (2), GFC_CONVERT_LITTLE (3).

Example:

```
int main (int argc, char *argv[])
{
  /* Initialize libgfortran.  */
  _gfortran_set_args (argc, argv);
  _gfortran_set_convert (1);
  return 0;
}
```

7.3.4 `_gfortran_set_record_marker` — Set length of record markers

Description:

`_gfortran_set_record_marker` sets the length of record markers for unformatted files.

Syntax: `void _gfortran_set_record_marker (int val)`

Arguments:

val Length of the record marker; valid values are 4 and 8. Default is 4.

Example:

```
int main (int argc, char *argv[])
{
  /* Initialize libgfortran.  */
  _gfortran_set_args (argc, argv);
  _gfortran_set_record_marker (8);
  return 0;
}
```

7.3.5 _gfortran_set_fpe — Enable floating point exception traps

Description:

_gfortran_set_fpe enables floating point exception traps for the specified exceptions. On most systems, this will result in a SIGFPE signal being sent and the program being aborted.

Syntax: `void _gfortran_set_fpe (int val)`

Arguments:

option[0]   IEEE exceptions. Possible values are (bitwise or-ed) zero (0, default) no trapping, `GFC_FPE_INVALID` (1), `GFC_FPE_DENORMAL` (2), `GFC_FPE_ZERO` (4), `GFC_FPE_OVERFLOW` (8), `GFC_FPE_UNDERFLOW` (16), and `GFC_FPE_INEXACT` (32).

Example:

```
int main (int argc, char *argv[])
{
  /* Initialize libgfortran.  */
  _gfortran_set_args (argc, argv);
  /* FPE for invalid operations such as SQRT(-1.0).  */
  _gfortran_set_fpe (1);
  return 0;
}
```

7.3.6 _gfortran_set_max_subrecord_length — Set subrecord length

Description:

_gfortran_set_max_subrecord_length set the maximum length for a subrecord. This option only makes sense for testing and debugging of unformatted I/O.

Syntax: `void _gfortran_set_max_subrecord_length (int val)`

Arguments:

val   the maximum length for a subrecord; the maximum permitted value is 2147483639, which is also the default.

Example:

```
int main (int argc, char *argv[])
{
  /* Initialize libgfortran.  */
  _gfortran_set_args (argc, argv);
  _gfortran_set_max_subrecord_length (8);
  return 0;
}
```

7.4 Naming and argument-passing conventions

This section gives an overview about the naming convention of procedures and global variables and about the argument passing conventions used by GNU Fortran. If a C binding has been specified, the naming convention and some of the argument-passing conventions change. If possible, mixed-language and mixed-compiler projects should use the better defined C binding for interoperability. See see Section 7.1 [Interoperability with C], page 55.

7.4.1 Naming conventions

According the Fortran standard, valid Fortran names consist of a letter between A to Z, a to z, digits 0, 1 to 9 and underscores (_) with the restriction that names may only start with a letter. As vendor extension, the dollar sign ($) is additionally permitted with the option '-fdollar-ok', but not as first character and only if the target system supports it.

By default, the procedure name is the lower-cased Fortran name with an appended underscore (_); using '-fno-underscoring' no underscore is appended while -fsecond-underscore appends two underscores. Depending on the target system and the calling convention, the procedure might be additionally dressed; for instance, on 32bit Windows with stdcall, an at-sign @ followed by an integer number is appended. For the changing the calling convention, see see Section 7.2 [GNU Fortran Compiler Directives], page 61.

For common blocks, the same convention is used, i.e. by default an underscore is appended to the lower-cased Fortran name. Blank commons have the name __BLNK__.

For procedures and variables declared in the specification space of a module, the name is formed by __, followed by the lower-cased module name, _MOD_, and the lower-cased Fortran name. Note that no underscore is appended.

7.4.2 Argument passing conventions

Subroutines do not return a value (matching C99's void) while functions either return a value as specified in the platform ABI or the result variable is passed as hidden argument to the function and no result is returned. A hidden result variable is used when the result variable is an array or of type CHARACTER.

Arguments are passed according to the platform ABI. In particular, complex arguments might not be compatible to a struct with two real components for the real and imaginary part. The argument passing matches the one of C99's _Complex. Functions with scalar complex result variables return their value and do not use a by-reference argument. Note that with the '-ff2c' option, the argument passing is modified and no longer completely matches the platform ABI. Some other Fortran compilers use f2c semantic by default; this might cause problems with interoperablility.

GNU Fortran passes most arguments by reference, i.e. by passing a pointer to the data. Note that the compiler might use a temporary variable into which the actual argument has been copied, if required semantically (copy-in/copy-out).

For arguments with ALLOCATABLE and POINTER attribute (including procedure pointers), a pointer to the pointer is passed such that the pointer address can be modified in the procedure.

For dummy arguments with the VALUE attribute: Scalar arguments of the type INTEGER, LOGICAL, REAL and COMPLEX are passed by value according to the platform ABI. (As vendor extension and not recommended, using %VAL() in the call to a procedure has the same effect.) For TYPE(C_PTR) and procedure pointers, the pointer itself is passed such that it can be modified without affecting the caller.

For Boolean (LOGICAL) arguments, please note that GCC expects only the integer value 0 and 1. If a GNU Fortran LOGICAL variable contains another integer value, the result is undefined. As some other Fortran compilers use −1 for .TRUE., extra care has to be taken – such as passing the value as INTEGER. (The same value restriction also applies to other front ends of GCC, e.g. to GCC's C99 compiler for _Bool or GCC's Ada compiler for Boolean.)

For arguments of **CHARACTER** type, the character length is passed as hidden argument. For deferred-length strings, the value is passed by reference, otherwise by value. The character length has the type **INTEGER(kind=4)**. Note with C binding, **CHARACTER(len=1)** result variables are returned according to the platform ABI and no hidden length argument is used for dummy arguments; with **VALUE**, those variables are passed by value.

For **OPTIONAL** dummy arguments, an absent argument is denoted by a NULL pointer, except for scalar dummy arguments of type **INTEGER**, **LOGICAL**, **REAL** and **COMPLEX** which have the **VALUE** attribute. For those, a hidden Boolean argument (**logical(kind=C_bool),value**) is used to indicate whether the argument is present.

Arguments which are assumed-shape, assumed-rank or deferred-rank arrays or, with '**-fcoarray=lib**', allocatable scalar coarrays use an array descriptor. All other arrays pass the address of the first element of the array. With '**-fcoarray=lib**', the token and the offset belonging to nonallocatable coarrays dummy arguments are passed as hidden argument along the character length hidden arguments. The token is an oparque pointer identifying the coarray and the offset is a passed-by-value integer of kind **C_PTRDIFF_T**, denoting the byte offset between the base address of the coarray and the passed scalar or first element of the passed array.

The arguments are passed in the following order

- Result variable, when the function result is passed by reference
- Character length of the function result, if it is a of type **CHARACTER** and no C binding is used
- The arguments in the order in which they appear in the Fortran declaration
- The the present status for optional arguments with value attribute, which are internally passed by value
- The character length and/or coarray token and offset for the first argument which is a **CHARACTER** or a nonallocatable coarray dummy argument, followed by the hidden arguments of the next dummy argument of such a type

8 Coarray Programming

8.1 Type and enum ABI Documentation

8.1.1 `caf_token_t`

Typedef of type `void *` on the compiler side. Can be any data type on the library side.

8.1.2 `caf_register_t`

Indicates which kind of coarray variable should be registered.

```
typedef enum caf_register_t {
  CAF_REGTYPE_COARRAY_STATIC,
  CAF_REGTYPE_COARRAY_ALLOC,
  CAF_REGTYPE_LOCK_STATIC,
  CAF_REGTYPE_LOCK_ALLOC,
  CAF_REGTYPE_CRITICAL,
  CAF_REGTYPE_EVENT_STATIC,
  CAF_REGTYPE_EVENT_ALLOC
}
caf_register_t;
```

8.2 Function ABI Documentation

8.2.1 `_gfortran_caf_init` — Initialiation function

Description:

> This function is called at startup of the program before the Fortran main program, if the latter has been compiled with '`-fcoarray=lib`'. It takes as arguments the command-line arguments of the program. It is permitted to pass to `NULL` pointers as argument; if non-`NULL`, the library is permitted to modify the arguments.

Syntax: `void _gfortran_caf_init (int *argc, char ***argv)`

Arguments:

> *argc*   intent(inout) An integer pointer with the number of arguments passed to the program or `NULL`.
>
> *argv*   intent(inout) A pointer to an array of strings with the command-line arguments or `NULL`.

NOTES   The function is modelled after the initialization function of the Message Passing Interface (MPI) specification. Due to the way coarray registration works, it might not be the first call to the libaray. If the main program is not written in Fortran and only a library uses coarrays, it can happen that this function is never called. Therefore, it is recommended that the library does not rely on the passed arguments and whether the call has been done.

8.2.2 _gfortran_caf_finish — Finalization function

Description:

This function is called at the end of the Fortran main program, if it has been compiled with the '-fcoarray=lib' option.

Syntax: void _gfortran_caf_finish (void)

NOTES   For non-Fortran programs, it is recommended to call the function at the end of the main program. To ensure that the shutdown is also performed for programs where this function is not explicitly invoked, for instance non-Fortran programs or calls to the system's exit() function, the library can use a destructor function. Note that programs can also be terminated using the STOP and ERROR STOP statements; those use different library calls.

8.2.3 _gfortran_caf_this_image — Querying the image number

Description:

This function returns the current image number, which is a positive number.

Syntax: int _gfortran_caf_this_image (int distance)

Arguments:

distance   As specified for the this_image intrinsic in TS18508. Shall be a nonnegative number.

NOTES   If the Fortran intrinsic this_image is invoked without an argument, which is the only permitted form in Fortran 2008, GCC passes 0 as first argument.

8.2.4 _gfortran_caf_num_images — Querying the maximal number of images

Description:

This function returns the number of images in the current team, if *distance* is 0 or the number of images in the parent team at the specified distance. If failed is -1, the function returns the number of all images at the specified distance; if it is 0, the function returns the number of nonfailed images, and if it is 1, it returns the number of failed images.

Syntax: int _gfortran_caf_num_images(int distance, int failed)

Arguments:

distance   the distance from this image to the ancestor. Shall be positive.
failed   shall be -1, 0, or 1

NOTES   This function follows TS18508. If the num_image intrinsic has no arguments, the the compiler passes distance=0 and failed=-1 to the function.

8.2.5 _gfortran_caf_register — Registering coarrays

Description:

Allocates memory for a coarray and creates a token to identify the coarray. The function is called for both coarrays with SAVE attribute and using an explicit ALLOCATE statement. If an error occurs and STAT is a NULL pointer, the function shall abort with printing an error message and starting the error termination. If no error occurs and *STAT* is present, it shall be set to zero. Otherwise, it shall be set to a positive value and, if not-NULL, *ERRMSG* shall be set to a string describing the failure. The function shall return a pointer to the requested memory for the local image as a call to `malloc` would do.

For `CAF_REGTYPE_COARRAY_STATIC` and `CAF_REGTYPE_COARRAY_ALLOC`, the passed size is the byte size requested. For `CAF_REGTYPE_LOCK_STATIC`, `CAF_REGTYPE_LOCK_ALLOC` and `CAF_REGTYPE_CRITICAL` it is the array size or one for a scalar.

Syntax: `void *caf_register (size_t size, caf_register_t type, caf_token_t *token, int *stat, char *errmsg, int errmsg_len)`

Arguments:

size	For normal coarrays, the byte size of the coarray to be allocated; for lock types and event types, the number of elements.
type	one of the caf_register_t types.
token	intent(out) An opaque pointer identifying the coarray.
stat	intent(out) For allocatable coarrays, stores the STAT=; may be NULL
errmsg	intent(out) When an error occurs, this will be set to an error message; may be NULL
errmsg_len	the buffer size of errmsg.

NOTES Nonalloatable coarrays have to be registered prior use from remote images. In order to guarantee this, they have to be registered before the main program. This can be achieved by creating constructor functions. That is what GCC does such that also nonallocatable coarrays the memory is allocated and no static memory is used. The token permits to identify the coarray; to the processor, the token is a nonaliasing pointer. The library can, for instance, store the base address of the coarray in the token, some handle or a more complicated struct.

For normal coarrays, the returned pointer is used for accesses on the local image. For lock types, the value shall only used for checking the allocation status. Note that for critical blocks, the locking is only required on one image; in the locking statement, the processor shall always pass always an image index of one for critical-block lock variables (`CAF_REGTYPE_CRITICAL`). For lock types and critical-block variables, the initial value shall be unlocked (or, respecitively, not in critical section) such as the value false; for event types, the initial state should be no event, e.g. zero.

8.2.6 _gfortran_caf_deregister — **Deregistering coarrays**

Description:

Called to free the memory of a coarray; the processor calls this function for automatic and explicit deallocation. In case of an error, this function shall fail with an error message, unless the *STAT* variable is not null.

Syntax: `void caf_deregister (const caf_token_t *token, int *stat, char *errmsg, int errmsg_len)`

Arguments:

stat	intent(out) Stores the STAT=; may be NULL
errmsg	intent(out) When an error occurs, this will be set to an error message; may be NULL
errmsg_len	the buffer size of errmsg.

NOTES   For nonalloatable coarrays this function is never called. If a cleanup is required, it has to be handled via the finish, stop and error stop functions, and via destructors.

8.2.7 `_gfortran_caf_send` — Sending data from a local image to a remote image

Description:

Called to send a scalar, an array section or whole array from a local to a remote image identified by the image_index.

Syntax: `void _gfortran_caf_send (caf_token_t token, size_t offset, int image_index, gfc_descriptor_t *dest, caf_vector_t *dst_vector, gfc_descriptor_t *src, int dst_kind, int src_kind, bool may_require_tmp)`

Arguments:

token	intent(in) An opaque pointer identifying the coarray.
offset	By which amount of bytes the actual data is shifted compared to the base address of the coarray.
image_index	The ID of the remote image; must be a positive number.
dest	intent(in) Array descriptor for the remote image for the bounds and the size. The base_addr shall not be accessed.
dst_vector	intent(int) If not NULL, it contains the vector subscript of the destination array; the values are relative to the dimension triplet of the dest argument.
src	intent(in) Array descriptor of the local array to be transferred to the remote image
dst_kind	Kind of the destination argument
src_kind	Kind of the source argument
may_require_tmp	The variable is false it is known at compile time that the *dest* and *src* either cannot overlap or overlap (fully or partially) such that walking *src* and *dest* in element wise element order (honoring the stride value) will not lead to wrong results. Otherwise, the value is true.

NOTES   It is permitted to have image_id equal the current image; the memory of the send-to and the send-from might (partially) overlap in that case. The implementation has to take care that it handles this case, e.g. using `memmove` which handles (partially) overlapping memory. If *may_require_tmp* is true, the library might additionally create a temporary variable, unless additional checks show that this is not required (e.g. because walking backward is possible or because both arrays are contiguous and `memmove` takes care of overlap issues).

Note that the assignment of a scalar to an array is permitted. In addition, the library has to handle numeric-type conversion and for strings, padding and different character kinds.

8.2.8 _gfortran_caf_get — Getting data from a remote image

Description:

Called to get an array section or whole array from a a remote, image identified by the image_index.

Syntax: void _gfortran_caf_get_desc (caf_token_t token, size_t offset, int image_index, gfc_descriptor_t *src, caf_vector_t *src_vector, gfc_descriptor_t *dest, int src_kind, int dst_kind, bool may_require_tmp)

Arguments:

token	intent(in) An opaque pointer identifying the coarray.
offset	By which amount of bytes the actual data is shifted compared to the base address of the coarray.
image_index	The ID of the remote image; must be a positive number.
dest	intent(in) Array descriptor of the local array to be transferred to the remote image
src	intent(in) Array descriptor for the remote image for the bounds and the size. The base_addr shall not be accessed.
src_vector	intent(int) If not NULL, it contains the vector subscript of the destination array; the values are relative to the dimension triplet of the dest argument.
dst_kind	Kind of the destination argument
src_kind	Kind of the source argument
may_require_tmp	The variable is false it is known at compile time that the *dest* and *src* either cannot overlap or overlap (fully or partially) such that walking *src* and *dest* in element wise element order (honoring the stride value) will not lead to wrong results. Otherwise, the value is true.

NOTES   It is permitted to have image_id equal the current image; the memory of the send-to and the send-from might (partially) overlap in that case. The implementation has to take care that it handles this case, e.g. using `memmove` which handles (partially) overlapping memory. If *may_require_tmp* is true, the library might additionally create a temporary variable, unless additional checks show that this is not required (e.g. because walking backward is possible or because both arrays are contiguous and `memmove` takes care of overlap issues).

Note that the library has to handle numeric-type conversion and for strings, padding and different character kinds.

8.2.9 _gfortran_caf_sendget — Sending data between remote images

Description:

Called to send a scalar, an array section or whole array from a remote image identified by the src_image_index to a remote image identified by the dst_image_index.

Syntax: void _gfortran_caf_sendget (caf_token_t dst_token, size_t dst_offset, int dst_image_index, gfc_descriptor_t *dest, caf_vector_t *dst_vector, caf_token_t src_token, size_t src_offset, int src_image_index, gfc_descriptor_t *src, caf_vector_t *src_vector, int dst_kind, int src_kind, bool may_require_tmp)

Arguments:

dst_token	intent(in) An opaque pointer identifying the destination coarray.
dst_offset	By which amount of bytes the actual data is shifted compared to the base address of the destination coarray.
dst_image_index	The ID of the destination remote image; must be a positive number.
dest	intent(in) Array descriptor for the destination remote image for the bounds and the size. The base_addr shall not be accessed.
dst_vector	intent(int) If not NULL, it contains the vector subscript of the destination array; the values are relative to the dimension triplet of the dest argument.
src_token	An opaque pointer identifying the source coarray.
src_offset	By which amount of bytes the actual data is shifted compared to the base address of the source coarray.
src_image_index	The ID of the source remote image; must be a positive number.
src	intent(in) Array descriptor of the local array to be transferred to the remote image.
src_vector	intent(in) Array descriptor of the local array to be transferred to the remote image
dst_kind	Kind of the destination argument
src_kind	Kind of the source argument
may_require_tmp	The variable is false it is known at compile time that the *dest* and *src* either cannot overlap or overlap (fully or partially) such that walking *src* and *dest* in element wise element order (honoring the stride value) will not lead to wrong results. Otherwise, the value is true.

NOTES   It is permitted to have image_ids equal; the memory of the send-to and the send-from might (partially) overlap in that case. The implementation has to take care that it handles this case, e.g. using memmove which handles (partially) overlapping memory. If *may_require_tmp* is true, the library might additionally create a temporary variable, unless additional checks show that this is not required (e.g. because walking backward is possible or because both arrays are contiguous and `memmove` takes care of overlap issues).

Note that the assignment of a scalar to an array is permitted. In addition, the library has to handle numeric-type conversion and for strings, padding and different character kinds.

8.2.10 `_gfortran_caf_lock` — Locking a lock variable

Description:

Acquire a lock on the given image on a scalar locking variable or for the given array element for an array-valued variable. If the *aquired_lock* is NULL, the function return after having obtained the lock. If it is nonnull, the result is is assigned the value true (one) when the lock could be obtained and false (zero) otherwise. Locking a lock variable which has already been locked by the same image is an error.

Syntax: `void _gfortran_caf_lock (caf_token_t token, size_t index, int image_index, int *aquired_lock, int *stat, char *errmsg, int errmsg_len)`

Arguments:

token	intent(in) An opaque pointer identifying the coarray.
index	Array index; first array index is 0. For scalars, it is always 0.
image_index	The ID of the remote image; must be a positive number.
aquired_lock	intent(out) If not NULL, it returns whether lock could be obtained
stat	intent(out) Stores the STAT=; may be NULL
errmsg	intent(out) When an error occurs, this will be set to an error message; may be NULL
errmsg_len	the buffer size of errmsg.

NOTES   This function is also called for critical blocks; for those, the array index is always zero and the image index is one. Libraries are permitted to use other images for critical-block locking variables.

8.2.11 `_gfortran_caf_lock` — Unlocking a lock variable

Description:

Release a lock on the given image on a scalar locking variable or for the given array element for an array-valued variable. Unlocking a lock variable which is unlocked or has been locked by a different image is an error.

Syntax: `void _gfortran_caf_unlock (caf_token_t token, size_t index, int image_index, int *stat, char *errmsg, int errmsg_len)`

Arguments:

token	intent(in) An opaque pointer identifying the coarray.
index	Array index; first array index is 0. For scalars, it is always 0.
image_index	The ID of the remote image; must be a positive number.
stat	intent(out) For allocatable coarrays, stores the STAT=; may be NULL

errmsg	intent(out) When an error occurs, this will be set to an error message; may be NULL
errmsg_len	the buffer size of errmsg.

NOTES   This function is also called for critical block; for those, the array index is always zero and the image index is one. Libraries are permitted to use other images for critical-block locking variables.

8.2.12 `_gfortran_caf_event_post` — **Post an event**

Description:

Increment the event count of the specified event variable.

Syntax: `void _gfortran_caf_event_post (caf_token_t token, size_t index, int image_index, int *stat, char *errmsg, int errmsg_len)`

Arguments:

token	intent(in) An opaque pointer identifying the coarray.
index	Array index; first array index is 0. For scalars, it is always 0.
image_index	The ID of the remote image; must be a positive number; zero indicates the current image when accessed noncoindexed.
stat	intent(out) Stores the STAT=; may be NULL
errmsg	intent(out) When an error occurs, this will be set to an error message; may be NULL
errmsg_len	the buffer size of errmsg.

NOTES   This acts like an atomic add of one to the remote image's event variable. The statement is an image-control statement but does not imply sync memory. Still, all preceeding push communications of this image to the specified remote image has to be completed before `event_wait` on the remote image returns.

8.2.13 `_gfortran_caf_event_wait` — **Wait that an event occurred**

Description:

Wait until the event count has reached at least the specified *until_count*; if so, atomically decrement the event variable by this amount and return.

Syntax: `void _gfortran_caf_event_wait (caf_token_t token, size_t index, int until_count, int *stat, char *errmsg, int errmsg_len)`

Arguments:

token	intent(in) An opaque pointer identifying the coarray.
index	Array index; first array index is 0. For scalars, it is always 0.
until_count	The number of events which have to be available before the function returns.
stat	intent(out) Stores the STAT=; may be NULL
errmsg	intent(out) When an error occurs, this will be set to an error message; may be NULL
errmsg_len	the buffer size of errmsg.

NOTES   This function only operates on a local coarray. It acts like a loop checking atomically the value of the event variable, breaking if the value is greater or equal the requested number of counts. Before the function returns, the event variable has to be decremented by the requested *until_count* value. A possible implementation would be a busy loop for a certain number of spins (possibly depending on the number of threads relative to the number of available cores) followed by other waiting strategy such as a sleeping wait (possibly with an increasing number of sleep time) or, if possible, a futex wait.

The statement is an image-control statement but does not imply sync memory. Still, all preceeding push communications to this image of images having issued a `event_push` have to be completed before this function returns.

8.2.14 `_gfortran_caf_event_query` — Query event count

Description:

Return the event count of the specified event count.

Syntax: `void _gfortran_caf_event_query (caf_token_t token, size_t index,`
`int image_index, int *count, int *stat)`

Arguments:

token	intent(in) An opaque pointer identifying the coarray.
index	Array index; first array index is 0. For scalars, it is always 0.
image_index	The ID of the remote image; must be a positive number; zero indicates the current image when accessed noncoindexed.
count	intent(out) The number of events currently posted to the event variable
stat	intent(out) Stores the STAT=; may be NULL

NOTES   The typical use is to check the local even variable to only call `event_wait` when the data is available. However, a coindexed variable is permitted; there is no ordering or synchronization implied. It acts like an atomic fetch of the value of the event variable.

8.2.15 `_gfortran_caf_sync_all` — All-image barrier

Description:

Synchronization of all images in the current team; the program only continues on a given image after this function has been called on all images of the current team. Additionally, it ensures that all pending data transfers of previous segment have completed.

Syntax: `void _gfortran_caf_sync_all (int *stat, char *errmsg, int errmsg_`
`len)`

Arguments:

stat	intent(out) Stores the status STAT= and may be NULL.
errmsg	intent(out) When an error occurs, this will be set to an error message; may be NULL
errmsg_len	the buffer size of errmsg.

8.2.16 _gfortran_caf_sync_images — Barrier for selected images

Description:

Synchronization between the specified images; the program only continues on a given image after this function has been called on all images specified for that image. Note that one image can wait for all other images in the current team (e.g. via `sync images(*)`) while those only wait for that specific image. Additionally, `sync images` it ensures that all pending data transfers of previous segment have completed.

Syntax: `void _gfortran_caf_sync_images (int count, int images[], int *stat, char *errmsg, int errmsg_len)`

Arguments:

count	the number of images which are provided in the next argument. For a zero-sized array, the value is zero. For `sync images (*)`, the value is −1.
images	intent(in) an array with the images provided by the user. If *count* is zero, a NULL pointer is passed.
stat	intent(out) Stores the status STAT= and may be NULL.
errmsg	intent(out) When an error occurs, this will be set to an error message; may be NULL
errmsg_len	the buffer size of errmsg.

8.2.17 _gfortran_caf_sync_memory — Wait for completion of segment-memory operations

Description:

Acts as optimization barrier between different segments. It also ensures that all pending memory operations of this image have been completed.

Syntax: `void _gfortran_caf_sync_memory (int *stat, char *errmsg, int errmsg_len)`

Arguments:

stat	intent(out) Stores the status STAT= and may be NULL.
errmsg	intent(out) When an error occurs, this will be set to an error message; may be NULL
errmsg_len	the buffer size of errmsg.

NOTE A simple implementation could be
`__asm__ __volatile__ (""::::"memory")` to prevent code movements.

8.2.18 _gfortran_caf_error_stop — Error termination with exit code

Description:

Invoked for an `ERROR STOP` statement which has an integer argument. The function should terminate the program with the specified exit code.

Syntax: `void _gfortran_caf_error_stop (int32_t error)`

Arguments:

        error   the exit status to be used.

8.2.19 `_gfortran_caf_error_stop_str` — Error termination with string

Description:

        Invoked for an **ERROR STOP** statement which has a string as argument. The function should terminate the program with a nonzero-exit code.

Syntax: `void _gfortran_caf_error_stop (const char *string, int32_t len)`

Arguments:

        string   the error message (not zero terminated)
        len   the length of the string

8.2.20 `_gfortran_caf_atomic_define` — Atomic variable assignment

Description:

        Assign atomically a value to an integer or logical variable.

Syntax: `void _gfortran_caf_atomic_define (caf_token_t token, size_t offset, int image_index, void *value, int *stat, int type, int kind)`

Arguments:

token	intent(in) An opaque pointer identifying the coarray.
offset	By which amount of bytes the actual data is shifted compared to the base address of the coarray.
image_index	The ID of the remote image; must be a positive number; zero indicates the current image when used noncoindexed.
value	intent(in) the value to be assigned, passed by reference.
stat	intent(out) Stores the status STAT= and may be NULL.
type	the data type, i.e. `BT_INTEGER` (1) or `BT_LOGICAL` (2).
kind	The kind value (only 4; always `int`)

8.2.21 `_gfortran_caf_atomic_ref` — Atomic variable reference

Description:

        Reference atomically a value of a kind-4 integer or logical variable.

Syntax: `void _gfortran_caf_atomic_ref (caf_token_t token, size_t offset, int image_index, void *value, int *stat, int type, int kind)`

Arguments:
Arguments:

token	intent(in) An opaque pointer identifying the coarray.
offset	By which amount of bytes the actual data is shifted compared to the base address of the coarray.
image_index	The ID of the remote image; must be a positive number; zero indicates the current image when used noncoindexed.
value	intent(out) The variable assigned the atomically referenced variable.

stat	intent(out) Stores the status STAT= and may be NULL.
type	the data type, i.e. `BT_INTEGER` (1) or `BT_LOGICAL` (2).
kind	The kind value (only 4; always `int`)

8.2.22 `_gfortran_caf_atomic_cas` — Atomic compare and swap

Description:

Atomic compare and swap of a kind-4 integer or logical variable. Assigns atomically the specified value to the atomic variable, if the latter has the value specified by the passed condition value.

Syntax:
```
void _gfortran_caf_atomic_cas (caf_token_t token, size_t offset,
int image_index, void *old, void *compare, void *new_val, int *stat,
int type, int kind)
```

Arguments:

token	intent(in) An opaque pointer identifying the coarray.
offset	By which amount of bytes the actual data is shifted compared to the base address of the coarray.
image_index	The ID of the remote image; must be a positive number; zero indicates the current image when used noncoindexed.
old	intent(out) the value which the atomic variable had just before the cas operation.
compare	intent(in) The value used for comparision.
new_val	intent(in) The new value for the atomic variable, assigned to the atomic variable, if `compare` equals the value of the atomic variable.
stat	intent(out) Stores the status STAT= and may be NULL.
type	the data type, i.e. `BT_INTEGER` (1) or `BT_LOGICAL` (2).
kind	The kind value (only 4; always `int`)

8.2.23 `_gfortran_caf_atomic_op` — Atomic operation

Description:

Apply an operation atomically to an atomic integer or logical variable. After the operation, *old* contains the value just before the operation, which, respectively, adds (GFC_CAF_ATOMIC_ADD) atomically the `value` to the atomic integer variable or does a bitwise AND, OR or exclusive OR of the between the atomic variable and *value*; the result is then stored in the atomic variable.

Syntax:
```
void _gfortran_caf_atomic_op (int op, caf_token_t token, size_t
offset, int image_index, void *value, void *old, int *stat, int type,
int kind)
```

Arguments:

op	the operation to be performed; possible values `GFC_CAF_ATOMIC_ADD` (1), `GFC_CAF_ATOMIC_AND` (2), `GFC_CAF_ATOMIC_OR` (3), `GFC_CAF_ATOMIC_XOR` (4).
token	intent(in) An opaque pointer identifying the coarray.

offset	By which amount of bytes the actual data is shifted compared to the base address of the coarray.
image_index	The ID of the remote image; must be a positive number; zero indicates the current image when used noncoindexed.
old	intent(out) the value which the atomic variable had just before the atomic operation.
val	intent(in) The new value for the atomic variable, assigned to the atomic variable, if `compare` equals the value of the atomic variable.
stat	intent(out) Stores the status STAT= and may be NULL.
type	the data type, i.e. `BT_INTEGER` (1) or `BT_LOGICAL` (2).
kind	The kind value (only 4; always `int`)

8.2.24 `_gfortran_caf_co_broadcast` — Sending data to all images

Description:

Distribute a value from a given image to all other images in the team. Has to be called collectively.

Syntax: `void _gfortran_caf_co_broadcast (gfc_descriptor_t *a, int source_image, int *stat, char *errmsg, int errmsg_len)`

Arguments:

a	intent(inout) And array descriptor with the data to be breoadcasted (on *source_image*) or to be received (other images).
source_image	The ID of the image from which the data should be taken.
stat	intent(out) Stores the status STAT= and may be NULL.
errmsg	intent(out) When an error occurs, this will be set to an error message; may be NULL
errmsg_len	the buffer size of errmsg.

8.2.25 `_gfortran_caf_co_max` — Collective maximum reduction

Description:

Calculates the for the each array element of the variable a the maximum value for that element in the current team; if *result_image* has the value 0, the result shall be stored on all images, otherwise, only on the specified image. This function operates on numeric values and character strings.

Syntax: `void _gfortran_caf_co_max (gfc_descriptor_t *a, int result_image, int *stat, char *errmsg, int a_len, int errmsg_len)`

Arguments:

a	intent(inout) And array descriptor with the data to be breoadcasted (on *source_image*) or to be received (other images).
result_image	The ID of the image to which the reduced value should be copied to; if zero, it has to be copied to all images.
stat	intent(out) Stores the status STAT= and may be NULL.
errmsg	intent(out) When an error occurs, this will be set to an error message; may be NULL

| a_len | The string length of argument a. |
| errmsg_len | the buffer size of errmsg. |

NOTES If *result_image* is nonzero, the value on all images except of the specified one become undefined; hence, the library may make use of this.

8.2.26 _gfortran_caf_co_min — Collective minimum reduction

Description:

Calculates the for the each array element of the variable a the minimum value for that element in the current team; if *result_image* has the value 0, the result shall be stored on all images, otherwise, only on the specified image. This function operates on numeric values and character strings.

Syntax: `void _gfortran_caf_co_min (gfc_descriptor_t *a, int result_image, int *stat, char *errmsg, int a_len, int errmsg_len)`

Arguments:

a	intent(inout) And array descriptor with the data to be breoadcasted (on *source_image*) or to be received (other images).
result_image	The ID of the image to which the reduced value should be copied to; if zero, it has to be copied to all images.
stat	intent(out) Stores the status STAT= and may be NULL.
errmsg	intent(out) When an error occurs, this will be set to an error message; may be NULL
a_len	The string length of argument a.
errmsg_len	the buffer size of errmsg.

NOTES If *result_image* is nonzero, the value on all images except of the specified one become undefined; hence, the library may make use of this.

8.2.27 _gfortran_caf_co_sum — Collective summing reduction

Description:

Calculates the for the each array element of the variable a the sum value for that element in the current team; if *result_image* has the value 0, the result shall be stored on all images, otherwise, only on the specified image. This function operates on numeric values.

Syntax: `void _gfortran_caf_co_sum (gfc_descriptor_t *a, int result_image, int *stat, char *errmsg, int errmsg_len)`

Arguments:

a	intent(inout) And array descriptor with the data to be breoadcasted (on *source_image*) or to be received (other images).
result_image	The ID of the image to which the reduced value should be copied to; if zero, it has to be copied to all images.
stat	intent(out) Stores the status STAT= and may be NULL.
errmsg	intent(out) When an error occurs, this will be set to an error message; may be NULL
errmsg_len	the buffer size of errmsg.

NOTES   If *result_image* is nonzero, the value on all images except of the specified one become undefined; hence, the library may make use of this.

8.2.28 `_gfortran_caf_co_reduce` — **Generic collective reduction**

Description:

Calculates the for the each array element of the variable *a* the reduction value for that element in the current team; if *result_image* has the value 0, the result shall be stored on all images, otherwise, only on the specified image. The *opr* is a pure function doing a mathematically commutative and associative operation.

The *opr_flags* denote the following; the values are bitwise ored. `GFC_CAF_BYREF` (1) if the result should be returned by value; `GFC_CAF_HIDDENLEN` (2) whether the result and argument string lengths shall be specified as hidden argument; `GFC_CAF_ARG_VALUE` (4) whether the arguments shall be passed by value, `GFC_CAF_ARG_DESC` (8) whether the arguments shall be passed by descriptor.

Syntax: `void _gfortran_caf_co_reduce (gfc_descriptor_t *a, void * (*opr) (void *, void *), int opr_flags, int result_image, int *stat, char *errmsg, int a_len, int errmsg_len)`

Arguments:

opr	Function pointer to the reduction function.
opr_flags	Flags regarding the reduction function
a	intent(inout) And array descriptor with the data to be breoadcasted (on *source_image*) or to be received (other images).
result_image	The ID of the image to which the reduced value should be copied to; if zero, it has to be copied to all images.
stat	intent(out) Stores the status STAT= and may be NULL.
errmsg	intent(out) When an error occurs, this will be set to an error message; may be NULL
a_len	The string length of argument a.
errmsg_len	the buffer size of errmsg.

NOTES   If *result_image* is nonzero, the value on all images except of the specified one become undefined; hence, the library may make use of this. For character arguments, the result is passed as first argument, followed by the result string length, next come the two string arguments, followed by the two hidden arguments. With C binding, there are no hidden arguments and by-reference passing and either only a single character is passed or an array descriptor.

9 Intrinsic Procedures

9.1 Introduction to intrinsic procedures

The intrinsic procedures provided by GNU Fortran include all of the intrinsic procedures required by the Fortran 95 standard, a set of intrinsic procedures for backwards compatibility with G77, and a selection of intrinsic procedures from the Fortran 2003 and Fortran 2008 standards. Any conflict between a description here and a description in either the Fortran 95 standard, the Fortran 2003 standard or the Fortran 2008 standard is unintentional, and the standard(s) should be considered authoritative.

The enumeration of the `KIND` type parameter is processor defined in the Fortran 95 standard. GNU Fortran defines the default integer type and default real type by `INTEGER(KIND=4)` and `REAL(KIND=4)`, respectively. The standard mandates that both data types shall have another kind, which have more precision. On typical target architectures supported by `gfortran`, this kind type parameter is `KIND=8`. Hence, `REAL(KIND=8)` and `DOUBLE PRECISION` are equivalent. In the description of generic intrinsic procedures, the kind type parameter will be specified by `KIND=*`, and in the description of specific names for an intrinsic procedure the kind type parameter will be explicitly given (e.g., `REAL(KIND=4)` or `REAL(KIND=8)`). Finally, for brevity the optional `KIND=` syntax will be omitted.

Many of the intrinsic procedures take one or more optional arguments. This document follows the convention used in the Fortran 95 standard, and denotes such arguments by square brackets.

GNU Fortran offers the '-std=f95' and '-std=gnu' options, which can be used to restrict the set of intrinsic procedures to a given standard. By default, `gfortran` sets the '-std=gnu' option, and so all intrinsic procedures described here are accepted. There is one caveat. For a select group of intrinsic procedures, `g77` implemented both a function and a subroutine. Both classes have been implemented in `gfortran` for backwards compatibility with `g77`. It is noted here that these functions and subroutines cannot be intermixed in a given subprogram. In the descriptions that follow, the applicable standard for each intrinsic procedure is noted.

9.2 `ABORT` — Abort the program

Description:

> `ABORT` causes immediate termination of the program. On operating systems that support a core dump, `ABORT` will produce a core dump. It will also print a backtrace, unless `-fno-backtrace` is given.

Standard: GNU extension

Class: Subroutine

Syntax: `CALL ABORT`

Return value:

> Does not return.

Example:

```
program test_abort
  integer :: i = 1, j = 2
  if (i /= j) call abort
end program test_abort
```

See also: Section 9.94 [EXIT], page 145, Section 9.154 [KILL], page 180, Section 9.35 [BACKTRACE], page 108

9.3 ABS — Absolute value

Description:

      ABS(A) computes the absolute value of A.

Standard: Fortran 77 and later, has overloads that are GNU extensions

Class: Elemental function

Syntax: RESULT = ABS(A)

Arguments:

    A   The type of the argument shall be an INTEGER, REAL, or COMPLEX.

Return value:

      The return value is of the same type and kind as the argument except the return value is REAL for a COMPLEX argument.

Example:

```
program test_abs
  integer :: i = -1
  real :: x = -1.e0
  complex :: z = (-1.e0,0.e0)
  i = abs(i)
  x = abs(x)
  x = abs(z)
end program test_abs
```

Specific names:

Name	Argument	Return type	Standard
ABS(A)	REAL(4) A	REAL(4)	Fortran 77 and later
CABS(A)	COMPLEX(4) A	REAL(4)	Fortran 77 and later
DABS(A)	REAL(8) A	REAL(8)	Fortran 77 and later
IABS(A)	INTEGER(4) A	INTEGER(4)	Fortran 77 and later
ZABS(A)	COMPLEX(8) A	COMPLEX(8)	GNU extension
CDABS(A)	COMPLEX(8) A	COMPLEX(8)	GNU extension

9.4 ACCESS — Checks file access modes

Description:

      ACCESS(NAME, MODE) checks whether the file *NAME* exists, is readable, writable or executable. Except for the executable check, ACCESS can be replaced by Fortran 95's INQUIRE.

Standard: GNU extension

Class: Inquiry function

Syntax: `RESULT = ACCESS(NAME, MODE)`

Arguments:

NAME	Scalar **CHARACTER** of default kind with the file name. Tailing blank are ignored unless the character **achar(0)** is present, then all characters up to and excluding **achar(0)** are used as file name.
MODE	Scalar **CHARACTER** of default kind with the file access mode, may be any concatenation of "**r**" (readable), "**w**" (writable) and "**x**" (executable), or " " to check for existence.

Return value:

Returns a scalar **INTEGER**, which is 0 if the file is accessible in the given mode; otherwise or if an invalid argument has been given for **MODE** the value 1 is returned.

Example:

```
program access_test
  implicit none
  character(len=*), parameter :: file  = 'test.dat'
  character(len=*), parameter :: file2 = 'test.dat  '//achar(0)
  if(access(file,' ') == 0) print *, trim(file),' is exists'
  if(access(file,'r') == 0) print *, trim(file),' is readable'
  if(access(file,'w') == 0) print *, trim(file),' is writable'
  if(access(file,'x') == 0) print *, trim(file),' is executable'
  if(access(file2,'rwx') == 0) &
    print *, trim(file2),' is readable, writable and executable'
end program access_test
```

Specific names:
See also:

9.5 ACHAR — Character in ASCII collating sequence

Description:

ACHAR(I) returns the character located at position I in the ASCII collating sequence.

Standard: Fortran 77 and later, with *KIND* argument Fortran 2003 and later

Class: Elemental function

Syntax: `RESULT = ACHAR(I [, KIND])`

Arguments:

I	The type shall be **INTEGER**.
KIND	(Optional) An **INTEGER** initialization expression indicating the kind parameter of the result.

Return value:

The return value is of type **CHARACTER** with a length of one. If the *KIND* argument is present, the return value is of the specified kind and of the default kind otherwise.

Example:

```
program test_achar
  character c
  c = achar(32)
end program test_achar
```

Note: See Section 9.135 [ICHAR], page 170 for a discussion of converting between numerical values and formatted string representations.

See also: Section 9.55 [CHAR], page 119, Section 9.127 [IACHAR], page 165, Section 9.135 [ICHAR], page 170

9.6 ACOS — Arccosine function

Description:

ACOS(X) computes the arccosine of X (inverse of COS(X)).

Standard: Fortran 77 and later, for a complex argument Fortran 2008 or later

Class: Elemental function

Syntax: RESULT = ACOS(X)

Arguments:

| X | The type shall either be REAL with a magnitude that is less than or equal to one - or the type shall be COMPLEX. |

Return value:

The return value is of the same type and kind as X. The real part of the result is in radians and lies in the range $0 \leq \Re\, acos(x) \leq \pi$.

Example:

```
program test_acos
  real(8) :: x = 0.866_8
  x = acos(x)
end program test_acos
```

Specific names:

Name	Argument	Return type	Standard
ACOS(X)	REAL(4) X	REAL(4)	Fortran 77 and later
DACOS(X)	REAL(8) X	REAL(8)	Fortran 77 and later

See also: Inverse function: Section 9.69 [COS], page 128

9.7 ACOSH — Inverse hyperbolic cosine function

Description:

ACOSH(X) computes the inverse hyperbolic cosine of X.

Standard: Fortran 2008 and later

Class: Elemental function

Syntax: RESULT = ACOSH(X)

Arguments:

| X | The type shall be REAL or COMPLEX. |

Return value:

> The return value has the same type and kind as X. If X is complex, the imaginary part of the result is in radians and lies between $0 \leq \Im \, acosh(x) \leq \pi$.

Example:

```
PROGRAM test_acosh
  REAL(8), DIMENSION(3) :: x = (/ 1.0, 2.0, 3.0 /)
  WRITE (*,*) ACOSH(x)
END PROGRAM
```

Specific names:

Name	Argument	Return type	Standard
DACOSH(X)	REAL(8) X	REAL(8)	GNU extension

See also: Inverse function: Section 9.70 [COSH], page 129

9.8 ADJUSTL — Left adjust a string

Description:

> ADJUSTL(STRING) will left adjust a string by removing leading spaces. Spaces are inserted at the end of the string as needed.

Standard: Fortran 90 and later

Class: Elemental function

Syntax: RESULT = ADJUSTL(STRING)

Arguments:

> *STRING*   The type shall be CHARACTER.

Return value:

> The return value is of type CHARACTER and of the same kind as *STRING* where leading spaces are removed and the same number of spaces are inserted on the end of *STRING*.

Example:

```
program test_adjustl
  character(len=20) :: str = '   gfortran'
  str = adjustl(str)
  print *, str
end program test_adjustl
```

See also: Section 9.9 [ADJUSTR], page 89, Section 9.264 [TRIM], page 243

9.9 ADJUSTR — Right adjust a string

Description:

> ADJUSTR(STRING) will right adjust a string by removing trailing spaces. Spaces are inserted at the start of the string as needed.

Standard: Fortran 95 and later

Class: Elemental function

Syntax: RESULT = ADJUSTR(STRING)

Arguments:

       STR   The type shall be **CHARACTER**.

Return value:

       The return value is of type **CHARACTER** and of the same kind as *STRING* where trailing spaces are removed and the same number of spaces are inserted at the start of *STRING*.

Example:

```
program test_adjustr
  character(len=20) :: str = 'gfortran'
  str = adjustr(str)
  print *, str
end program test_adjustr
```

See also: Section 9.8 [ADJUSTL], page 89, Section 9.264 [TRIM], page 243

9.10 AIMAG — Imaginary part of complex number

Description:

       AIMAG(Z) yields the imaginary part of complex argument **Z**. The **IMAG(Z)** and **IMAGPART(Z)** intrinsic functions are provided for compatibility with **g77**, and their use in new code is strongly discouraged.

Standard: Fortran 77 and later, has overloads that are GNU extensions

Class: Elemental function

Syntax: **RESULT = AIMAG(Z)**

Arguments:

       Z   The type of the argument shall be **COMPLEX**.

Return value:

       The return value is of type **REAL** with the kind type parameter of the argument.

Example:

```
program test_aimag
  complex(4) z4
  complex(8) z8
  z4 = cmplx(1.e0_4, 0.e0_4)
  z8 = cmplx(0.e0_8, 1.e0_8)
  print *, aimag(z4), dimag(z8)
end program test_aimag
```

Specific names:

Name	Argument	Return type	Standard
AIMAG(Z)	COMPLEX Z	REAL	GNU extension
DIMAG(Z)	COMPLEX(8) Z	REAL(8)	GNU extension
IMAG(Z)	COMPLEX Z	REAL	GNU extension
IMAGPART(Z)	COMPLEX Z	REAL	GNU extension

9.11 AINT — Truncate to a whole number

Description:

AINT(A [, KIND]) truncates its argument to a whole number.

Standard: Fortran 77 and later

Class: Elemental function

Syntax: RESULT = AINT(A [, KIND])

Arguments:

A	The type of the argument shall be REAL.
KIND	(Optional) An INTEGER initialization expression indicating the kind parameter of the result.

Return value:

The return value is of type REAL with the kind type parameter of the argument if the optional *KIND* is absent; otherwise, the kind type parameter will be given by *KIND*. If the magnitude of X is less than one, AINT(X) returns zero. If the magnitude is equal to or greater than one then it returns the largest whole number that does not exceed its magnitude. The sign is the same as the sign of X.

Example:

```
program test_aint
  real(4) x4
  real(8) x8
  x4 = 1.234E0_4
  x8 = 4.321_8
  print *, aint(x4), dint(x8)
  x8 = aint(x4,8)
end program test_aint
```

Specific names:

Name	Argument	Return type	Standard
AINT(A)	REAL(4) A	REAL(4)	Fortran 77 and later
DINT(A)	REAL(8) A	REAL(8)	Fortran 77 and later

9.12 ALARM — Execute a routine after a given delay

Description:

ALARM(SECONDS, HANDLER [, STATUS]) causes external subroutine *HANDLER* to be executed after a delay of *SECONDS* by using alarm(2) to set up a signal and signal(2) to catch it. If *STATUS* is supplied, it will be returned with the number of seconds remaining until any previously scheduled alarm was due to be delivered, or zero if there was no previously scheduled alarm.

Standard: GNU extension

Class: Subroutine

Syntax: CALL ALARM(SECONDS, HANDLER [, STATUS])

Arguments:

SECONDS	The type of the argument shall be a scalar `INTEGER`. It is `INTENT(IN)`.
HANDLER	Signal handler (`INTEGER FUNCTION` or `SUBROUTINE`) or dummy/global `INTEGER` scalar. The scalar values may be either `SIG_IGN=1` to ignore the alarm generated or `SIG_DFL=0` to set the default action. It is `INTENT(IN)`.
STATUS	(Optional) *STATUS* shall be a scalar variable of the default `INTEGER` kind. It is `INTENT(OUT)`.

Example:

```
program test_alarm
  external handler_print
  integer i
  call alarm (3, handler_print, i)
  print *, i
  call sleep(10)
end program test_alarm
```

This will cause the external routine *handler_print* to be called after 3 seconds.

9.13 ALL — All values in *MASK* along *DIM* are true

Description:

ALL(MASK [, DIM]) determines if all the values are true in *MASK* in the array along dimension *DIM*.

Standard: Fortran 95 and later

Class: Transformational function

Syntax: `RESULT = ALL(MASK [, DIM])`

Arguments:

MASK	The type of the argument shall be `LOGICAL` and it shall not be scalar.
DIM	(Optional) *DIM* shall be a scalar integer with a value that lies between one and the rank of *MASK*.

Return value:

ALL(MASK) returns a scalar value of type `LOGICAL` where the kind type parameter is the same as the kind type parameter of *MASK*. If *DIM* is present, then `ALL(MASK, DIM)` returns an array with the rank of *MASK* minus 1. The shape is determined from the shape of *MASK* where the *DIM* dimension is elided.

(A)	`ALL(MASK)` is true if all elements of *MASK* are true. It also is true if *MASK* has zero size; otherwise, it is false.
(B)	If the rank of *MASK* is one, then `ALL(MASK,DIM)` is equivalent to `ALL(MASK)`. If the rank is greater than one, then `ALL(MASK,DIM)` is determined by applying `ALL` to the array sections.

Example:

```
program test_all
  logical l
  l = all((/.true., .true., .true./))
  print *, l
  call section
  contains
    subroutine section
      integer a(2,3), b(2,3)
      a = 1
      b = 1
      b(2,2) = 2
      print *, all(a .eq. b, 1)
      print *, all(a .eq. b, 2)
    end subroutine section
end program test_all
```

9.14 ALLOCATED — Status of an allocatable entity

Description:

ALLOCATED(ARRAY) and ALLOCATED(SCALAR) check the allocation status of *AR-RAY* and *SCALAR*, respectively.

Standard: Fortran 95 and later. Note, the SCALAR= keyword and allocatable scalar entities are available in Fortran 2003 and later.

Class: Inquiry function

Syntax:

RESULT = ALLOCATED(ARRAY)
RESULT = ALLOCATED(SCALAR)

Arguments:

ARRAY	The argument shall be an ALLOCATABLE array.
SCALAR	The argument shall be an ALLOCATABLE scalar.

Return value:

The return value is a scalar LOGICAL with the default logical kind type parameter. If the argument is allocated, then the result is .TRUE.; otherwise, it returns .FALSE.

Example:

```
program test_allocated
  integer :: i = 4
  real(4), allocatable :: x(:)
  if (.not. allocated(x)) allocate(x(i))
end program test_allocated
```

9.15 AND — Bitwise logical AND

Description:

Bitwise logical AND.

This intrinsic routine is provided for backwards compatibility with GNU Fortran 77. For integer arguments, programmers should consider the use of the Section 9.129 [IAND], page 167 intrinsic defined by the Fortran standard.

Standard: GNU extension

Class: Function

Syntax: RESULT = AND(I, J)

Arguments:

    I   The type shall be either a scalar `INTEGER` type or a scalar `LOGICAL` type.

    J   The type shall be the same as the type of *I*.

Return value:

The return type is either a scalar `INTEGER` or a scalar `LOGICAL`. If the kind type parameters differ, then the smaller kind type is implicitly converted to larger kind, and the return has the larger kind.

Example:

```
PROGRAM test_and
  LOGICAL :: T = .TRUE., F = .FALSE.
  INTEGER :: a, b
  DATA a / Z'F' /, b / Z'3' /

  WRITE (*,*) AND(T, T), AND(T, F), AND(F, T), AND(F, F)
  WRITE (*,*) AND(a, b)
END PROGRAM
```

See also: Fortran 95 elemental function: Section 9.129 [IAND], page 167

9.16 `ANINT` — Nearest whole number

Description:

`ANINT(A [, KIND])` rounds its argument to the nearest whole number.

Standard: Fortran 77 and later

Class: Elemental function

Syntax: RESULT = ANINT(A [, KIND])

Arguments:

    A   The type of the argument shall be `REAL`.

    KIND   (Optional) An `INTEGER` initialization expression indicating the kind parameter of the result.

Return value:

The return value is of type real with the kind type parameter of the argument if the optional *KIND* is absent; otherwise, the kind type parameter will be given by *KIND*. If *A* is greater than zero, `ANINT(A)` returns `AINT(X+0.5)`. If *A* is less than or equal to zero then it returns `AINT(X-0.5)`.

Example:

```
program test_anint
  real(4) x4
  real(8) x8
  x4 = 1.234E0_4
  x8 = 4.321_8
```

```
            print *, anint(x4), dnint(x8)
            x8 = anint(x4,8)
        end program test_anint
```

Specific names:

Name	Argument	Return type	Standard
AINT(A)	REAL(4) A	REAL(4)	Fortran 77 and later
DNINT(A)	REAL(8) A	REAL(8)	Fortran 77 and later

9.17 ANY — Any value in *MASK* along *DIM* is true

Description:

ANY(MASK [, DIM]) determines if any of the values in the logical array *MASK* along dimension *DIM* are .TRUE..

Standard: Fortran 95 and later

Class: Transformational function

Syntax: RESULT = ANY(MASK [, DIM])

Arguments:

MASK   The type of the argument shall be LOGICAL and it shall not be scalar.

DIM   (Optional) *DIM* shall be a scalar integer with a value that lies between one and the rank of *MASK*.

Return value:

ANY(MASK) returns a scalar value of type LOGICAL where the kind type parameter is the same as the kind type parameter of *MASK*. If *DIM* is present, then ANY(MASK, DIM) returns an array with the rank of *MASK* minus 1. The shape is determined from the shape of *MASK* where the *DIM* dimension is elided.

(A)   ANY(MASK) is true if any element of *MASK* is true; otherwise, it is false. It also is false if *MASK* has zero size.

(B)   If the rank of *MASK* is one, then ANY(MASK,DIM) is equivalent to ANY(MASK). If the rank is greater than one, then ANY(MASK,DIM) is determined by applying ANY to the array sections.

Example:

```
        program test_any
          logical l
          l = any((/.true., .true., .true./))
          print *, l
          call section
          contains
            subroutine section
              integer a(2,3), b(2,3)
              a = 1
              b = 1
              b(2,2) = 2
              print *, any(a .eq. b, 1)
              print *, any(a .eq. b, 2)
            end subroutine section
        end program test_any
```

9.18 ASIN — Arcsine function

Description:

ASIN(X) computes the arcsine of its X (inverse of SIN(X)).

Standard: Fortran 77 and later, for a complex argument Fortran 2008 or later

Class: Elemental function

Syntax: RESULT = ASIN(X)

Arguments:

X   The type shall be either REAL and a magnitude that is less than or equal to one - or be COMPLEX.

Return value:

The return value is of the same type and kind as X. The real part of the result is in radians and lies in the range $-\pi/2 \le \Re\, asin(x) \le \pi/2$.

Example:

```
program test_asin
  real(8) :: x = 0.866_8
  x = asin(x)
end program test_asin
```

Specific names:

Name	Argument	Return type	Standard
ASIN(X)	REAL(4) X	REAL(4)	Fortran 77 and later
DASIN(X)	REAL(8) X	REAL(8)	Fortran 77 and later

See also: Inverse function: Section 9.240 [SIN], page 228

9.19 ASINH — Inverse hyperbolic sine function

Description:

ASINH(X) computes the inverse hyperbolic sine of X.

Standard: Fortran 2008 and later

Class: Elemental function

Syntax: RESULT = ASINH(X)

Arguments:

X   The type shall be REAL or COMPLEX.

Return value:

The return value is of the same type and kind as X. If X is complex, the imaginary part of the result is in radians and lies between $-\pi/2 \le \Im\, asinh(x) \le \pi/2$.

Example:

```
PROGRAM test_asinh
  REAL(8), DIMENSION(3) :: x = (/ -1.0, 0.0, 1.0 /)
  WRITE (*,*) ASINH(x)
END PROGRAM
```

Specific names:

Name	Argument	Return type	Standard
DASINH(X)	REAL(8) X	REAL(8)	GNU extension.

See also: Inverse function: Section 9.241 [SINH], page 229

9.20 ASSOCIATED — Status of a pointer or pointer/target pair

Description:

ASSOCIATED(POINTER [, TARGET]) determines the status of the pointer *POINTER* or if *POINTER* is associated with the target *TARGET*.

Standard: Fortran 95 and later

Class: Inquiry function

Syntax: RESULT = ASSOCIATED(POINTER [, TARGET])

Arguments:

POINTER	*POINTER* shall have the POINTER attribute and it can be of any type.
TARGET	(Optional) *TARGET* shall be a pointer or a target. It must have the same type, kind type parameter, and array rank as *POINTER*.

The association status of neither *POINTER* nor *TARGET* shall be undefined.

Return value:

ASSOCIATED(POINTER) returns a scalar value of type LOGICAL(4). There are several cases:

(A) When the optional *TARGET* is not present then
ASSOCIATED(POINTER) is true if *POINTER* is associated with a target; otherwise, it returns false.

(B) If *TARGET* is present and a scalar target, the result is true if *TARGET* is not a zero-sized storage sequence and the target associated with *POINTER* occupies the same storage units. If *POINTER* is disassociated, the result is false.

(C) If *TARGET* is present and an array target, the result is true if *TARGET* and *POINTER* have the same shape, are not zero-sized arrays, are arrays whose elements are not zero-sized storage sequences, and *TARGET* and *POINTER* occupy the same storage units in array element order. As in case(B), the result is false, if *POINTER* is disassociated.

(D) If *TARGET* is present and an scalar pointer, the result is true if *TARGET* is associated with *POINTER*, the target associated with *TARGET* are not zero-sized storage sequences and occupy the same storage units. The result is false, if either *TARGET* or *POINTER* is disassociated.

(E) If *TARGET* is present and an array pointer, the result is true if target associated with *POINTER* and the target associated with *TARGET* have the same shape, are not zero-sized arrays, are arrays whose elements are not zero-sized storage sequences, and *TARGET* and *POINTER* occupy the same storage units in array element order. The result is false, if either *TARGET* or *POINTER* is disassociated.

Example:

```
program test_associated
  implicit none
  real, target  :: tgt(2) = (/1., 2./)
  real, pointer :: ptr(:)
  ptr => tgt
  if (associated(ptr)     .eqv. .false.) call abort
  if (associated(ptr,tgt) .eqv. .false.) call abort
end program test_associated
```

See also: Section 9.201 [NULL], page 206

9.21 ATAN — Arctangent function

Description:

ATAN(X) computes the arctangent of *X*.

Standard: Fortran 77 and later, for a complex argument and for two arguments Fortran 2008 or later

Class: Elemental function

Syntax:

```
RESULT = ATAN(X)
RESULT = ATAN(Y, X)
```

Arguments:

X   The type shall be **REAL** or **COMPLEX**; if *Y* is present, *X* shall be REAL.

Y shall be of the same type and kind as *X*.

Return value:

The return value is of the same type and kind as *X*. If *Y* is present, the result is identical to ATAN2(Y,X). Otherwise, it the arcus tangent of *X*, where the real part of the result is in radians and lies in the range $-\pi/2 \le \Re\mathrm{atan}(x) \le \pi/2$.

Example:

```
program test_atan
  real(8) :: x = 2.866_8
  x = atan(x)
end program test_atan
```

Specific names:

Name	Argument	Return type	Standard
`ATAN(X)`	`REAL(4) X`	`REAL(4)`	Fortran 77 and later
`DATAN(X)`	`REAL(8) X`	`REAL(8)`	Fortran 77 and later

See also: Inverse function: Section 9.255 [TAN], page 238

9.22 `ATAN2` — **Arctangent function**

Description:

`ATAN2(Y, X)` computes the principal value of the argument function of the complex number $X+iY$. This function can be used to transform from Cartesian into polar coordinates and allows to determine the angle in the correct quadrant.

Standard: Fortran 77 and later

Class: Elemental function

Syntax: `RESULT = ATAN2(Y, X)`

Arguments:

Y	The type shall be `REAL`.
X	The type and kind type parameter shall be the same as Y. If Y is zero, then X must be nonzero.

Return value:

The return value has the same type and kind type parameter as Y. It is the principal value of the complex number $X + iY$. If X is nonzero, then it lies in the range $-\pi \le \mathrm{atan}(x) \le \pi$. The sign is positive if Y is positive. If Y is zero, then the return value is zero if X is strictly positive, π if X is negative and Y is positive zero (or the processor does not handle signed zeros), and $-\pi$ if X is negative and Y is negative zero. Finally, if X is zero, then the magnitude of the result is $\pi/2$.

Example:

```
program test_atan2
  real(4) :: x = 1.e0_4, y = 0.5e0_4
  x = atan2(y,x)
end program test_atan2
```

Specific names:

Name	Argument	Return type	Standard
`ATAN2(X, Y)`	`REAL(4) X, Y`	`REAL(4)`	Fortran 77 and later
`DATAN2(X, Y)`	`REAL(8) X, Y`	`REAL(8)`	Fortran 77 and later

9.23 `ATANH` — **Inverse hyperbolic tangent function**

Description:

`ATANH(X)` computes the inverse hyperbolic tangent of X.

Standard: Fortran 2008 and later

Class: Elemental function

Syntax: RESULT = ATANH(X)

Arguments:

X   The type shall be REAL or COMPLEX.

Return value:

The return value has same type and kind as X. If X is complex, the imaginary part of the result is in radians and lies between $-\pi/2 \leq \Im\,\mathrm{atanh}(x) \leq \pi/2$.

Example:

```
PROGRAM test_atanh
  REAL, DIMENSION(3) :: x = (/ -1.0, 0.0, 1.0 /)
  WRITE (*,*) ATANH(x)
END PROGRAM
```

Specific names:

Name	Argument	Return type	Standard
DATANH(X)	REAL(8) X	REAL(8)	GNU extension

See also: Inverse function: Section 9.256 [TANH], page 238

9.24 ATOMIC_ADD — Atomic ADD operation

Description:

ATOMIC_ADD(ATOM, VALUE) atomically adds the value of *VAR* to the variable *ATOM*. When *STAT* is present and the invokation was successful, it is assigned the value 0. If it is present and the invokation has failed, it is assigned a positive value; in particular, for a coindexed *ATOM*, if the remote image has stopped, it is assigned the value of ISO_FORTRAN_ENV's STAT_STOPPED_IMAGE and if the remote image has failed, the value STAT_FAILED_IMAGE.

Standard: TS 18508 or later

Class: Atomic subroutine

Syntax: CALL ATOMIC_ADD (ATOM, VALUE [, STAT])

Arguments:

ATOM   Scalar coarray or coindexed variable of integer type with ATOMIC_INT_KIND kind.

VALUE   Scalar of the same type as *ATOM*. If the kind is different, the value is converted to the kind of *ATOM*.

STAT   (optional) Scalar default-kind integer variable.

Example:

```
program atomic
  use iso_fortran_env
  integer(atomic_int_kind) :: atom[*]
  call atomic_add (atom[1], this_image())
end program atomic
```

See also: Section 9.27 [ATOMIC_DEFINE], page 102, Section 9.28 [ATOMIC_FETCH_ADD], page 103, Section 10.1 [ISO_FORTRAN_ENV], page 249, Section 9.25 [ATOMIC_AND], page 101, Section 9.32 [ATOMIC_OR], page 106, Section 9.34 [ATOMIC_XOR], page 107

9.25 ATOMIC_AND — Atomic bitwise AND operation

Description:

ATOMIC_AND(ATOM, VALUE) atomically defines *ATOM* with the bitwise AND between the values of *ATOM* and *VALUE*. When *STAT* is present and the invokation was successful, it is assigned the value 0. If it is present and the invokation has failed, it is assigned a positive value; in particular, for a coindexed *ATOM*, if the remote image has stopped, it is assigned the value of ISO_FORTRAN_ENV's STAT_STOPPED_IMAGE and if the remote image has failed, the value STAT_FAILED_IMAGE.

Standard: TS 18508 or later

Class: Atomic subroutine

Syntax: CALL ATOMIC_AND (ATOM, VALUE [, STAT])

Arguments:

ATOM	Scalar coarray or coindexed variable of integer type with ATOMIC_INT_KIND kind.
VALUE	Scalar of the same type as *ATOM*. If the kind is different, the value is converted to the kind of *ATOM*.
STAT	(optional) Scalar default-kind integer variable.

Example:

```
program atomic
  use iso_fortran_env
  integer(atomic_int_kind) :: atom[*]
  call atomic_and (atom[1], int(b'10100011101'))
end program atomic
```

See also: Section 9.27 [ATOMIC_DEFINE], page 102, Section 9.29 [ATOMIC_FETCH_AND], page 103, Section 10.1 [ISO_FORTRAN_ENV], page 249, Section 9.24 [ATOMIC_ADD], page 100, Section 9.32 [ATOMIC_OR], page 106, Section 9.34 [ATOMIC_XOR], page 107

9.26 ATOMIC_CAS — Atomic compare and swap

Description:

ATOMIC_CAS compares the variable *ATOM* with the value of *COMPARE*; if the value is the same, *ATOM* is set to the value of *NEW*. Additionally, *OLD* is set to the value of *ATOM* that was used for the comparison. When *STAT* is present and the invokation was successful, it is assigned the value 0. If it is present and the invokation has failed, it is assigned a positive value; in particular, for a coindexed *ATOM*, if the remote image has stopped, it is assigned the value of ISO_FORTRAN_ENV's STAT_STOPPED_IMAGE and if the remote image has failed, the value STAT_FAILED_IMAGE.

Standard: TS 18508 or later

Class: Atomic subroutine

Syntax: CALL ATOMIC_CAS (ATOM, OLD, COMPARE, NEW [, STAT])

Arguments:

ATOM	Scalar coarray or coindexed variable of either integer type with `ATOMIC_INT_KIND` kind or logical type with `ATOMIC_LOGICAL_KIND` kind.
OLD	Scalar of the same type and kind as *ATOM*.
COMPARE	Scalar variable of the same type and kind as *ATOM*.
NEW	Scalar variable of the same type as *ATOM*. If kind is different, the value is converted to the kind of *ATOM*.
STAT	(optional) Scalar default-kind integer variable.

Example:

```
program atomic
  use iso_fortran_env
  logical(atomic_logical_kind) :: atom[*], prev
  call atomic_cas (atom[1], prev, .false., .true.))
end program atomic
```

See also: Section 9.27 [ATOMIC_DEFINE], page 102, Section 9.33 [ATOMIC_REF], page 106, Section 10.1 [ISO_FORTRAN_ENV], page 249

9.27 `ATOMIC_DEFINE` — **Setting a variable atomically**

Description:

ATOMIC_DEFINE(ATOM, VALUE) defines the variable *ATOM* with the value *VALUE* atomically. When *STAT* is present and the invokation was successful, it is assigned the value 0. If it is present and the invokation has failed, it is assigned a positive value; in particular, for a coindexed *ATOM*, if the remote image has stopped, it is assigned the value of `ISO_FORTRAN_ENV`'s `STAT_STOPPED_IMAGE` and if the remote image has failed, the value `STAT_FAILED_IMAGE`.

Standard: Fortran 2008 and later; with *STAT*, TS 18508 or later

Class: Atomic subroutine

Syntax: `CALL ATOMIC_DEFINE (ATOM, VALUE [, STAT])`

Arguments:

ATOM	Scalar coarray or coindexed variable of either integer type with `ATOMIC_INT_KIND` kind or logical type with `ATOMIC_LOGICAL_KIND` kind.
VALUE	Scalar of the same type as *ATOM*. If the kind is different, the value is converted to the kind of *ATOM*.
STAT	(optional) Scalar default-kind integer variable.

Example:

```
program atomic
  use iso_fortran_env
  integer(atomic_int_kind) :: atom[*]
  call atomic_define (atom[1], this_image())
end program atomic
```

See also: Section 9.33 [ATOMIC_REF], page 106, Section 9.26 [ATOMIC_CAS], page 101, Section 10.1 [ISO_FORTRAN_ENV], page 249, Section 9.24 [ATOMIC_ADD], page 100, Section 9.25 [ATOMIC_AND], page 101, Section 9.32 [ATOMIC_OR], page 106, Section 9.34 [ATOMIC_XOR], page 107

9.28 `ATOMIC_FETCH_ADD` — Atomic ADD operation with prior fetch

Description:

ATOMIC_FETCH_ADD(ATOM, VALUE, OLD) atomically stores the value of *ATOM* in *OLD* and adds the value of *VAR* to the variable *ATOM*. When *STAT* is present and the invokation was successful, it is assigned the value 0. If it is present and the invokation has failed, it is assigned a positive value; in particular, for a coindexed *ATOM*, if the remote image has stopped, it is assigned the value of ISO_FORTRAN_ENV's STAT_STOPPED_IMAGE and if the remote image has failed, the value STAT_FAILED_IMAGE.

Standard: TS 18508 or later

Class: Atomic subroutine

Syntax: `CALL ATOMIC_FETCH_ADD (ATOM, VALUE, old [, STAT])`

Arguments:

ATOM	Scalar coarray or coindexed variable of integer type with ATOMIC_INT_KIND kind. ATOMIC_LOGICAL_KIND kind.
VALUE	Scalar of the same type as *ATOM*. If the kind is different, the value is converted to the kind of *ATOM*.
OLD	Scalar of the same type and kind as *ATOM*.
STAT	(optional) Scalar default-kind integer variable.

Example:

```
program atomic
  use iso_fortran_env
  integer(atomic_int_kind) :: atom[*], old
  call atomic_add (atom[1], this_image(), old)
end program atomic
```

See also: Section 9.27 [ATOMIC_DEFINE], page 102, Section 9.24 [ATOMIC_ADD], page 100, Section 10.1 [ISO_FORTRAN_ENV], page 249, Section 9.29 [ATOMIC_FETCH_AND], page 103, Section 9.30 [ATOMIC_FETCH_OR], page 104, Section 9.31 [ATOMIC_FETCH_XOR], page 105

9.29 `ATOMIC_FETCH_AND` — Atomic bitwise AND operation with prior fetch

Description:

ATOMIC_AND(ATOM, VALUE) atomically stores the value of *ATOM* in *OLD* and defines *ATOM* with the bitwise AND between the values of *ATOM* and *VALUE*. When *STAT* is present and the invokation was successful, it is

assigned the value 0. If it is present and the invocation has failed, it is assigned
a positive value; in particular, for a coindexed *ATOM*, if the remote image has
stopped, it is assigned the value of `ISO_FORTRAN_ENV`'s `STAT_STOPPED_IMAGE`
and if the remote image has failed, the value `STAT_FAILED_IMAGE`.

Standard: TS 18508 or later

Class: Atomic subroutine

Syntax: `CALL ATOMIC_FETCH_AND (ATOM, VALUE, OLD [, STAT])`

Arguments:

ATOM	Scalar coarray or coindexed variable of integer type with `ATOMIC_INT_KIND` kind.
VALUE	Scalar of the same type as *ATOM*. If the kind is different, the value is converted to the kind of *ATOM*.
OLD	Scalar of the same type and kind as *ATOM*.
STAT	(optional) Scalar default-kind integer variable.

Example:

```
program atomic
  use iso_fortran_env
  integer(atomic_int_kind) :: atom[*], old
  call atomic_fetch_and (atom[1], int(b'10100011101'), old)
end program atomic
```

See also: Section 9.27 [ATOMIC_DEFINE], page 102, Section 9.25 [ATOMIC_AND],
                page 101, Section 10.1 [ISO_FORTRAN_ENV], page 249, Section 9.28
                [ATOMIC_FETCH_ADD], page 103, Section 9.30 [ATOMIC_FETCH_OR],
                page 104, Section 9.31 [ATOMIC_FETCH_XOR], page 105

9.30 `ATOMIC_FETCH_OR` — Atomic bitwise OR operation with prior fetch

Description:

`ATOMIC_OR(ATOM, VALUE)` atomically stores the value of *ATOM* in *OLD* and
defines *ATOM* with the bitwise OR between the values of *ATOM* and *VALUE*.
When *STAT* is present and the invokation was successful, it is assigned the
value 0. If it is present and the invokation has failed, it is assigned a positive
value; in particular, for a coindexed *ATOM*, if the remote image has stopped,
it is assigned the value of `ISO_FORTRAN_ENV`'s `STAT_STOPPED_IMAGE` and if the
remote image has failed, the value `STAT_FAILED_IMAGE`.

Standard: TS 18508 or later

Class: Atomic subroutine

Syntax: `CALL ATOMIC_FETCH_OR (ATOM, VALUE, OLD [, STAT])`

Arguments:

ATOM	Scalar coarray or coindexed variable of integer type with `ATOMIC_INT_KIND` kind.
VALUE	Scalar of the same type as *ATOM*. If the kind is different, the value is converted to the kind of *ATOM*.

OLD	Scalar of the same type and kind as *ATOM*.
STAT	(optional) Scalar default-kind integer variable.

Example:

```
program atomic
  use iso_fortran_env
  integer(atomic_int_kind) :: atom[*], old
  call atomic_fetch_or (atom[1], int(b'10100011101'), old)
end program atomic
```

See also: Section 9.27 [ATOMIC_DEFINE], page 102, Section 9.32 [ATOMIC_OR], page 106, Section 10.1 [ISO_FORTRAN_ENV], page 249, Section 9.28 [ATOMIC_FETCH_ADD], page 103, Section 9.29 [ATOMIC_FETCH_AND], page 103, Section 9.31 [ATOMIC_FETCH_XOR], page 105

9.31 ATOMIC_FETCH_XOR — Atomic bitwise XOR operation with prior fetch

Description:

ATOMIC_XOR(ATOM, VALUE) atomically stores the value of *ATOM* in *OLD* and defines *ATOM* with the bitwise XOR between the values of *ATOM* and *VALUE*. When *STAT* is present and the invokation was successful, it is assigned the value 0. If it is present and the invokation has failed, it is assigned a positive value; in particular, for a coindexed *ATOM*, if the remote image has stopped, it is assigned the value of ISO_FORTRAN_ENV's STAT_STOPPED_IMAGE and if the remote image has failed, the value STAT_FAILED_IMAGE.

Standard: TS 18508 or later

Class: Atomic subroutine

Syntax: CALL ATOMIC_FETCH_XOR (ATOM, VALUE, OLD [, STAT])

Arguments:

ATOM	Scalar coarray or coindexed variable of integer type with ATOMIC_INT_KIND kind.
VALUE	Scalar of the same type as *ATOM*. If the kind is different, the value is converted to the kind of *ATOM*.
OLD	Scalar of the same type and kind as *ATOM*.
STAT	(optional) Scalar default-kind integer variable.

Example:

```
program atomic
  use iso_fortran_env
  integer(atomic_int_kind) :: atom[*], old
  call atomic_fetch_xor (atom[1], int(b'10100011101'), old)
end program atomic
```

See also: Section 9.27 [ATOMIC_DEFINE], page 102, Section 9.34 [ATOMIC_XOR], page 107, Section 10.1 [ISO_FORTRAN_ENV], page 249, Section 9.28 [ATOMIC_FETCH_ADD], page 103, Section 9.29 [ATOMIC_FETCH_AND], page 103, Section 9.30 [ATOMIC_FETCH_OR], page 104

9.32 `ATOMIC_OR` — Atomic bitwise OR operation

Description:

ATOMIC_OR(ATOM, VALUE) atomically defines *ATOM* with the bitwise AND between the values of *ATOM* and *VALUE*. When *STAT* is present and the invokation was successful, it is assigned the value 0. If it is present and the invokation has failed, it is assigned a positive value; in particular, for a coindexed *ATOM*, if the remote image has stopped, it is assigned the value of `ISO_FORTRAN_ENV`'s `STAT_STOPPED_IMAGE` and if the remote image has failed, the value `STAT_FAILED_IMAGE`.

Standard: TS 18508 or later

Class: Atomic subroutine

Syntax: `CALL ATOMIC_OR (ATOM, VALUE [, STAT])`

Arguments:

ATOM	Scalar coarray or coindexed variable of integer type with `ATOMIC_INT_KIND` kind.
VALUE	Scalar of the same type as *ATOM*. If the kind is different, the value is converted to the kind of *ATOM*.
STAT	(optional) Scalar default-kind integer variable.

Example:

```
program atomic
  use iso_fortran_env
  integer(atomic_int_kind) :: atom[*]
  call atomic_or (atom[1], int(b'10100011101'))
end program atomic
```

See also: Section 9.27 [ATOMIC_DEFINE], page 102, Section 9.30 [ATOMIC_FETCH_OR], page 104, Section 10.1 [ISO_FORTRAN_ENV], page 249, Section 9.24 [ATOMIC_ADD], page 100, Section 9.32 [ATOMIC_OR], page 106, Section 9.34 [ATOMIC_XOR], page 107

9.33 `ATOMIC_REF` — Obtaining the value of a variable atomically

Description:

ATOMIC_DEFINE(ATOM, VALUE) atomically assigns the value of the variable *ATOM* to *VALUE*. When *STAT* is present and the invokation was successful, it is assigned the value 0. If it is present and the invokation has failed, it is assigned a positive value; in particular, for a coindexed *ATOM*, if the remote image has stopped, it is assigned the value of `ISO_FORTRAN_ENV`'s `STAT_STOPPED_IMAGE` and if the remote image has failed, the value `STAT_FAILED_IMAGE`.

Standard: Fortran 2008 and later; with *STAT*, TS 18508 or later

Class: Atomic subroutine

Syntax: `CALL ATOMIC_REF(VALUE, ATOM [, STAT])`

Arguments:

VALUE	Scalar of the same type as *ATOM*. If the kind is different, the value is converted to the kind of *ATOM*.
ATOM	Scalar coarray or coindexed variable of either integer type with `ATOMIC_INT_KIND` kind or logical type with `ATOMIC_LOGICAL_KIND` kind.
STAT	(optional) Scalar default-kind integer variable.

Example:

```
program atomic
  use iso_fortran_env
  logical(atomic_logical_kind) :: atom[*]
  logical :: val
  call atomic_ref (atom, .false.)
  ! ...
  call atomic_ref (atom, val)
  if (val) then
    print *, "Obtained"
  end if
end program atomic
```

See also: Section 9.27 [ATOMIC_DEFINE], page 102, Section 9.26 [ATOMIC_CAS], page 101, Section 10.1 [ISO_FORTRAN_ENV], page 249, Section 9.28 [ATOMIC_FETCH_ADD], page 103, Section 9.29 [ATOMIC_FETCH_AND], page 103, Section 9.30 [ATOMIC_FETCH_OR], page 104, Section 9.31 [ATOMIC_FETCH_XOR], page 105

9.34 `ATOMIC_XOR` — Atomic bitwise OR operation

Description:

ATOMIC_AND(ATOM, VALUE) atomically defines *ATOM* with the bitwise XOR between the values of *ATOM* and *VALUE*. When *STAT* is present and the invokation was successful, it is assigned the value 0. If it is present and the invokation has failed, it is assigned a positive value; in particular, for a coindexed *ATOM*, if the remote image has stopped, it is assigned the value of `ISO_FORTRAN_ENV`'s `STAT_STOPPED_IMAGE` and if the remote image has failed, the value `STAT_FAILED_IMAGE`.

Standard: TS 18508 or later

Class: Atomic subroutine

Syntax: `CALL ATOMIC_XOR (ATOM, VALUE [, STAT])`

Arguments:

ATOM	Scalar coarray or coindexed variable of integer type with `ATOMIC_INT_KIND` kind.
VALUE	Scalar of the same type as *ATOM*. If the kind is different, the value is converted to the kind of *ATOM*.
STAT	(optional) Scalar default-kind integer variable.

Example:

```
program atomic
  use iso_fortran_env
  integer(atomic_int_kind) :: atom[*]
  call atomic_xor (atom[1], int(b'10100011101'))
end program atomic
```

See also: Section 9.27 [ATOMIC_DEFINE], page 102, Section 9.31 [ATOMIC_FETCH_XOR],
                page 105, Section 10.1 [ISO_FORTRAN_ENV], page 249, Section 9.24
                [ATOMIC_ADD], page 100, Section 9.32 [ATOMIC_OR], page 106,
                Section 9.34 [ATOMIC_XOR], page 107

9.35 BACKTRACE — Show a backtrace

Description:

BACKTRACE shows a backtrace at an arbitrary place in user code. Program
execution continues normally afterwards. The backtrace information is printed
to the unit corresponding to ERROR_UNIT in ISO_FORTRAN_ENV.

Standard: GNU Extension

Class: Subroutine

Syntax: CALL BACKTRACE

Arguments:
              None

See also: Section 9.2 [ABORT], page 85

9.36 BESSEL_J0 — Bessel function of the first kind of order 0

Description:

BESSEL_J0(X) computes the Bessel function of the first kind of order 0 of X.
This function is available under the name BESJ0 as a GNU extension.

Standard: Fortran 2008 and later

Class: Elemental function

Syntax: RESULT = BESSEL_J0(X)

Arguments:
              X The type shall be REAL.

Return value:

The return value is of type REAL and lies in the range $-0.4027... \leq Bessel(0,x) \leq 1$. It has the same kind as X.

Example:
```
program test_besj0
  real(8) :: x = 0.0_8
  x = bessel_j0(x)
end program test_besj0
```

Specific names:

Name	Argument	Return type	Standard
DBESJ0(X)	REAL(8) X	REAL(8)	GNU extension

9.37 BESSEL_J1 — Bessel function of the first kind of order 1

Description:

BESSEL_J1(X) computes the Bessel function of the first kind of order 1 of X. This function is available under the name BESJ1 as a GNU extension.

Standard: Fortran 2008

Class: Elemental function

Syntax: RESULT = BESSEL_J1(X)

Arguments:

X   The type shall be REAL.

Return value:

The return value is of type REAL and lies in the range $-0.5818... \leq Bessel(0, x) \leq 0.5818$. It has the same kind as X.

Example:

```
program test_besj1
  real(8) :: x = 1.0_8
  x = bessel_j1(x)
end program test_besj1
```

Specific names:

Name	Argument	Return type	Standard
DBESJ1(X)	REAL(8) X	REAL(8)	GNU extension

9.38 BESSEL_JN — Bessel function of the first kind

Description:

BESSEL_JN(N, X) computes the Bessel function of the first kind of order N of X. This function is available under the name BESJN as a GNU extension. If N and X are arrays, their ranks and shapes shall conform.

BESSEL_JN(N1, N2, X) returns an array with the Bessel functions of the first kind of the orders N1 to N2.

Standard: Fortran 2008 and later, negative N is allowed as GNU extension

Class: Elemental function, except for the transformational function BESSEL_JN(N1, N2, X)

Syntax:

RESULT = BESSEL_JN(N, X)
RESULT = BESSEL_JN(N1, N2, X)

Arguments:

N   Shall be a scalar or an array of type INTEGER.
N1   Shall be a non-negative scalar of type INTEGER.
N2   Shall be a non-negative scalar of type INTEGER.
X   Shall be a scalar or an array of type REAL; for BESSEL_JN(N1, N2, X) it shall be scalar.

Return value:

The return value is a scalar of type **REAL**. It has the same kind as *X*.

Note: The transformational function uses a recurrence algorithm which might, for some values of *X*, lead to different results than calls to the elemental function.

Example:

```
program test_besjn
  real(8) :: x = 1.0_8
  x = bessel_jn(5,x)
end program test_besjn
```

Specific names:

Name	Argument	Return type	Standard
DBESJN(N, X)	INTEGER N	REAL(8)	GNU extension
	REAL(8) X		

9.39 BESSEL_Y0 — Bessel function of the second kind of order 0

Description:

BESSEL_Y0(X) computes the Bessel function of the second kind of order 0 of *X*. This function is available under the name BESY0 as a GNU extension.

Standard: Fortran 2008 and later

Class: Elemental function

Syntax: RESULT = BESSEL_Y0(X)

Arguments:

X   The type shall be **REAL**.

Return value:

The return value is of type **REAL**. It has the same kind as *X*.

Example:

```
program test_besy0
  real(8) :: x = 0.0_8
  x = bessel_y0(x)
end program test_besy0
```

Specific names:

Name	Argument	Return type	Standard
DBESY0(X)	REAL(8) X	REAL(8)	GNU extension

9.40 BESSEL_Y1 — Bessel function of the second kind of order 1

Description:

BESSEL_Y1(X) computes the Bessel function of the second kind of order 1 of *X*. This function is available under the name BESY1 as a GNU extension.

Standard: Fortran 2008 and later

Class: Elemental function

Syntax: `RESULT = BESSEL_Y1(X)`

Arguments:

        X The type shall be `REAL`.

Return value:

        The return value is of type `REAL`. It has the same kind as X.

Example:

```
program test_besy1
  real(8) :: x = 1.0_8
  x = bessel_y1(x)
end program test_besy1
```

Specific names:

Name	Argument	Return type	Standard
DBESY1(X)	REAL(8) X	REAL(8)	GNU extension

9.41 BESSEL_YN — Bessel function of the second kind

Description:

        `BESSEL_YN(N, X)` computes the Bessel function of the second kind of order N of X. This function is available under the name `BESYN` as a GNU extension. If N and X are arrays, their ranks and shapes shall conform.

        `BESSEL_YN(N1, N2, X)` returns an array with the Bessel functions of the first kind of the orders $N1$ to $N2$.

Standard: Fortran 2008 and later, negative N is allowed as GNU extension

Class: Elemental function, except for the transformational function `BESSEL_YN(N1, N2, X)`

Syntax:

        `RESULT = BESSEL_YN(N, X)`
        `RESULT = BESSEL_YN(N1, N2, X)`

Arguments:

N	Shall be a scalar or an array of type `INTEGER` .
$N1$	Shall be a non-negative scalar of type `INTEGER`.
$N2$	Shall be a non-negative scalar of type `INTEGER`.
X	Shall be a scalar or an array of type `REAL`; for `BESSEL_YN(N1, N2, X)` it shall be scalar.

Return value:

        The return value is a scalar of type `REAL`. It has the same kind as X.

Note: The transformational function uses a recurrence algorithm which might, for some values of X, lead to different results than calls to the elemental function.

Example:

```
program test_besyn
  real(8) :: x = 1.0_8
  x = bessel_yn(5,x)
end program test_besyn
```

Specific names:

Name	Argument	Return type	Standard
DBESYN(N,X)	INTEGER N	REAL(8)	GNU extension
	REAL(8) X		

9.42 BGE — Bitwise greater than or equal to

Description:

Determines whether an integral is a bitwise greater than or equal to another.

Standard: Fortran 2008 and later

Class: Elemental function

Syntax: RESULT = BGE(I, J)

Arguments:

I	Shall be of INTEGER type.
J	Shall be of INTEGER type, and of the same kind as *I*.

Return value:

The return value is of type LOGICAL and of the default kind.

See also: Section 9.43 [BGT], page 112, Section 9.45 [BLE], page 113, Section 9.46 [BLT], page 113

9.43 BGT — Bitwise greater than

Description:

Determines whether an integral is a bitwise greater than another.

Standard: Fortran 2008 and later

Class: Elemental function

Syntax: RESULT = BGT(I, J)

Arguments:

I	Shall be of INTEGER type.
J	Shall be of INTEGER type, and of the same kind as *I*.

Return value:

The return value is of type LOGICAL and of the default kind.

See also: Section 9.42 [BGE], page 112, Section 9.45 [BLE], page 113, Section 9.46 [BLT], page 113

9.44 BIT_SIZE — Bit size inquiry function

Description:

BIT_SIZE(I) returns the number of bits (integer precision plus sign bit) represented by the type of *I*. The result of BIT_SIZE(I) is independent of the actual value of *I*.

Standard: Fortran 95 and later

Class: Inquiry function

Syntax: RESULT = BIT_SIZE(I)

Arguments:

I   The type shall be INTEGER.

Return value:

The return value is of type INTEGER

Example:

```
program test_bit_size
    integer :: i = 123
    integer :: size
    size = bit_size(i)
    print *, size
end program test_bit_size
```

9.45 BLE — Bitwise less than or equal to

Description:

Determines whether an integral is a bitwise less than or equal to another.

Standard: Fortran 2008 and later

Class: Elemental function

Syntax: RESULT = BLE(I, J)

Arguments:

I   Shall be of INTEGER type.

J   Shall be of INTEGER type, and of the same kind as *I*.

Return value:

The return value is of type LOGICAL and of the default kind.

See also: Section 9.43 [BGT], page 112, Section 9.42 [BGE], page 112, Section 9.46 [BLT], page 113

9.46 BLT — Bitwise less than

Description:

Determines whether an integral is a bitwise less than another.

Standard: Fortran 2008 and later

Class: Elemental function

Syntax: RESULT = BLT(I, J)

Arguments:

I   Shall be of INTEGER type.

J   Shall be of INTEGER type, and of the same kind as *I*.

Return value:

The return value is of type LOGICAL and of the default kind.

See also: Section 9.42 [BGE], page 112, Section 9.43 [BGT], page 112, Section 9.45 [BLE], page 113

9.47 BTEST — Bit test function

Description:

BTEST(I,POS) returns logical .TRUE. if the bit at *POS* in *I* is set. The counting of the bits starts at 0.

Standard: Fortran 95 and later

Class: Elemental function

Syntax: RESULT = BTEST(I, POS)

Arguments:

I	The type shall be INTEGER.
POS	The type shall be INTEGER.

Return value:

The return value is of type LOGICAL

Example:

```
program test_btest
    integer :: i = 32768 + 1024 + 64
    integer :: pos
    logical :: bool
    do pos=0,16
        bool = btest(i, pos)
        print *, pos, bool
    end do
end program test_btest
```

9.48 C_ASSOCIATED — Status of a C pointer

Description:

C_ASSOCIATED(c_ptr_1[, c_ptr_2]) determines the status of the C pointer *c_ptr_1* or if *c_ptr_1* is associated with the target *c_ptr_2*.

Standard: Fortran 2003 and later

Class: Inquiry function

Syntax: RESULT = C_ASSOCIATED(c_ptr_1[, c_ptr_2])

Arguments:

c_ptr_1	Scalar of the type C_PTR or C_FUNPTR.
c_ptr_2	(Optional) Scalar of the same type as *c_ptr_1*.

Return value:

The return value is of type LOGICAL; it is .false. if either *c_ptr_1* is a C NULL pointer or if *c_ptr1* and *c_ptr_2* point to different addresses.

Example:

```
subroutine association_test(a,b)
  use iso_c_binding, only: c_associated, c_loc, c_ptr
  implicit none
  real, pointer :: a
  type(c_ptr) :: b
  if(c_associated(b, c_loc(a))) &
```

```
            stop 'b and a do not point to same target'
        end subroutine association_test
```

See also: Section 9.52 [C_LOC], page 117, Section 9.51 [C_FUNLOC], page 116

9.49 C_F_POINTER — Convert C into Fortran pointer

Description:

C_F_POINTER(CPTR, FPTR[, SHAPE]) assigns the target of the C pointer *CPTR* to the Fortran pointer *FPTR* and specifies its shape.

Standard: Fortran 2003 and later

Class: Subroutine

Syntax: CALL C_F_POINTER(CPTR, FPTR[, SHAPE])

Arguments:

CPTR	scalar of the type C_PTR. It is INTENT(IN).
FPTR	pointer interoperable with *cptr*. It is INTENT(OUT).
SHAPE	(Optional) Rank-one array of type INTEGER with INTENT(IN). It shall be present if and only if *fptr* is an array. The size must be equal to the rank of *fptr*.

Example:

```
program main
  use iso_c_binding
  implicit none
  interface
    subroutine my_routine(p) bind(c,name='myC_func')
      import :: c_ptr
      type(c_ptr), intent(out) :: p
    end subroutine
  end interface
  type(c_ptr) :: cptr
  real,pointer :: a(:)
  call my_routine(cptr)
  call c_f_pointer(cptr, a, [12])
end program main
```

See also: Section 9.52 [C_LOC], page 117, Section 9.50 [C_F_PROCPOINTER], page 115

9.50 C_F_PROCPOINTER — Convert C into Fortran procedure pointer

Description:

C_F_PROCPOINTER(CPTR, FPTR) Assign the target of the C function pointer *CPTR* to the Fortran procedure pointer *FPTR*.

Standard: Fortran 2003 and later

Class: Subroutine

Syntax: CALL C_F_PROCPOINTER(cptr, fptr)

Arguments:

CPTR	scalar of the type C_FUNPTR. It is INTENT(IN).
FPTR	procedure pointer interoperable with *cptr*. It is INTENT(OUT).

Example:

```
program main
  use iso_c_binding
  implicit none
  abstract interface
    function func(a)
      import :: c_float
      real(c_float), intent(in) :: a
      real(c_float) :: func
    end function
  end interface
  interface
    function getIterFunc() bind(c,name="getIterFunc")
      import :: c_funptr
      type(c_funptr) :: getIterFunc
    end function
  end interface
  type(c_funptr) :: cfunptr
  procedure(func), pointer :: myFunc
  cfunptr = getIterFunc()
  call c_f_procpointer(cfunptr, myFunc)
end program main
```

See also: Section 9.52 [C_LOC], page 117, Section 9.49 [C_F_POINTER], page 115

9.51 C_FUNLOC — Obtain the C address of a procedure

Description:

C_FUNLOC(x) determines the C address of the argument.

Standard: Fortran 2003 and later

Class: Inquiry function

Syntax: RESULT = C_FUNLOC(x)

Arguments:

x	Interoperable function or pointer to such function.

Return value:

The return value is of type C_FUNPTR and contains the C address of the argument.

Example:

```
module x
  use iso_c_binding
  implicit none
contains
  subroutine sub(a) bind(c)
    real(c_float) :: a
    a = sqrt(a)+5.0
  end subroutine sub
end module x
```

```
program main
  use iso_c_binding
  use x
  implicit none
  interface
    subroutine my_routine(p) bind(c,name='myC_func')
      import :: c_funptr
      type(c_funptr), intent(in) :: p
    end subroutine
  end interface
  call my_routine(c_funloc(sub))
end program main
```

See also: Section 9.48 [C_ASSOCIATED], page 114, Section 9.52 [C_LOC], page 117, Section 9.49 [C_F_POINTER], page 115, Section 9.50 [C_F_PROCPOINTER], page 115

9.52 C_LOC — Obtain the C address of an object

Description:
C_LOC(X) determines the C address of the argument.

Standard: Fortran 2003 and later

Class: Inquiry function

Syntax: RESULT = C_LOC(X)

Arguments:

X   Shall have either the POINTER or TARGET attribute. It shall not be a coindexed object. It shall either be a variable with interoperable type and kind type parameters, or be a scalar, nonpolymorphic variable with no length type parameters.

Return value:
The return value is of type C_PTR and contains the C address of the argument.

Example:
```
subroutine association_test(a,b)
  use iso_c_binding, only: c_associated, c_loc, c_ptr
  implicit none
  real, pointer :: a
  type(c_ptr) :: b
  if(c_associated(b, c_loc(a))) &
     stop 'b and a do not point to same target'
end subroutine association_test
```

See also: Section 9.48 [C_ASSOCIATED], page 114, Section 9.51 [C_FUNLOC], page 116, Section 9.49 [C_F_POINTER], page 115, Section 9.50 [C_F_PROCPOINTER], page 115

9.53 C_SIZEOF — Size in bytes of an expression

Description:
C_SIZEOF(X) calculates the number of bytes of storage the expression X occupies.

Standard: Fortran 2008

Class: Inquiry function of the module `ISO_C_BINDING`

Syntax: `N = C_SIZEOF(X)`

Arguments:

        X   The argument shall be an interoperable data entity.

Return value:

    The return value is of type integer and of the system-dependent kind `C_SIZE_T` (from the `ISO_C_BINDING` module). Its value is the number of bytes occupied by the argument. If the argument has the `POINTER` attribute, the number of bytes of the storage area pointed to is returned. If the argument is of a derived type with `POINTER` or `ALLOCATABLE` components, the return value does not account for the sizes of the data pointed to by these components.

Example:

```
use iso_c_binding
integer(c_int) :: i
real(c_float) :: r, s(5)
print *, (c_sizeof(s)/c_sizeof(r) == 5)
end
```

    The example will print `.TRUE.` unless you are using a platform where default `REAL` variables are unusually padded.

See also: Section 9.243 [SIZEOF], page 230, Section 9.250 [STORAGE_SIZE], page 234

9.54 `CEILING` — Integer ceiling function

Description:

    `CEILING(A)` returns the least integer greater than or equal to *A*.

Standard: Fortran 95 and later

Class: Elemental function

Syntax: `RESULT = CEILING(A [, KIND])`

Arguments:

    A   The type shall be `REAL`.

    KIND   (Optional) An `INTEGER` initialization expression indicating the kind parameter of the result.

Return value:

    The return value is of type `INTEGER(KIND)` if *KIND* is present and a default-kind `INTEGER` otherwise.

Example:

```
program test_ceiling
    real :: x = 63.29
    real :: y = -63.59
    print *, ceiling(x) ! returns 64
    print *, ceiling(y) ! returns -63
end program test_ceiling
```

See also: Section 9.101 [FLOOR], page 150, Section 9.198 [NINT], page 204

9.55 CHAR — Character conversion function

Description:

CHAR(I [, KIND]) returns the character represented by the integer *I*.

Standard: Fortran 77 and later

Class: Elemental function

Syntax: RESULT = CHAR(I [, KIND])

Arguments:

I	The type shall be INTEGER.
KIND	(Optional) An INTEGER initialization expression indicating the kind parameter of the result.

Return value:

The return value is of type CHARACTER(1)

Example:

```
program test_char
    integer :: i = 74
    character(1) :: c
    c = char(i)
    print *, i, c ! returns 'J'
end program test_char
```

Specific names:

Name	Argument	Return type	Standard
CHAR(I)	INTEGER I	CHARACTER(LEN=1)	F77 and later

Note: See Section 9.135 [ICHAR], page 170 for a discussion of converting between numerical values and formatted string representations.

See also: Section 9.5 [ACHAR], page 87, Section 9.127 [IACHAR], page 165, Section 9.135 [ICHAR], page 170

9.56 CHDIR — Change working directory

Description:

Change current working directory to a specified path.

This intrinsic is provided in both subroutine and function forms; however, only one form can be used in any given program unit.

Standard: GNU extension

Class: Subroutine, function

Syntax:

CALL CHDIR(NAME [, STATUS])
STATUS = CHDIR(NAME)

Arguments:

NAME	The type shall be CHARACTER of default kind and shall specify a valid path within the file system.

  STATUS   (Optional) `INTEGER` status flag of the default kind. Returns 0 on success, and a system specific and nonzero error code otherwise.

Example:

```
PROGRAM test_chdir
  CHARACTER(len=255) :: path
  CALL getcwd(path)
  WRITE(*,*) TRIM(path)
  CALL chdir("/tmp")
  CALL getcwd(path)
  WRITE(*,*) TRIM(path)
END PROGRAM
```

See also: Section 9.116 [GETCWD], page 160

9.57 CHMOD — Change access permissions of files

Description:

  `CHMOD` changes the permissions of a file.

  This intrinsic is provided in both subroutine and function forms; however, only one form can be used in any given program unit.

Standard: GNU extension

Class: Subroutine, function

Syntax:

```
CALL CHMOD(NAME, MODE[, STATUS])
STATUS = CHMOD(NAME, MODE)
```

Arguments:

  NAME   Scalar `CHARACTER` of default kind with the file name. Trailing blanks are ignored unless the character `achar(0)` is present, then all characters up to and excluding `achar(0)` are used as the file name.

  MODE   Scalar `CHARACTER` of default kind giving the file permission. *MODE* uses the same syntax as the `chmod` utility as defined by the POSIX standard. The argument shall either be a string of a nonnegative octal number or a symbolic mode.

  STATUS   (optional) scalar `INTEGER`, which is 0 on success and nonzero otherwise.

Return value:

  In either syntax, *STATUS* is set to 0 on success and nonzero otherwise.

Example: `CHMOD` as subroutine

```
program chmod_test
  implicit none
  integer :: status
```

```
      call chmod('test.dat','u+x',status)
      print *, 'Status: ', status
   end program chmod_test
```

CHMOD as function:

```
program chmod_test
  implicit none
  integer :: status
  status = chmod('test.dat','u+x')
  print *, 'Status: ', status
end program chmod_test
```

9.58 CMPLX — Complex conversion function

Description:

CMPLX(X [, Y [, KIND]]) returns a complex number where X is converted to the real component. If Y is present it is converted to the imaginary component. If Y is not present then the imaginary component is set to 0.0. If X is complex then Y must not be present.

Standard: Fortran 77 and later

Class: Elemental function

Syntax: RESULT = CMPLX(X [, Y [, KIND]])

Arguments:

X	The type may be INTEGER, REAL, or COMPLEX.
Y	(Optional; only allowed if X is not COMPLEX.) May be INTEGER or REAL.
KIND	(Optional) An INTEGER initialization expression indicating the kind parameter of the result.

Return value:

The return value is of COMPLEX type, with a kind equal to *KIND* if it is specified. If *KIND* is not specified, the result is of the default COMPLEX kind, regardless of the kinds of X and Y.

Example:

```
program test_cmplx
    integer :: i = 42
    real :: x = 3.14
    complex :: z
    z = cmplx(i, x)
    print *, z, cmplx(x)
end program test_cmplx
```

See also: Section 9.67 [COMPLEX], page 127

9.59 CO_BROADCAST — Copy a value to all images the current set of images

Description:

CO_BROADCAST copies the value of argument A on the image with image index SOURCE_IMAGE to all images in the current team. A becomes defined as if by intrinsic assignment. If the execution was successful and *STAT* is present, it is assigned the value zero. If the execution failed, *STAT* gets assigned a nonzero value and, if present, *ERRMSG* gets assigned a value describing the occurred error.

Standard: Technical Specification (TS) 18508 or later

Class: Collective subroutine

Syntax: CALL CO_BROADCAST(A, SOURCE_IMAGE [, STAT, ERRMSG])

Arguments:

A	INTENT(INOUT) argument; shall have the same dynamic type and type paramters on all images of the current team. If it is an array, it shall have the same shape on all images.
SOURCE_IMAGE	a scalar integer expression. It shall have the same the same value on all images and refer to an image of the current team.
STAT	(optional) a scalar integer variable
ERRMSG	(optional) a scalar character variable

Example:

```
program test
  integer :: val(3)
  if (this_image() == 1) then
    val = [1, 5, 3]
  end if
  call co_broadcast (val, source_image=1)
  print *, this_image, ":", val
end program test
```

See also: Section 9.60 [CO_MAX], page 122, Section 9.61 [CO_MIN], page 123, Section 9.63 [CO_SUM], page 125, Section 9.62 [CO_REDUCE], page 124

9.60 CO_MAX — Maximal value on the current set of images

Description:

CO_MAX determines element-wise the maximal value of *A* on all images of the current team. If *RESULT_IMAGE* is present, the maximum values are returned in *A* on the specified image only and the value of *A* on the other images become undefined. If *RESULT_IMAGE* is not present, the value is returned on all images. If the execution was successful and *STAT* is present, it is assigned the value zero. If the execution failed, *STAT* gets assigned a nonzero value and, if present, *ERRMSG* gets assigned a value describing the occurred error.

Standard: Technical Specification (TS) 18508 or later

Class: Collective subroutine

Syntax: CALL CO_MAX(A [, RESULT_IMAGE, STAT, ERRMSG])

Arguments:

A	shall be an integer, real or character variable, which has the same type and type parameters on all images of the team.

RESULT_IMAGE(optional) a scalar integer expression; if present, it shall have the same the same value on all images and refer to an image of the current team.

STAT   (optional) a scalar integer variable

ERRMSG   (optional) a scalar character variable

Example:

```
program test
  integer :: val
  val = this_image ()
  call co_max (val, result_image=1)
  if (this_image() == 1) then
    write(*,*) "Maximal value", val  ! prints num_images()
  end if
end program test
```

See also: Section 9.61 [CO_MIN], page 123, Section 9.63 [CO_SUM], page 125, Section 9.62 [CO_REDUCE], page 124, Section 9.59 [CO_BROADCAST], page 121

9.61 CO_MIN — Minimal value on the current set of images

Description:

CO_MIN determines element-wise the minimal value of A on all images of the current team. If *RESULT_IMAGE* is present, the minimal values are returned in A on the specified image only and the value of A on the other images become undefined. If *RESULT_IMAGE* is not present, the value is returned on all images. If the execution was successful and *STAT* is present, it is assigned the value zero. If the execution failed, *STAT* gets assigned a nonzero value and, if present, *ERRMSG* gets assigned a value describing the occurred error.

Standard: Technical Specification (TS) 18508 or later

Class: Collective subroutine

Syntax: CALL CO_MIN(A [, RESULT_IMAGE, STAT, ERRMSG])

Arguments:

A shall be an integer, real or character variable, which has the same type and type parameters on all images of the team.

RESULT_IMAGE(optional) a scalar integer expression; if present, it shall have the same the same value on all images and refer to an image of the current team.

STAT   (optional) a scalar integer variable

ERRMSG   (optional) a scalar character variable

Example:

```
program test
  integer :: val
  val = this_image ()
  call co_min (val, result_image=1)
  if (this_image() == 1) then
    write(*,*) "Minimal value", val  ! prints 1
```

```
            end if
        end program test
```

See also: Section 9.60 [CO_MAX], page 122, Section 9.63 [CO_SUM], page 125, Section 9.62 [CO_REDUCE], page 124, Section 9.59 [CO_BROADCAST], page 121

9.62 CO_REDUCE — Reduction of values on the current set of images

Description:

CO_REDUCE determines element-wise the reduction of the value of *A* on all images of the current team. The pure function passed as *OPERATOR* is used to pairwise reduce the values of *A* by passing either the value of *A* of different images or the result values of such a reduction as argument. If *A* is an array, the deduction is done element wise. If *RESULT_IMAGE* is present, the result values are returned in *A* on the specified image only and the value of *A* on the other images become undefined. If *RESULT_IMAGE* is not present, the value is returned on all images. If the execution was successful and *STAT* is present, it is assigned the value zero. If the execution failed, *STAT* gets assigned a nonzero value and, if present, *ERRMSG* gets assigned a value describing the occurred error.

Standard: Technical Specification (TS) 18508 or later

Class: Collective subroutine

Syntax: CALL CO_REDUCE(A, OPERATOR, [, RESULT_IMAGE, STAT, ERRMSG])

Arguments:

A	is an INTENT(INOUT) argument and shall be nonpolymorphic. If it is allocatable, it shall be allocated; if it is a pointer, it shall be associated. *A* shall have the same type and type parameters on all images of the team; if it is an array, it shall have the same shape on all images.
OPERATOR	pure function with two scalar nonallocatable arguments, which shall be nonpolymorphic and have the same type and type parameters as *A*. The function shall return a nonallocatable scalar of the same type and type parameters as *A*. The function shall be the same on all images and with regards to the arguments mathematically commutative and associative. Note that *OPERATOR* may not be an elemental function, unless it is an intrisic function.
RESULT_IMAGE	(optional) a scalar integer expression; if present, it shall have the same the same value on all images and refer to an image of the current team.
STAT	(optional) a scalar integer variable
ERRMSG	(optional) a scalar character variable

Example:

```
program test
  integer :: val
  val = this_image ()
  call co_reduce (val, result_image=1, operator=myprod)
  if (this_image() == 1) then
    write(*,*) "Product value", val  ! prints num_images() factorial
  end if
contains
  pure function myprod(a, b)
    integer, value :: a, b
    integer :: myprod
    myprod = a * b
  end function myprod
end program test
```

Note: While the rules permit in principle an intrinsic function, none of the intrinsics in the standard fulfill the criteria of having a specific function, which takes two arguments of the same type and returning that type as result.

See also: Section 9.61 [CO_MIN], page 123, Section 9.60 [CO_MAX], page 122, Section 9.63 [CO_SUM], page 125, Section 9.59 [CO_BROADCAST], page 121

9.63 CO_SUM — Sum of values on the current set of images

Description:

CO_SUM sums up the values of each element of *A* on all images of the current team. If *RESULT_IMAGE* is present, the summed-up values are returned in *A* on the specified image only and the value of *A* on the other images become undefined. If *RESULT_IMAGE* is not present, the value is returned on all images. If the execution was successful and *STAT* is present, it is assigned the value zero. If the execution failed, *STAT* gets assigned a nonzero value and, if present, *ERRMSG* gets assigned a value describing the occurred error.

Standard: Technical Specification (TS) 18508 or later

Class: Collective subroutine

Syntax: CALL CO_MIN(A [, RESULT_IMAGE, STAT, ERRMSG])

Arguments:

A	shall be an integer, real or complex variable, which has the same type and type parameters on all images of the team.
RESULT_IMAGE	(optional) a scalar integer expression; if present, it shall have the same the same value on all images and refer to an image of the current team.
STAT	(optional) a scalar integer variable
ERRMSG	(optional) a scalar character variable

Example:

```
program test
  integer :: val
  val = this_image ()
  call co_sum (val, result_image=1)
  if (this_image() == 1) then
```

```
      write(*,*) "The sum is ", val ! prints (n**2 + n)/2, with n = num_images()▮
    end if
end program test
```

See also: Section 9.60 [CO_MAX], page 122, Section 9.61 [CO_MIN], page 123, Section 9.62 [CO_REDUCE], page 124, Section 9.59 [CO_BROADCAST], page 121

9.64 COMMAND_ARGUMENT_COUNT — Get number of command line arguments

Description:

COMMAND_ARGUMENT_COUNT returns the number of arguments passed on the command line when the containing program was invoked.

Standard: Fortran 2003 and later

Class: Inquiry function

Syntax: RESULT = COMMAND_ARGUMENT_COUNT()

Arguments:

None

Return value:

The return value is an INTEGER of default kind.

Example:

```
program test_command_argument_count
    integer :: count
    count = command_argument_count()
    print *, count
end program test_command_argument_count
```

See   also: Section   9.114   [GET_COMMAND],   page   158,   Section   9.115 [GET_COMMAND_ARGUMENT], page 159

9.65 COMPILER_OPTIONS — Options passed to the compiler

Description:

COMPILER_OPTIONS returns a string with the options used for compiling.

Standard: Fortran 2008

Class: Inquiry function of the module ISO_FORTRAN_ENV

Syntax: STR = COMPILER_OPTIONS()

Arguments:

None.

Return value:

The return value is a default-kind string with system-dependent length. It contains the compiler flags used to compile the file, which called the COMPILER_OPTIONS intrinsic.

Example:

```
use iso_fortran_env
print '(4a)', 'This file was compiled by ', &
              compiler_version(), ' using the options ', &
              compiler_options()
end
```

See also: Section   9.66   [COMPILER_VERSION],   page   127,   Section   10.1
[ISO_FORTRAN_ENV], page 249

9.66 COMPILER_VERSION — Compiler version string

Description:

COMPILER_VERSION returns a string with the name and the version of the compiler.

Standard: Fortran 2008

Class: Inquiry function of the module ISO_FORTRAN_ENV

Syntax: STR = COMPILER_VERSION()

Arguments:

None.

Return value:

The return value is a default-kind string with system-dependent length. It
contains the name of the compiler and its version number.

Example:

```
use iso_fortran_env
print '(4a)', 'This file was compiled by ', &
              compiler_version(), ' using the options ', &
              compiler_options()
end
```

See also: Section   9.65   [COMPILER_OPTIONS],   page   126,   Section   10.1
[ISO_FORTRAN_ENV], page 249

9.67 COMPLEX — Complex conversion function

Description:

COMPLEX(X, Y) returns a complex number where X is converted to the real
component and Y is converted to the imaginary component.

Standard: GNU extension

Class: Elemental function

Syntax: RESULT = COMPLEX(X, Y)

Arguments:

X	The type may be INTEGER or REAL.
Y	The type may be INTEGER or REAL.

Return value:

If X and Y are both of `INTEGER` type, then the return value is of default `COMPLEX` type.

If X and Y are of `REAL` type, or one is of `REAL` type and one is of `INTEGER` type, then the return value is of `COMPLEX` type with a kind equal to that of the `REAL` argument with the highest precision.

Example:

```
program test_complex
    integer :: i = 42
    real :: x = 3.14
    print *, complex(i, x)
end program test_complex
```

See also: Section 9.58 [CMPLX], page 121

9.68 `CONJG` — Complex conjugate function

Description:

`CONJG(Z)` returns the conjugate of Z. If Z is `(x, y)` then the result is `(x, -y)`

Standard: Fortran 77 and later, has overloads that are GNU extensions

Class: Elemental function

Syntax: `Z = CONJG(Z)`

Arguments:

Z The type shall be `COMPLEX`.

Return value:

The return value is of type `COMPLEX`.

Example:

```
program test_conjg
    complex :: z = (2.0, 3.0)
    complex(8) :: dz = (2.71_8, -3.14_8)
    z= conjg(z)
    print *, z
    dz = dconjg(dz)
    print *, dz
end program test_conjg
```

Specific names:

Name	Argument	Return type	Standard
CONJG(Z)	COMPLEX Z	COMPLEX	GNU extension
DCONJG(Z)	COMPLEX(8) Z	COMPLEX(8)	GNU extension

9.69 `COS` — Cosine function

Description:

`COS(X)` computes the cosine of X.

Standard: Fortran 77 and later, has overloads that are GNU extensions

Class: Elemental function

Syntax: `RESULT = COS(X)`

Arguments:

        X   The type shall be `REAL` or `COMPLEX`.

Return value:

        The return value is of the same type and kind as *X*. The real part of the result is in radians. If *X* is of the type `REAL`, the return value lies in the range $-1 \le \cos(x) \le 1$.

Example:

```
program test_cos
  real :: x = 0.0
  x = cos(x)
end program test_cos
```

Specific names:

Name	Argument	Return type	Standard
COS(X)	REAL(4) X	REAL(4)	Fortran 77 and later
DCOS(X)	REAL(8) X	REAL(8)	Fortran 77 and later
CCOS(X)	COMPLEX(4) X	COMPLEX(4)	Fortran 77 and later
ZCOS(X)	COMPLEX(8) X	COMPLEX(8)	GNU extension
CDCOS(X)	COMPLEX(8) X	COMPLEX(8)	GNU extension

See also: Inverse function: Section 9.6 [ACOS], page 88

9.70 `COSH` — Hyperbolic cosine function

Description:

        `COSH(X)` computes the hyperbolic cosine of *X*.

Standard: Fortran 77 and later, for a complex argument Fortran 2008 or later

Class: Elemental function

Syntax: `X = COSH(X)`

Arguments:

        X   The type shall be `REAL` or `COMPLEX`.

Return value:

        The return value has same type and kind as *X*. If *X* is complex, the imaginary part of the result is in radians. If *X* is `REAL`, the return value has a lower bound of one, $\cosh(x) \ge 1$.

Example:

```
program test_cosh
  real(8) :: x = 1.0_8
  x = cosh(x)
end program test_cosh
```

Specific names:

Name	Argument	Return type	Standard
COSH(X)	REAL(4) X	REAL(4)	Fortran 77 and later
DCOSH(X)	REAL(8) X	REAL(8)	Fortran 77 and later

See also: Inverse function: Section 9.7 [ACOSH], page 88

9.71 COUNT — Count function

Description:

Counts the number of .TRUE. elements in a logical *MASK*, or, if the *DIM* argument is supplied, counts the number of elements along each row of the array in the *DIM* direction. If the array has zero size, or all of the elements of *MASK* are .FALSE., then the result is 0.

Standard: Fortran 95 and later, with *KIND* argument Fortran 2003 and later

Class: Transformational function

Syntax: RESULT = COUNT(MASK [, DIM, KIND])

Arguments:

MASK	The type shall be LOGICAL.
DIM	(Optional) The type shall be INTEGER.
KIND	(Optional) An INTEGER initialization expression indicating the kind parameter of the result.

Return value:

The return value is of type INTEGER and of kind *KIND*. If *KIND* is absent, the return value is of default integer kind. If *DIM* is present, the result is an array with a rank one less than the rank of *ARRAY*, and a size corresponding to the shape of *ARRAY* with the *DIM* dimension removed.

Example:

```
program test_count
    integer, dimension(2,3) :: a, b
    logical, dimension(2,3) :: mask
    a = reshape( (/ 1, 2, 3, 4, 5, 6 /), (/ 2, 3 /))
    b = reshape( (/ 0, 7, 3, 4, 5, 8 /), (/ 2, 3 /))
    print '(3i3)', a(1,:)
    print '(3i3)', a(2,:)
    print *
    print '(3i3)', b(1,:)
    print '(3i3)', b(2,:)
    print *
    mask = a.ne.b
    print '(3l3)', mask(1,:)
    print '(3l3)', mask(2,:)
    print *
    print '(3i3)', count(mask)
    print *
    print '(3i3)', count(mask, 1)
    print *
    print '(3i3)', count(mask, 2)
end program test_count
```

9.72 CPU_TIME — CPU elapsed time in seconds

Description:

Returns a REAL value representing the elapsed CPU time in seconds. This is useful for testing segments of code to determine execution time.

If a time source is available, time will be reported with microsecond resolution. If no time source is available, *TIME* is set to `-1.0`.

Note that *TIME* may contain a, system dependent, arbitrary offset and may not start with `0.0`. For `CPU_TIME`, the absolute value is meaningless, only differences between subsequent calls to this subroutine, as shown in the example below, should be used.

Standard: Fortran 95 and later

Class: Subroutine

Syntax: `CALL CPU_TIME(TIME)`

Arguments:

      TIME   The type shall be `REAL` with `INTENT(OUT)`.

Return value:

      None

Example:

```
program test_cpu_time
    real :: start, finish
    call cpu_time(start)
        ! put code to test here
    call cpu_time(finish)
    print '("Time = ",f6.3," seconds.")',finish-start
end program test_cpu_time
```

See also: Section 9.254 [SYSTEM_CLOCK], page 237, Section 9.75 [DATE_AND_TIME], page 133

9.73 CSHIFT — Circular shift elements of an array

Description:

CSHIFT(ARRAY, SHIFT [, DIM]) performs a circular shift on elements of *ARRAY* along the dimension of *DIM*. If *DIM* is omitted it is taken to be `1`. *DIM* is a scalar of type `INTEGER` in the range of $1 \leq DIM \leq n$) where n is the rank of *ARRAY*. If the rank of *ARRAY* is one, then all elements of *ARRAY* are shifted by *SHIFT* places. If rank is greater than one, then all complete rank one sections of *ARRAY* along the given dimension are shifted. Elements shifted out one end of each rank one section are shifted back in the other end.

Standard: Fortran 95 and later

Class: Transformational function

Syntax: `RESULT = CSHIFT(ARRAY, SHIFT [, DIM])`

Arguments:

      ARRAY   Shall be an array of any type.
      SHIFT   The type shall be `INTEGER`.
      DIM   The type shall be `INTEGER`.

Return value:

      Returns an array of same type and rank as the *ARRAY* argument.

Example:

```
program test_cshift
    integer, dimension(3,3) :: a
    a = reshape( (/ 1, 2, 3, 4, 5, 6, 7, 8, 9 /), (/ 3, 3 /))
    print '(3i3)', a(1,:)
    print '(3i3)', a(2,:)
    print '(3i3)', a(3,:)
    a = cshift(a, SHIFT=(/1, 2, -1/), DIM=2)
    print *
    print '(3i3)', a(1,:)
    print '(3i3)', a(2,:)
    print '(3i3)', a(3,:)
end program test_cshift
```

9.74 CTIME — Convert a time into a string

Description:

CTIME converts a system time value, such as returned by TIME8, to a string. The output will be of the form 'Sat Aug 19 18:13:14 1995'.

This intrinsic is provided in both subroutine and function forms; however, only one form can be used in any given program unit.

Standard: GNU extension

Class: Subroutine, function

Syntax:

CALL CTIME(TIME, RESULT).
RESULT = CTIME(TIME).

Arguments:

TIME	The type shall be of type INTEGER.
RESULT	The type shall be of type CHARACTER and of default kind. It is an INTENT(OUT) argument. If the length of this variable is too short for the time and date string to fit completely, it will be blank on procedure return.

Return value:

The converted date and time as a string.

Example:

```
program test_ctime
    integer(8) :: i
    character(len=30) :: date
    i = time8()

    ! Do something, main part of the program

    call ctime(i,date)
    print *, 'Program was started on ', date
end program test_ctime
```

See Also: Section 9.75 [DATE_AND_TIME], page 133, Section 9.123 [GMTIME], page 163, Section 9.175 [LTIME], page 191, Section 9.258 [TIME], page 240, Section 9.259 [TIME8], page 240

9.75 DATE_AND_TIME — Date and time subroutine

Description:

DATE_AND_TIME(DATE, TIME, ZONE, VALUES) gets the corresponding date and time information from the real-time system clock. *DATE* is INTENT(OUT) and has form ccyymmdd. *TIME* is INTENT(OUT) and has form hhmmss.sss. *ZONE* is INTENT(OUT) and has form (+-)hhmm, representing the difference with respect to Coordinated Universal Time (UTC). Unavailable time and date parameters return blanks.

VALUES is INTENT(OUT) and provides the following:

VALUE(1):	The year
VALUE(2):	The month
VALUE(3):	The day of the month
VALUE(4):	Time difference with UTC in minutes
VALUE(5):	The hour of the day
VALUE(6):	The minutes of the hour
VALUE(7):	The seconds of the minute
VALUE(8):	The milliseconds of the second

Standard: Fortran 95 and later

Class: Subroutine

Syntax: CALL DATE_AND_TIME([DATE, TIME, ZONE, VALUES])

Arguments:

DATE	(Optional) The type shall be CHARACTER(LEN=8) or larger, and of default kind.
TIME	(Optional) The type shall be CHARACTER(LEN=10) or larger, and of default kind.
ZONE	(Optional) The type shall be CHARACTER(LEN=5) or larger, and of default kind.
VALUES	(Optional) The type shall be INTEGER(8).

Return value:

None

Example:

```
program test_time_and_date
    character(8)  :: date
    character(10) :: time
    character(5)  :: zone
    integer,dimension(8) :: values
    ! using keyword arguments
    call date_and_time(date,time,zone,values)
    call date_and_time(DATE=date,ZONE=zone)
    call date_and_time(TIME=time)
    call date_and_time(VALUES=values)
    print '(a,2x,a,2x,a)', date, time, zone
    print '(8i5)', values
end program test_time_and_date
```

See also: Section 9.72 [CPU_TIME], page 130, Section 9.254 [SYSTEM_CLOCK], page 237

9.76 DBLE — Double conversion function

Description:

DBLE(A) Converts *A* to double precision real type.

Standard: Fortran 77 and later

Class: Elemental function

Syntax: RESULT = DBLE(A)

Arguments:

A   The type shall be INTEGER, REAL, or COMPLEX.

Return value:

The return value is of type double precision real.

Example:

```
program test_dble
    real    :: x = 2.18
    integer :: i = 5
    complex :: z = (2.3,1.14)
    print *, dble(x), dble(i), dble(z)
end program test_dble
```

See also: Section 9.219 [REAL], page 216

9.77 DCMPLX — Double complex conversion function

Description:

DCMPLX(X [,Y]) returns a double complex number where *X* is converted to the real component. If *Y* is present it is converted to the imaginary component. If *Y* is not present then the imaginary component is set to 0.0. If *X* is complex then *Y* must not be present.

Standard: GNU extension

Class: Elemental function

Syntax: RESULT = DCMPLX(X [, Y])

Arguments:

X   The type may be INTEGER, REAL, or COMPLEX.

Y   (Optional if *X* is not COMPLEX.) May be INTEGER or REAL.

Return value:

The return value is of type COMPLEX(8)

Example:

```
program test_dcmplx
    integer :: i = 42
    real :: x = 3.14
    complex :: z
```

```
            z = cmplx(i, x)
            print *, dcmplx(i)
            print *, dcmplx(x)
            print *, dcmplx(z)
            print *, dcmplx(x,i)
        end program test_dcmplx
```

9.78 DIGITS — Significant binary digits function

Description:

DIGITS(X) returns the number of significant binary digits of the internal model representation of X. For example, on a system using a 32-bit floating point representation, a default real number would likely return 24.

Standard: Fortran 95 and later

Class: Inquiry function

Syntax: RESULT = DIGITS(X)

Arguments:

X   The type may be INTEGER or REAL.

Return value:

The return value is of type INTEGER.

Example:

```
        program test_digits
            integer :: i = 12345
            real :: x = 3.143
            real(8) :: y = 2.33
            print *, digits(i)
            print *, digits(x)
            print *, digits(y)
        end program test_digits
```

9.79 DIM — Positive difference

Description:

DIM(X,Y) returns the difference X-Y if the result is positive; otherwise returns zero.

Standard: Fortran 77 and later

Class: Elemental function

Syntax: RESULT = DIM(X, Y)

Arguments:

X   The type shall be INTEGER or REAL.
Y   The type shall be the same type and kind as X.

Return value:

The return value is of type INTEGER or REAL.

Example:

```
program test_dim
    integer :: i
    real(8) :: x
    i = dim(4, 15)
    x = dim(4.345_8, 2.111_8)
    print *, i
    print *, x
end program test_dim
```

Specific names:

Name	Argument	Return type	Standard
DIM(X,Y)	REAL(4) X, Y	REAL(4)	Fortran 77 and later
IDIM(X,Y)	INTEGER(4) X, Y	INTEGER(4)	Fortran 77 and later
DDIM(X,Y)	REAL(8) X, Y	REAL(8)	Fortran 77 and later

9.80 DOT_PRODUCT — Dot product function

Description:

DOT_PRODUCT(VECTOR_A, VECTOR_B) computes the dot product multiplication of two vectors *VECTOR_A* and *VECTOR_B*. The two vectors may be either numeric or logical and must be arrays of rank one and of equal size. If the vectors are INTEGER or REAL, the result is SUM(VECTOR_A*VECTOR_B). If the vectors are COMPLEX, the result is SUM(CONJG(VECTOR_A)*VECTOR_B). If the vectors are LOGICAL, the result is ANY(VECTOR_A .AND. VECTOR_B).

Standard: Fortran 95 and later

Class: Transformational function

Syntax: RESULT = DOT_PRODUCT(VECTOR_A, VECTOR_B)

Arguments:

VECTOR_A The type shall be numeric or LOGICAL, rank 1.
VECTOR_B The type shall be numeric if *VECTOR_A* is of numeric type or LOGICAL if *VECTOR_A* is of type LOGICAL. *VECTOR_B* shall be a rank-one array.

Return value:

If the arguments are numeric, the return value is a scalar of numeric type, INTEGER, REAL, or COMPLEX. If the arguments are LOGICAL, the return value is .TRUE. or .FALSE..

Example:

```
program test_dot_prod
    integer, dimension(3) :: a, b
    a = (/ 1, 2, 3 /)
    b = (/ 4, 5, 6 /)
    print '(3i3)', a
    print *
    print '(3i3)', b
    print *
    print *, dot_product(a,b)
end program test_dot_prod
```

9.81 DPROD — Double product function

Description:
DPROD(X,Y) returns the product X*Y.

Standard: Fortran 77 and later

Class: Elemental function

Syntax: RESULT = DPROD(X, Y)

Arguments:

X	The type shall be REAL.
Y	The type shall be REAL.

Return value:
The return value is of type REAL(8).

Example:

```
program test_dprod
    real :: x = 5.2
    real :: y = 2.3
    real(8) :: d
    d = dprod(x,y)
    print *, d
end program test_dprod
```

Specific names:

Name	Argument	Return type	Standard
DPROD(X,Y)	REAL(4) X, Y	REAL(8)	Fortran 77 and later

9.82 DREAL — Double real part function

Description:
DREAL(Z) returns the real part of complex variable Z.

Standard: GNU extension

Class: Elemental function

Syntax: RESULT = DREAL(A)

Arguments:

A	The type shall be COMPLEX(8).

Return value:
The return value is of type REAL(8).

Example:

```
program test_dreal
    complex(8) :: z = (1.3_8,7.2_8)
    print *, dreal(z)
end program test_dreal
```

See also: Section 9.10 [AIMAG], page 90

9.83 `DSHIFTL` — Combined left shift

Description:

DSHIFTL(I, J, SHIFT) combines bits of *I* and *J*. The rightmost *SHIFT* bits of the result are the leftmost *SHIFT* bits of *J*, and the remaining bits are the rightmost bits of *I*.

Standard: Fortran 2008 and later

Class: Elemental function

Syntax: RESULT = DSHIFTL(I, J, SHIFT)

Arguments:

I	Shall be of type `INTEGER` or a BOZ constant.
J	Shall be of type `INTEGER` or a BOZ constant. If both *I* and *J* have integer type, then they shall have the same kind type parameter. *I* and *J* shall not both be BOZ constants.
SHIFT	Shall be of type `INTEGER`. It shall be nonnegative. If *I* is not a BOZ constant, then *SHIFT* shall be less than or equal to `BIT_SIZE(I)`; otherwise, *SHIFT* shall be less than or equal to `BIT_SIZE(J)`.

Return value:

If either *I* or *J* is a BOZ constant, it is first converted as if by the intrinsic function `INT` to an integer type with the kind type parameter of the other.

See also: Section 9.84 [DSHIFTR], page 138

9.84 `DSHIFTR` — Combined right shift

Description:

DSHIFTR(I, J, SHIFT) combines bits of *I* and *J*. The leftmost *SHIFT* bits of the result are the rightmost *SHIFT* bits of *I*, and the remaining bits are the leftmost bits of *J*.

Standard: Fortran 2008 and later

Class: Elemental function

Syntax: RESULT = DSHIFTR(I, J, SHIFT)

Arguments:

I	Shall be of type `INTEGER` or a BOZ constant.
J	Shall be of type `INTEGER` or a BOZ constant. If both *I* and *J* have integer type, then they shall have the same kind type parameter. *I* and *J* shall not both be BOZ constants.
SHIFT	Shall be of type `INTEGER`. It shall be nonnegative. If *I* is not a BOZ constant, then *SHIFT* shall be less than or equal to `BIT_SIZE(I)`; otherwise, *SHIFT* shall be less than or equal to `BIT_SIZE(J)`.

Return value:

If either *I* or *J* is a BOZ constant, it is first converted as if by the intrinsic function `INT` to an integer type with the kind type parameter of the other.

See also: Section 9.83 [DSHIFTL], page 138

9.85 DTIME — Execution time subroutine (or function)

Description:

DTIME(VALUES, TIME) initially returns the number of seconds of runtime since the start of the process's execution in *TIME*. *VALUES* returns the user and system components of this time in VALUES(1) and VALUES(2) respectively. *TIME* is equal to VALUES(1) + VALUES(2).

Subsequent invocations of DTIME return values accumulated since the previous invocation.

On some systems, the underlying timings are represented using types with sufficiently small limits that overflows (wrap around) are possible, such as 32-bit types. Therefore, the values returned by this intrinsic might be, or become, negative, or numerically less than previous values, during a single run of the compiled program.

Please note, that this implementation is thread safe if used within OpenMP directives, i.e., its state will be consistent while called from multiple threads. However, if DTIME is called from multiple threads, the result is still the time since the last invocation. This may not give the intended results. If possible, use CPU_TIME instead.

This intrinsic is provided in both subroutine and function forms; however, only one form can be used in any given program unit.

VALUES and *TIME* are INTENT(OUT) and provide the following:

VALUES(1):	User time in seconds.
VALUES(2):	System time in seconds.
TIME:	Run time since start in seconds.

Standard: GNU extension

Class: Subroutine, function

Syntax:

CALL DTIME(VALUES, TIME).
TIME = DTIME(VALUES), (not recommended).

Arguments:

VALUES	The type shall be REAL(4), DIMENSION(2).
TIME	The type shall be REAL(4).

Return value:

Elapsed time in seconds since the last invocation or since the start of program execution if not called before.

Example:

```
program test_dtime
    integer(8) :: i, j
    real, dimension(2) :: tarray
    real :: result
    call dtime(tarray, result)
```

```
                print *, result
                print *, tarray(1)
                print *, tarray(2)
                do i=1,100000000     ! Just a delay
                    j = i * i - i
                end do
                call dtime(tarray, result)
                print *, result
                print *, tarray(1)
                print *, tarray(2)
            end program test_dtime
```

See also: Section 9.72 [CPU_TIME], page 130

9.86 EOSHIFT — End-off shift elements of an array

Description:

EOSHIFT(ARRAY, SHIFT[, BOUNDARY, DIM]) performs an end-off shift on elements of *ARRAY* along the dimension of *DIM*. If *DIM* is omitted it is taken to be 1. *DIM* is a scalar of type INTEGER in the range of $1 \le DIM \le n$) where n is the rank of *ARRAY*. If the rank of *ARRAY* is one, then all elements of *ARRAY* are shifted by *SHIFT* places. If rank is greater than one, then all complete rank one sections of *ARRAY* along the given dimension are shifted. Elements shifted out one end of each rank one section are dropped. If *BOUNDARY* is present then the corresponding value of from *BOUNDARY* is copied back in the other end. If *BOUNDARY* is not present then the following are copied in depending on the type of *ARRAY*.

Array Type	Boundary Value
Numeric	0 of the type and kind of *ARRAY*.
Logical	.FALSE..
Character(*len*)	*len* blanks.

Standard: Fortran 95 and later

Class: Transformational function

Syntax: RESULT = EOSHIFT(ARRAY, SHIFT [, BOUNDARY, DIM])

Arguments:

ARRAY	May be any type, not scalar.
SHIFT	The type shall be INTEGER.
BOUNDARY	Same type as *ARRAY*.
DIM	The type shall be INTEGER.

Return value:

Returns an array of same type and rank as the *ARRAY* argument.

Example:

```
program test_eoshift
    integer, dimension(3,3) :: a
    a = reshape( (/ 1, 2, 3, 4, 5, 6, 7, 8, 9 /), (/ 3, 3 /))
    print '(3i3)', a(1,:)
    print '(3i3)', a(2,:)
    print '(3i3)', a(3,:)
```

```
        a = EOSHIFT(a, SHIFT=(/1, 2, 1/), BOUNDARY=-5, DIM=2)
        print *
        print '(3i3)', a(1,:)
        print '(3i3)', a(2,:)
        print '(3i3)', a(3,:)
    end program test_eoshift
```

9.87 EPSILON — Epsilon function

Description:

EPSILON(X) returns the smallest number E of the same kind as X such that $1 + E > 1$.

Standard: Fortran 95 and later

Class: Inquiry function

Syntax: RESULT = EPSILON(X)

Arguments:

X   The type shall be REAL.

Return value:

The return value is of same type as the argument.

Example:

```
        program test_epsilon
            real :: x = 3.143
            real(8) :: y = 2.33
            print *, EPSILON(x)
            print *, EPSILON(y)
        end program test_epsilon
```

9.88 ERF — Error function

Description:

ERF(X) computes the error function of X.

Standard: Fortran 2008 and later

Class: Elemental function

Syntax: RESULT = ERF(X)

Arguments:

X   The type shall be REAL.

Return value:

The return value is of type REAL, of the same kind as X and lies in the range $-1 \leq erf(x) \leq 1$.

Example:

```
        program test_erf
          real(8) :: x = 0.17_8
          x = erf(x)
        end program test_erf
```

Specific names:

Name	Argument	Return type	Standard
DERF(X)	REAL(8) X	REAL(8)	GNU extension

9.89 ERFC — Error function

Description:

ERFC(X) computes the complementary error function of X.

Standard: Fortran 2008 and later

Class: Elemental function

Syntax: RESULT = ERFC(X)

Arguments:

X   The type shall be **REAL**.

Return value:

The return value is of type **REAL** and of the same kind as X. It lies in the range $0 \le erfc(x) \le 2$.

Example:

```
program test_erfc
  real(8) :: x = 0.17_8
  x = erfc(x)
end program test_erfc
```

Specific names:

Name	Argument	Return type	Standard
DERFC(X)	REAL(8) X	REAL(8)	GNU extension

9.90 ERFC_SCALED — Error function

Description:

ERFC_SCALED(X) computes the exponentially-scaled complementary error function of X.

Standard: Fortran 2008 and later

Class: Elemental function

Syntax: RESULT = ERFC_SCALED(X)

Arguments:

X   The type shall be **REAL**.

Return value:

The return value is of type **REAL** and of the same kind as X.

Example:

```
program test_erfc_scaled
  real(8) :: x = 0.17_8
  x = erfc_scaled(x)
end program test_erfc_scaled
```

9.91 ETIME — Execution time subroutine (or function)

Description:

ETIME(VALUES, TIME) returns the number of seconds of runtime since the start of the process's execution in *TIME*. *VALUES* returns the user and system components of this time in VALUES(1) and VALUES(2) respectively. *TIME* is equal to VALUES(1) + VALUES(2).

On some systems, the underlying timings are represented using types with sufficiently small limits that overflows (wrap around) are possible, such as 32-bit types. Therefore, the values returned by this intrinsic might be, or become, negative, or numerically less than previous values, during a single run of the compiled program.

This intrinsic is provided in both subroutine and function forms; however, only one form can be used in any given program unit.

VALUES and *TIME* are INTENT(OUT) and provide the following:

VALUES(1):	User time in seconds.
VALUES(2):	System time in seconds.
TIME:	Run time since start in seconds.

Standard: GNU extension

Class: Subroutine, function

Syntax:

CALL ETIME(VALUES, TIME).
TIME = ETIME(VALUES), (not recommended).

Arguments:

VALUES	The type shall be REAL(4), DIMENSION(2).
TIME	The type shall be REAL(4).

Return value:

Elapsed time in seconds since the start of program execution.

Example:

```
program test_etime
    integer(8) :: i, j
    real, dimension(2) :: tarray
    real :: result
    call ETIME(tarray, result)
    print *, result
    print *, tarray(1)
    print *, tarray(2)
    do i=1,100000000      ! Just a delay
        j = i * i - i
    end do
    call ETIME(tarray, result)
    print *, result
    print *, tarray(1)
    print *, tarray(2)
end program test_etime
```

See also: Section 9.72 [CPU_TIME], page 130

9.92 EVENT_QUERY — Query whether a coarray event has occurred

Description:

EVENT_QUERY assignes the number of events to *COUNT* which have been posted to the *EVENT* variable and not yet been removed by calling EVENT WAIT. When *STAT* is present and the invokation was successful, it is assigned the value 0. If it is present and the invokation has failed, it is assigned a positive value and *COUNT* is assigned the value −1.

Standard: TS 18508 or later

Class: subroutine

Syntax: CALL EVENT_QUERY (EVENT, COUNT [, STAT])

Arguments:

EVENT	(intent(IN)) Scalar of type EVENT_TYPE, defined in ISO_FORTRAN_ENV; shall not be coindexed.
COUNT	(intent(out))Scalar integer with at least the precision of default integer.
STAT	(optional) Scalar default-kind integer variable.

Example:

```
program atomic
  use iso_fortran_env
  implicit none
  type(event_type) :: event_value_has_been_set[*]
  integer :: cnt
  if (this_image() == 1) then
    call event_query (event_value_has_been_set, cnt)
    if (cnt > 0) write(*,*) "Value has been set"
  elseif (this_image() == 2) then
    event post (event_value_has_been_set[1])
  end if
end program atomic
```

9.93 EXECUTE_COMMAND_LINE — Execute a shell command

Description:

EXECUTE_COMMAND_LINE runs a shell command, synchronously or asynchronously.

The COMMAND argument is passed to the shell and executed, using the C library's system call. (The shell is sh on Unix systems, and cmd.exe on Windows.) If WAIT is present and has the value false, the execution of the command is asynchronous if the system supports it; otherwise, the command is executed synchronously.

The three last arguments allow the user to get status information. After synchronous execution, EXITSTAT contains the integer exit code of the command, as returned by system. CMDSTAT is set to zero if the command line was executed (whatever its exit status was). CMDMSG is assigned an error message if an error has occurred.

Note that the **system** function need not be thread-safe. It is the responsibility of the user to ensure that **system** is not called concurrently.

Standard: Fortran 2008 and later

Class: Subroutine

Syntax: `CALL EXECUTE_COMMAND_LINE(COMMAND [, WAIT, EXITSTAT, CMDSTAT, CMDMSG ])`

Arguments:

COMMAND	Shall be a default **CHARACTER** scalar.
WAIT	(Optional) Shall be a default **LOGICAL** scalar.
EXITSTAT	(Optional) Shall be an **INTEGER** of the default kind.
CMDSTAT	(Optional) Shall be an **INTEGER** of the default kind.
CMDMSG	(Optional) Shall be an **CHARACTER** scalar of the default kind.

Example:

```
program test_exec
  integer :: i

  call execute_command_line ("external_prog.exe", exitstat=i)
  print *, "Exit status of external_prog.exe was ", i

  call execute_command_line ("reindex_files.exe", wait=.false.)
  print *, "Now reindexing files in the background"

end program test_exec
```

Note:

Because this intrinsic is implemented in terms of the **system** function call, its behavior with respect to signaling is processor dependent. In particular, on POSIX-compliant systems, the SIGINT and SIGQUIT signals will be ignored, and the SIGCHLD will be blocked. As such, if the parent process is terminated, the child process might not be terminated alongside.

See also: Section 9.253 [SYSTEM], page 236

9.94 EXIT — Exit the program with status.

Description:

EXIT causes immediate termination of the program with status. If status is omitted it returns the canonical *success* for the system. All Fortran I/O units are closed.

Standard: GNU extension

Class: Subroutine

Syntax: `CALL EXIT([STATUS])`

Arguments:

STATUS	Shall be an **INTEGER** of the default kind.

Return value:

STATUS is passed to the parent process on exit.

Example:

```
program test_exit
  integer :: STATUS = 0
  print *, 'This program is going to exit.'
  call EXIT(STATUS)
end program test_exit
```

See also: Section 9.2 [ABORT], page 85, Section 9.154 [KILL], page 180

9.95 EXP — Exponential function

Description:

EXP(X) computes the base *e* exponential of *X*.

Standard: Fortran 77 and later, has overloads that are GNU extensions

Class: Elemental function

Syntax: RESULT = EXP(X)

Arguments:

X   The type shall be REAL or COMPLEX.

Return value:

The return value has same type and kind as *X*.

Example:

```
program test_exp
  real :: x = 1.0
  x = exp(x)
end program test_exp
```

Specific names:

Name	Argument	Return type	Standard
EXP(X)	REAL(4) X	REAL(4)	Fortran 77 and later
DEXP(X)	REAL(8) X	REAL(8)	Fortran 77 and later
CEXP(X)	COMPLEX(4) X	COMPLEX(4)	Fortran 77 and later
ZEXP(X)	COMPLEX(8) X	COMPLEX(8)	GNU extension
CDEXP(X)	COMPLEX(8) X	COMPLEX(8)	GNU extension

9.96 EXPONENT — Exponent function

Description:

EXPONENT(X) returns the value of the exponent part of *X*. If *X* is zero the value returned is zero.

Standard: Fortran 95 and later

Class: Elemental function

Syntax: RESULT = EXPONENT(X)

Arguments:

X   The type shall be REAL.

Return value:

The return value is of type default INTEGER.

Example:

```
program test_exponent
  real :: x = 1.0
  integer :: i
  i = exponent(x)
  print *, i
  print *, exponent(0.0)
end program test_exponent
```

9.97 EXTENDS_TYPE_OF — Query dynamic type for extension

Description:

Query dynamic type for extension.

Standard: Fortran 2003 and later

Class: Inquiry function

Syntax: RESULT = EXTENDS_TYPE_OF(A, MOLD)

Arguments:

A	Shall be an object of extensible declared type or unlimited polymorphic.
MOLD	Shall be an object of extensible declared type or unlimited polymorphic.

Return value:

The return value is a scalar of type default logical. It is true if and only if the dynamic type of A is an extension type of the dynamic type of MOLD.

See also: Section 9.225 [SAME_TYPE_AS], page 219

9.98 FDATE — Get the current time as a string

Description:

FDATE(DATE) returns the current date (using the same format as CTIME) in *DATE*. It is equivalent to CALL CTIME(DATE, TIME()).

This intrinsic is provided in both subroutine and function forms; however, only one form can be used in any given program unit.

Standard: GNU extension

Class: Subroutine, function

Syntax:

CALL FDATE(DATE).
DATE = FDATE().

Arguments:

DATE	The type shall be of type **CHARACTER** of the default kind. It is an **INTENT(OUT)** argument. If the length of this variable is too short for the date and time string to fit completely, it will be blank on procedure return.

Return value:

> The current date and time as a string.

Example:

```
program test_fdate
    integer(8) :: i, j
    character(len=30) :: date
    call fdate(date)
    print *, 'Program started on ', date
    do i = 1, 100000000 ! Just a delay
        j = i * i - i
    end do
    call fdate(date)
    print *, 'Program ended on ', date
end program test_fdate
```

See also: Section 9.75 [DATE_AND_TIME], page 133, Section 9.74 [CTIME], page 132

9.99 FGET — Read a single character in stream mode from stdin

Description:

> Read a single character in stream mode from stdin by bypassing normal formatted output. Stream I/O should not be mixed with normal record-oriented (formatted or unformatted) I/O on the same unit; the results are unpredictable.
>
> This intrinsic is provided in both subroutine and function forms; however, only one form can be used in any given program unit.
>
> Note that the FGET intrinsic is provided for backwards compatibility with g77. GNU Fortran provides the Fortran 2003 Stream facility. Programmers should consider the use of new stream IO feature in new code for future portability. See also Section 4.1 [Fortran 2003 status], page 35.

Standard: GNU extension

Class: Subroutine, function

Syntax:

```
CALL FGET(C [, STATUS])
STATUS = FGET(C)
```

Arguments:

> | | |
> |---|---|
> | C | The type shall be CHARACTER and of default kind. |
> | STATUS | (Optional) status flag of type INTEGER. Returns 0 on success, -1 on end-of-file, and a system specific positive error code otherwise. |

Example:

```
PROGRAM test_fget
    INTEGER, PARAMETER :: strlen = 100
    INTEGER :: status, i = 1
    CHARACTER(len=strlen) :: str = ""

    WRITE (*,*) 'Enter text:'
```

```
      DO
        CALL fget(str(i:i), status)
        if (status /= 0 .OR. i > strlen) exit
        i = i + 1
      END DO
      WRITE (*,*) TRIM(str)
    END PROGRAM
```

See also: Section 9.100 [FGETC], page 149, Section 9.104 [FPUT], page 152, Section 9.105 [FPUTC], page 152

9.100 FGETC — Read a single character in stream mode

Description:

Read a single character in stream mode by bypassing normal formatted output. Stream I/O should not be mixed with normal record-oriented (formatted or unformatted) I/O on the same unit; the results are unpredictable.

This intrinsic is provided in both subroutine and function forms; however, only one form can be used in any given program unit.

Note that the FGET intrinsic is provided for backwards compatibility with g77. GNU Fortran provides the Fortran 2003 Stream facility. Programmers should consider the use of new stream IO feature in new code for future portability. See also Section 4.1 [Fortran 2003 status], page 35.

Standard: GNU extension

Class: Subroutine, function

Syntax:

```
CALL FGETC(UNIT, C [, STATUS])
STATUS = FGETC(UNIT, C)
```

Arguments:

UNIT	The type shall be INTEGER.
C	The type shall be CHARACTER and of default kind.
STATUS	(Optional) status flag of type INTEGER. Returns 0 on success, -1 on end-of-file and a system specific positive error code otherwise.

Example:

```
PROGRAM test_fgetc
  INTEGER :: fd = 42, status
  CHARACTER :: c

  OPEN(UNIT=fd, FILE="/etc/passwd", ACTION="READ", STATUS = "OLD")
  DO
    CALL fgetc(fd, c, status)
    IF (status /= 0) EXIT
    call fput(c)
  END DO
  CLOSE(UNIT=fd)
END PROGRAM
```

See also: Section 9.99 [FGET], page 148, Section 9.104 [FPUT], page 152, Section 9.105 [FPUTC], page 152

9.101 FLOOR — Integer floor function

Description:

FLOOR(A) returns the greatest integer less than or equal to *X*.

Standard: Fortran 95 and later

Class: Elemental function

Syntax: RESULT = FLOOR(A [, KIND])

Arguments:

A   The type shall be **REAL**.

KIND   (Optional) An **INTEGER** initialization expression indicating the kind parameter of the result.

Return value:

The return value is of type **INTEGER(KIND)** if *KIND* is present and of default-kind **INTEGER** otherwise.

Example:

```
program test_floor
    real :: x = 63.29
    real :: y = -63.59
    print *, floor(x) ! returns 63
    print *, floor(y) ! returns -64
end program test_floor
```

See also: Section 9.54 [CEILING], page 118, Section 9.198 [NINT], page 204

9.102 FLUSH — Flush I/O unit(s)

Description:

Flushes Fortran unit(s) currently open for output. Without the optional argument, all units are flushed, otherwise just the unit specified.

Standard: GNU extension

Class: Subroutine

Syntax: CALL FLUSH(UNIT)

Arguments:

UNIT   (Optional) The type shall be **INTEGER**.

Note: Beginning with the Fortran 2003 standard, there is a **FLUSH** statement that should be preferred over the **FLUSH** intrinsic.

The **FLUSH** intrinsic and the Fortran 2003 **FLUSH** statement have identical effect: they flush the runtime library's I/O buffer so that the data becomes visible to other processes. This does not guarantee that the data is committed to disk.

On POSIX systems, you can request that all data is transferred to the storage device by calling the **fsync** function, with the POSIX file descriptor of the I/O unit as argument (retrieved with GNU intrinsic **FNUM**). The following example shows how:

```
! Declare the interface for POSIX fsync function
interface
  function fsync (fd) bind(c,name="fsync")
  use iso_c_binding, only: c_int
    integer(c_int), value :: fd
    integer(c_int) :: fsync
  end function fsync
end interface

! Variable declaration
integer :: ret

! Opening unit 10
open (10,file="foo")

! ...
! Perform I/O on unit 10
! ...

! Flush and sync
flush(10)
ret = fsync(fnum(10))

! Handle possible error
if (ret /= 0) stop "Error calling FSYNC"
```

9.103 FNUM — File number function

Description:

FNUM(UNIT) returns the POSIX file descriptor number corresponding to the open Fortran I/O unit UNIT.

Standard: GNU extension

Class: Function

Syntax: RESULT = FNUM(UNIT)

Arguments:

UNIT   The type shall be INTEGER.

Return value:

The return value is of type INTEGER

Example:

```
program test_fnum
  integer :: i
  open (unit=10, status = "scratch")
  i = fnum(10)
  print *, i
  close (10)
end program test_fnum
```

9.104 FPUT — Write a single character in stream mode to stdout

Description:

Write a single character in stream mode to stdout by bypassing normal formatted output. Stream I/O should not be mixed with normal record-oriented (formatted or unformatted) I/O on the same unit; the results are unpredictable.

This intrinsic is provided in both subroutine and function forms; however, only one form can be used in any given program unit.

Note that the **FGET** intrinsic is provided for backwards compatibility with **g77**. GNU Fortran provides the Fortran 2003 Stream facility. Programmers should consider the use of new stream IO feature in new code for future portability. See also Section 4.1 [Fortran 2003 status], page 35.

Standard: GNU extension

Class: Subroutine, function

Syntax:

```
CALL FPUT(C [, STATUS])
STATUS = FPUT(C)
```

Arguments:

C	The type shall be **CHARACTER** and of default kind.
STATUS	(Optional) status flag of type **INTEGER**. Returns 0 on success, -1 on end-of-file and a system specific positive error code otherwise.

Example:

```
PROGRAM test_fput
  CHARACTER(len=10) :: str = "gfortran"
  INTEGER :: i
  DO i = 1, len_trim(str)
    CALL fput(str(i:i))
  END DO
END PROGRAM
```

See also: Section 9.105 [FPUTC], page 152, Section 9.99 [FGET], page 148, Section 9.100 [FGETC], page 149

9.105 FPUTC — Write a single character in stream mode

Description:

Write a single character in stream mode by bypassing normal formatted output. Stream I/O should not be mixed with normal record-oriented (formatted or unformatted) I/O on the same unit; the results are unpredictable.

This intrinsic is provided in both subroutine and function forms; however, only one form can be used in any given program unit.

Note that the **FGET** intrinsic is provided for backwards compatibility with **g77**. GNU Fortran provides the Fortran 2003 Stream facility. Programmers should consider the use of new stream IO feature in new code for future portability. See also Section 4.1 [Fortran 2003 status], page 35.

Standard: GNU extension

Class: Subroutine, function

Syntax:

```
CALL FPUTC(UNIT, C [, STATUS])
STATUS = FPUTC(UNIT, C)
```

Arguments:

UNIT	The type shall be **INTEGER**.
C	The type shall be **CHARACTER** and of default kind.
STATUS	(Optional) status flag of type **INTEGER**. Returns 0 on success, -1 on end-of-file and a system specific positive error code otherwise.

Example:

```
PROGRAM test_fputc
  CHARACTER(len=10) :: str = "gfortran"
  INTEGER :: fd = 42, i

  OPEN(UNIT = fd, FILE = "out", ACTION = "WRITE", STATUS="NEW")
  DO i = 1, len_trim(str)
    CALL fputc(fd, str(i:i))
  END DO
  CLOSE(fd)
END PROGRAM
```

See also: Section 9.104 [FPUT], page 152, Section 9.99 [FGET], page 148, Section 9.100 [FGETC], page 149

9.106 FRACTION — Fractional part of the model representation

Description:

FRACTION(X) returns the fractional part of the model representation of X.

Standard: Fortran 95 and later

Class: Elemental function

Syntax: Y = FRACTION(X)

Arguments:

X	The type of the argument shall be a **REAL**.

Return value:

The return value is of the same type and kind as the argument. The fractional part of the model representation of X is returned; it is X * RADIX(X)**(-EXPONENT(X)).

Example:

```
program test_fraction
  real :: x
  x = 178.1387e-4
  print *, fraction(x), x * radix(x)**(-exponent(x))
end program test_fraction
```

9.107 FREE — Frees memory

Description:

Frees memory previously allocated by `MALLOC`. The `FREE` intrinsic is an extension intended to be used with Cray pointers, and is provided in GNU Fortran to allow user to compile legacy code. For new code using Fortran 95 pointers, the memory de-allocation intrinsic is `DEALLOCATE`.

Standard: GNU extension

Class: Subroutine

Syntax: `CALL FREE(PTR)`

Arguments:

    PTR   The type shall be `INTEGER`. It represents the location of the memory that should be de-allocated.

Return value:

    None

Example: See `MALLOC` for an example.

See also: Section 9.176 [MALLOC], page 192

9.108 FSEEK — Low level file positioning subroutine

Description:

Moves *UNIT* to the specified *OFFSET*. If *WHENCE* is set to 0, the *OFFSET* is taken as an absolute value `SEEK_SET`, if set to 1, *OFFSET* is taken to be relative to the current position `SEEK_CUR`, and if set to 2 relative to the end of the file `SEEK_END`. On error, *STATUS* is set to a nonzero value. If *STATUS* the seek fails silently.

This intrinsic routine is not fully backwards compatible with **g77**. In **g77**, the `FSEEK` takes a statement label instead of a *STATUS* variable. If FSEEK is used in old code, change

```
CALL FSEEK(UNIT, OFFSET, WHENCE, *label)
```

to

```
INTEGER :: status
CALL FSEEK(UNIT, OFFSET, WHENCE, status)
IF (status /= 0) GOTO label
```

Please note that GNU Fortran provides the Fortran 2003 Stream facility. Programmers should consider the use of new stream IO feature in new code for future portability. See also Section 4.1 [Fortran 2003 status], page 35.

Standard: GNU extension

Class: Subroutine

Syntax: `CALL FSEEK(UNIT, OFFSET, WHENCE[, STATUS])`

Arguments:

    UNIT   Shall be a scalar of type `INTEGER`.

OFFSET	Shall be a scalar of type `INTEGER`.
WHENCE	Shall be a scalar of type `INTEGER`. Its value shall be either 0, 1 or 2.
STATUS	(Optional) shall be a scalar of type `INTEGER(4)`.

Example:

```
PROGRAM test_fseek
    INTEGER, PARAMETER :: SEEK_SET = 0, SEEK_CUR = 1, SEEK_END = 2
    INTEGER :: fd, offset, ierr

    ierr   = 0
    offset = 5
    fd     = 10

    OPEN(UNIT=fd, FILE="fseek.test")
    CALL FSEEK(fd, offset, SEEK_SET, ierr)  ! move to OFFSET
    print *, FTELL(fd), ierr

    CALL FSEEK(fd, 0, SEEK_END, ierr)        ! move to end
    print *, FTELL(fd), ierr

    CALL FSEEK(fd, 0, SEEK_SET, ierr)        ! move to beginning
    print *, FTELL(fd), ierr

    CLOSE(UNIT=fd)
END PROGRAM
```

See also: Section 9.110 [FTELL], page 156

9.109 `FSTAT` — Get file status

Description:

FSTAT is identical to Section 9.249 [STAT], page 233, except that information about an already opened file is obtained.

The elements in **VALUES** are the same as described by Section 9.249 [STAT], page 233.

This intrinsic is provided in both subroutine and function forms; however, only one form can be used in any given program unit.

Standard: GNU extension

Class: Subroutine, function

Syntax:

```
CALL FSTAT(UNIT, VALUES [, STATUS])
STATUS = FSTAT(UNIT, VALUES)
```

Arguments:

UNIT	An open I/O unit number of type `INTEGER`.
VALUES	The type shall be `INTEGER(4)`, `DIMENSION(13)`.
STATUS	(Optional) status flag of type `INTEGER(4)`. Returns 0 on success and a system specific error code otherwise.

Example: See Section 9.249 [STAT], page 233 for an example.

See also: To stat a link: Section 9.174 [LSTAT], page 191, to stat a file: Section 9.249
                [STAT], page 233

9.110 FTELL — Current stream position

Description:

Retrieves the current position within an open file.

This intrinsic is provided in both subroutine and function forms; however, only
one form can be used in any given program unit.

Standard: GNU extension

Class: Subroutine, function

Syntax:

```
CALL FTELL(UNIT, OFFSET)
OFFSET = FTELL(UNIT)
```

Arguments:

OFFSET	Shall of type INTEGER.
UNIT	Shall of type INTEGER.

Return value:

In either syntax, *OFFSET* is set to the current offset of unit number *UNIT*, or
to −1 if the unit is not currently open.

Example:

```
PROGRAM test_ftell
  INTEGER :: i
  OPEN(10, FILE="temp.dat")
  CALL ftell(10,i)
  WRITE(*,*) i
END PROGRAM
```

See also: Section 9.108 [FSEEK], page 154

9.111 GAMMA — Gamma function

Description:

GAMMA(X) computes Gamma (Γ) of X. For positive, integer values of X the
Gamma function simplifies to the factorial function $\Gamma(x) = (x - 1)!$.

$$\Gamma(x) = \int_0^\infty t^{x-1} e^{-t}\, \mathrm{d}t$$

Standard: Fortran 2008 and later

Class: Elemental function

Syntax: X = GAMMA(X)

Arguments:

X	Shall be of type REAL and neither zero nor a negative integer.

Return value:

The return value is of type **REAL** of the same kind as *X*.

Example:

```
program test_gamma
  real :: x = 1.0
  x = gamma(x) ! returns 1.0
end program test_gamma
```

Specific names:

Name	Argument	Return type	Standard
GAMMA(X)	REAL(4) X	REAL(4)	GNU Extension
DGAMMA(X)	REAL(8) X	REAL(8)	GNU Extension

See also: Logarithm of the Gamma function: Section 9.170 [LOG_GAMMA], page 189

9.112 GERROR — Get last system error message

Description:

Returns the system error message corresponding to the last system error. This resembles the functionality of **strerror(3)** in C.

Standard: GNU extension

Class: Subroutine

Syntax: CALL GERROR(RESULT)

Arguments:

RESULT   Shall of type **CHARACTER** and of default

Example:

```
PROGRAM test_gerror
  CHARACTER(len=100) :: msg
  CALL gerror(msg)
  WRITE(*,*) msg
END PROGRAM
```

See also: Section 9.138 [IERRNO], page 172, Section 9.206 [PERROR], page 209

9.113 GETARG — Get command line arguments

Description:

Retrieve the *POS*-th argument that was passed on the command line when the containing program was invoked.

This intrinsic routine is provided for backwards compatibility with GNU Fortran 77. In new code, programmers should consider the use of the Section 9.115 [GET_COMMAND_ARGUMENT], page 159 intrinsic defined by the Fortran 2003 standard.

Standard: GNU extension

Class: Subroutine

Syntax: CALL GETARG(POS, VALUE)

Arguments:

POS	Shall be of type `INTEGER` and not wider than the default integer kind; $POS \geq 0$
VALUE	Shall be of type `CHARACTER` and of default kind.
VALUE	Shall be of type `CHARACTER`.

Return value:

After `GETARG` returns, the *VALUE* argument holds the *POS*th command line argument. If *VALUE* can not hold the argument, it is truncated to fit the length of *VALUE*. If there are less than *POS* arguments specified at the command line, *VALUE* will be filled with blanks. If *POS* = 0, *VALUE* is set to the name of the program (on systems that support this feature).

Example:

```
PROGRAM test_getarg
  INTEGER :: i
  CHARACTER(len=32) :: arg

  DO i = 1, iargc()
    CALL getarg(i, arg)
    WRITE (*,*) arg
  END DO
END PROGRAM
```

See also: GNU Fortran 77 compatibility function: Section 9.131 [IARGC], page 168

Fortran 2003 functions and subroutines: Section 9.114 [GET_COMMAND], page 158, Section 9.115 [GET_COMMAND_ARGUMENT], page 159, Section 9.64 [COMMAND_ARGUMENT_COUNT], page 126

9.114 GET_COMMAND — Get the entire command line

Description:

Retrieve the entire command line that was used to invoke the program.

Standard: Fortran 2003 and later

Class: Subroutine

Syntax: `CALL GET_COMMAND([COMMAND, LENGTH, STATUS])`

Arguments:

COMMAND	(Optional) shall be of type `CHARACTER` and of default kind.
LENGTH	(Optional) Shall be of type `INTEGER` and of default kind.
STATUS	(Optional) Shall be of type `INTEGER` and of default kind.

Return value:

If *COMMAND* is present, stores the entire command line that was used to invoke the program in *COMMAND*. If *LENGTH* is present, it is assigned the length of the command line. If *STATUS* is present, it is assigned 0 upon success of the command, -1 if *COMMAND* is too short to store the command line, or a positive value in case of an error.

Example:

```
PROGRAM test_get_command
  CHARACTER(len=255) :: cmd
  CALL get_command(cmd)
  WRITE (*,*) TRIM(cmd)
END PROGRAM
```

See also: Section 9.115 [GET_COMMAND_ARGUMENT], page 159, Section 9.64 [COMMAND_ARGUMENT_COUNT], page 126

9.115 GET_COMMAND_ARGUMENT — Get command line arguments

Description:

Retrieve the *NUMBER*-th argument that was passed on the command line when the containing program was invoked.

Standard: Fortran 2003 and later

Class: Subroutine

Syntax: `CALL GET_COMMAND_ARGUMENT(NUMBER [, VALUE, LENGTH, STATUS])`

Arguments:

NUMBER	Shall be a scalar of type `INTEGER` and of default kind, $NUMBER \geq 0$
VALUE	(Optional) Shall be a scalar of type `CHARACTER` and of default kind.
LENGTH	(Optional) Shall be a scalar of type `INTEGER` and of default kind.
STATUS	(Optional) Shall be a scalar of type `INTEGER` and of default kind.

Return value:

After `GET_COMMAND_ARGUMENT` returns, the *VALUE* argument holds the *NUMBER*-th command line argument. If *VALUE* can not hold the argument, it is truncated to fit the length of *VALUE*. If there are less than *NUMBER* arguments specified at the command line, *VALUE* will be filled with blanks. If *NUMBER* = 0, *VALUE* is set to the name of the program (on systems that support this feature). The *LENGTH* argument contains the length of the *NUMBER*-th command line argument. If the argument retrieval fails, *STATUS* is a positive number; if *VALUE* contains a truncated command line argument, *STATUS* is -1; and otherwise the *STATUS* is zero.

Example:

```
PROGRAM test_get_command_argument
  INTEGER :: i
  CHARACTER(len=32) :: arg

  i = 0
  DO
    CALL get_command_argument(i, arg)
    IF (LEN_TRIM(arg) == 0) EXIT

    WRITE (*,*) TRIM(arg)
    i = i+1
```

```
      END DO
      END PROGRAM
```

See also: Section 9.114 [GET_COMMAND], page 158, Section 9.64 [COM-MAND_ARGUMENT_COUNT], page 126

9.116 GETCWD — Get current working directory

Description:

Get current working directory.

This intrinsic is provided in both subroutine and function forms; however, only one form can be used in any given program unit.

Standard: GNU extension

Class: Subroutine, function

Syntax:

```
CALL GETCWD(C [, STATUS])
STATUS = GETCWD(C)
```

Arguments:

C	The type shall be **CHARACTER** and of default kind.
STATUS	(Optional) status flag. Returns 0 on success, a system specific and nonzero error code otherwise.

Example:

```
PROGRAM test_getcwd
  CHARACTER(len=255) :: cwd
  CALL getcwd(cwd)
  WRITE(*,*) TRIM(cwd)
END PROGRAM
```

See also: Section 9.56 [CHDIR], page 119

9.117 GETENV — Get an environmental variable

Description:

Get the *VALUE* of the environmental variable *NAME*.

This intrinsic routine is provided for backwards compatibility with GNU Fortran 77. In new code, programmers should consider the use of the Section 9.118 [GET_ENVIRONMENT_VARIABLE], page 161 intrinsic defined by the Fortran 2003 standard.

Note that **GETENV** need not be thread-safe. It is the responsibility of the user to ensure that the environment is not being updated concurrently with a call to the **GETENV** intrinsic.

Standard: GNU extension

Class: Subroutine

Syntax: CALL GETENV(NAME, VALUE)

Arguments:

NAME	Shall be of type **CHARACTER** and of default kind.
VALUE	Shall be of type **CHARACTER** and of default kind.

Return value:

Stores the value of *NAME* in *VALUE*. If *VALUE* is not large enough to hold the data, it is truncated. If *NAME* is not set, *VALUE* will be filled with blanks.

Example:

```
PROGRAM test_getenv
  CHARACTER(len=255) :: homedir
  CALL getenv("HOME", homedir)
  WRITE (*,*) TRIM(homedir)
END PROGRAM
```

See also: Section 9.118 [GET_ENVIRONMENT_VARIABLE], page 161

9.118 GET_ENVIRONMENT_VARIABLE — Get an environmental variable

Description:

Get the *VALUE* of the environmental variable *NAME*.

Note that **GET_ENVIRONMENT_VARIABLE** need not be thread-safe. It is the responsibility of the user to ensure that the environment is not being updated concurrently with a call to the **GET_ENVIRONMENT_VARIABLE** intrinsic.

Standard: Fortran 2003 and later

Class: Subroutine

Syntax: CALL GET_ENVIRONMENT_VARIABLE(NAME[, VALUE, LENGTH, STATUS, TRIM_NAME)

Arguments:

NAME	Shall be a scalar of type **CHARACTER** and of default kind.
VALUE	(Optional) Shall be a scalar of type **CHARACTER** and of default kind.
LENGTH	(Optional) Shall be a scalar of type **INTEGER** and of default kind.
STATUS	(Optional) Shall be a scalar of type **INTEGER** and of default kind.
TRIM_NAME	(Optional) Shall be a scalar of type **LOGICAL** and of default kind.

Return value:

Stores the value of *NAME* in *VALUE*. If *VALUE* is not large enough to hold the data, it is truncated. If *NAME* is not set, *VALUE* will be filled with blanks. Argument *LENGTH* contains the length needed for storing the environment variable *NAME* or zero if it is not present. *STATUS* is -1 if *VALUE* is present but too short for the environment variable; it is 1 if the environment variable does not exist and 2 if the processor does not support environment variables; in all other cases *STATUS* is zero. If *TRIM_NAME* is present with the value

.FALSE., the trailing blanks in *NAME* are significant; otherwise they are not part of the environment variable name.

Example:

```
PROGRAM test_getenv
  CHARACTER(len=255) :: homedir
  CALL get_environment_variable("HOME", homedir)
  WRITE (*,*) TRIM(homedir)
END PROGRAM
```

9.119 GETGID — Group ID function

Description:
          Returns the numerical group ID of the current process.

Standard: GNU extension

Class: Function

Syntax: RESULT = GETGID()

Return value:
          The return value of GETGID is an INTEGER of the default kind.

Example: See GETPID for an example.

See also: Section 9.121 [GETPID], page 163, Section 9.122 [GETUID], page 163

9.120 GETLOG — Get login name

Description:
          Gets the username under which the program is running.

Standard: GNU extension

Class: Subroutine

Syntax: CALL GETLOG(C)

Arguments:
          C   Shall be of type CHARACTER and of default kind.

Return value:
          Stores the current user name in *LOGIN*. (On systems where POSIX functions geteuid and getpwuid are not available, and the getlogin function is not implemented either, this will return a blank string.)

Example:

```
PROGRAM TEST_GETLOG
  CHARACTER(32) :: login
  CALL GETLOG(login)
  WRITE(*,*) login
END PROGRAM
```

See also: Section 9.122 [GETUID], page 163

9.121 GETPID — Process ID function

Description:

Returns the numerical process identifier of the current process.

Standard: GNU extension

Class: Function

Syntax: `RESULT = GETPID()`

Return value:

The return value of `GETPID` is an `INTEGER` of the default kind.

Example:

```
program info
  print *, "The current process ID is ", getpid()
  print *, "Your numerical user ID is ", getuid()
  print *, "Your numerical group ID is ", getgid()
end program info
```

See also: Section 9.119 [GETGID], page 162, Section 9.122 [GETUID], page 163

9.122 GETUID — User ID function

Description:

Returns the numerical user ID of the current process.

Standard: GNU extension

Class: Function

Syntax: `RESULT = GETUID()`

Return value:

The return value of `GETUID` is an `INTEGER` of the default kind.

Example: See `GETPID` for an example.

See also: Section 9.121 [GETPID], page 163, Section 9.120 [GETLOG], page 162

9.123 GMTIME — Convert time to GMT info

Description:

Given a system time value *TIME* (as provided by the `TIME8` intrinsic), fills *VALUES* with values extracted from it appropriate to the UTC time zone (Universal Coordinated Time, also known in some countries as GMT, Greenwich Mean Time), using `gmtime(3)`.

Standard: GNU extension

Class: Subroutine

Syntax: `CALL GMTIME(TIME, VALUES)`

Arguments:

TIME	An `INTEGER` scalar expression corresponding to a system time, with `INTENT(IN)`.
VALUES	A default `INTEGER` array with 9 elements, with `INTENT(OUT)`.

Return value:

> The elements of *VALUES* are assigned as follows:
>
> 1. Seconds after the minute, range 0–59 or 0–61 to allow for leap seconds
> 2. Minutes after the hour, range 0–59
> 3. Hours past midnight, range 0–23
> 4. Day of month, range 0–31
> 5. Number of months since January, range 0–12
> 6. Years since 1900
> 7. Number of days since Sunday, range 0–6
> 8. Days since January 1
> 9. Daylight savings indicator: positive if daylight savings is in effect, zero if not, and negative if the information is not available.

See also: Section 9.74 [CTIME], page 132, Section 9.175 [LTIME], page 191, Section 9.258 [TIME], page 240, Section 9.259 [TIME8], page 240

9.124 HOSTNM — Get system host name

Description:

> Retrieves the host name of the system on which the program is running.
>
> This intrinsic is provided in both subroutine and function forms; however, only one form can be used in any given program unit.

Standard: GNU extension

Class: Subroutine, function

Syntax:

```
CALL HOSTNM(C [, STATUS])
STATUS = HOSTNM(NAME)
```

Arguments:

C	Shall of type CHARACTER and of default kind.
STATUS	(Optional) status flag of type INTEGER. Returns 0 on success, or a system specific error code otherwise.

Return value:

> In either syntax, *NAME* is set to the current hostname if it can be obtained, or to a blank string otherwise.

9.125 HUGE — Largest number of a kind

Description:

> HUGE(X) returns the largest number that is not an infinity in the model of the type of X.

Standard: Fortran 95 and later

Class: Inquiry function

Syntax: RESULT = HUGE(X)

Arguments:

X	Shall be of type REAL or INTEGER.

Return value:

The return value is of the same type and kind as X

Example:

```
program test_huge_tiny
  print *, huge(0), huge(0.0), huge(0.0d0)
  print *, tiny(0.0), tiny(0.0d0)
end program test_huge_tiny
```

9.126 HYPOT — Euclidean distance function

Description:

HYPOT(X,Y) is the Euclidean distance function. It is equal to $\sqrt{X^2 + Y^2}$, without undue underflow or overflow.

Standard: Fortran 2008 and later

Class: Elemental function

Syntax: RESULT = HYPOT(X, Y)

Arguments:

X	The type shall be REAL.
Y	The type and kind type parameter shall be the same as X.

Return value:

The return value has the same type and kind type parameter as X.

Example:

```
program test_hypot
  real(4) :: x = 1.e0_4, y = 0.5e0_4
  x = hypot(x,y)
end program test_hypot
```

9.127 IACHAR — Code in ASCII collating sequence

Description:

IACHAR(C) returns the code for the ASCII character in the first character position of C.

Standard: Fortran 95 and later, with *KIND* argument Fortran 2003 and later

Class: Elemental function

Syntax: RESULT = IACHAR(C [, KIND])

Arguments:

C	Shall be a scalar CHARACTER, with INTENT(IN)
KIND	(Optional) An INTEGER initialization expression indicating the kind parameter of the result.

Return value:

> The return value is of type INTEGER and of kind *KIND*. If *KIND* is absent, the return value is of default integer kind.

Example:

```
program test_iachar
  integer i
  i = iachar(' ')
end program test_iachar
```

Note: See Section 9.135 [ICHAR], page 170 for a discussion of converting between numerical values and formatted string representations.

See also: Section 9.5 [ACHAR], page 87, Section 9.55 [CHAR], page 119, Section 9.135 [ICHAR], page 170

9.128 IALL — Bitwise AND of array elements

Description:

> Reduces with bitwise AND the elements of *ARRAY* along dimension *DIM* if the corresponding element in *MASK* is TRUE.

Standard: Fortran 2008 and later

Class: Transformational function

Syntax:

```
RESULT = IALL(ARRAY[, MASK])
RESULT = IALL(ARRAY, DIM[, MASK])
```

Arguments:

ARRAY	Shall be an array of type INTEGER
DIM	(Optional) shall be a scalar of type INTEGER with a value in the range from 1 to n, where n equals the rank of *ARRAY*.
MASK	(Optional) shall be of type LOGICAL and either be a scalar or an array of the same shape as *ARRAY*.

Return value:

> The result is of the same type as *ARRAY*.
>
> If *DIM* is absent, a scalar with the bitwise ALL of all elements in *ARRAY* is returned. Otherwise, an array of rank n-1, where n equals the rank of *ARRAY*, and a shape similar to that of *ARRAY* with dimension *DIM* dropped is returned.

Example:

```
PROGRAM test_iall
  INTEGER(1) :: a(2)

  a(1) = b'00100100'
  a(2) = b'01101010'

  ! prints 00100000
  PRINT '(b8.8)', IALL(a)
END PROGRAM
```

See also: Section 9.130 [IANY], page 167, Section 9.145 [IPARITY], page 175, Section 9.129 [IAND], page 167

9.129 `IAND` — **Bitwise logical and**

Description:

Bitwise logical `AND`.

Standard: Fortran 95 and later

Class: Elemental function

Syntax: `RESULT = IAND(I, J)`

Arguments:

I	The type shall be `INTEGER`.
J	The type shall be `INTEGER`, of the same kind as *I*. (As a GNU extension, different kinds are also permitted.)

Return value:

The return type is `INTEGER`, of the same kind as the arguments. (If the argument kinds differ, it is of the same kind as the larger argument.)

Example:

```
PROGRAM test_iand
  INTEGER :: a, b
  DATA a / Z'F' /, b / Z'3' /
  WRITE (*,*) IAND(a, b)
END PROGRAM
```

See also: Section 9.144 [IOR], page 175, Section 9.137 [IEOR], page 171, Section 9.133 [IBITS], page 169, Section 9.134 [IBSET], page 169, Section 9.132 [IBCLR], page 169, Section 9.200 [NOT], page 205

9.130 `IANY` — **Bitwise OR of array elements**

Description:

Reduces with bitwise OR (inclusive or) the elements of *ARRAY* along dimension *DIM* if the corresponding element in *MASK* is `TRUE`.

Standard: Fortran 2008 and later

Class: Transformational function

Syntax:

```
RESULT = IANY(ARRAY[, MASK])
RESULT = IANY(ARRAY, DIM[, MASK])
```

Arguments:

ARRAY	Shall be an array of type `INTEGER`
DIM	(Optional) shall be a scalar of type `INTEGER` with a value in the range from 1 to n, where n equals the rank of *ARRAY*.
MASK	(Optional) shall be of type `LOGICAL` and either be a scalar or an array of the same shape as *ARRAY*.

Return value:

The result is of the same type as *ARRAY*.

If *DIM* is absent, a scalar with the bitwise OR of all elements in *ARRAY* is returned. Otherwise, an array of rank n-1, where n equals the rank of *ARRAY*, and a shape similar to that of *ARRAY* with dimension *DIM* dropped is returned.

Example:

```
PROGRAM test_iany
  INTEGER(1) :: a(2)

  a(1) = b'00100100'
  a(2) = b'01101010'

  ! prints 01101110
  PRINT '(b8.8)', IANY(a)
END PROGRAM
```

See also: Section 9.145 [IPARITY], page 175, Section 9.128 [IALL], page 166, Section 9.144 [IOR], page 175

9.131 IARGC — Get the number of command line arguments

Description:

IARGC returns the number of arguments passed on the command line when the containing program was invoked.

This intrinsic routine is provided for backwards compatibility with GNU Fortran 77. In new code, programmers should consider the use of the Section 9.64 [COMMAND_ARGUMENT_COUNT], page 126 intrinsic defined by the Fortran 2003 standard.

Standard: GNU extension

Class: Function

Syntax: RESULT = IARGC()

Arguments:

None.

Return value:

The number of command line arguments, type INTEGER(4).

Example: See Section 9.113 [GETARG], page 157

See also: GNU Fortran 77 compatibility subroutine: Section 9.113 [GETARG], page 157

Fortran 2003 functions and subroutines: Section 9.114 [GET_COMMAND], page 158, Section 9.115 [GET_COMMAND_ARGUMENT], page 159, Section 9.64 [COMMAND_ARGUMENT_COUNT], page 126

9.132 `IBCLR` — **Clear bit**

Description:

IBCLR returns the value of *I* with the bit at position *POS* set to zero.

Standard: Fortran 95 and later

Class: Elemental function

Syntax: `RESULT = IBCLR(I, POS)`

Arguments:

I	The type shall be `INTEGER`.
POS	The type shall be `INTEGER`.

Return value:

The return value is of type `INTEGER` and of the same kind as *I*.

See also: Section 9.133 [IBITS], page 169, Section 9.134 [IBSET], page 169, Section 9.129 [IAND], page 167, Section 9.144 [IOR], page 175, Section 9.137 [IEOR], page 171, Section 9.195 [MVBITS], page 202

9.133 `IBITS` — **Bit extraction**

Description:

IBITS extracts a field of length *LEN* from *I*, starting from bit position *POS* and extending left for *LEN* bits. The result is right-justified and the remaining bits are zeroed. The value of POS+LEN must be less than or equal to the value `BIT_SIZE(I)`.

Standard: Fortran 95 and later

Class: Elemental function

Syntax: `RESULT = IBITS(I, POS, LEN)`

Arguments:

I	The type shall be `INTEGER`.
POS	The type shall be `INTEGER`.
LEN	The type shall be `INTEGER`.

Return value:

The return value is of type `INTEGER` and of the same kind as *I*.

See also: Section 9.44 [BIT_SIZE], page 112, Section 9.132 [IBCLR], page 169, Section 9.134 [IBSET], page 169, Section 9.129 [IAND], page 167, Section 9.144 [IOR], page 175, Section 9.137 [IEOR], page 171

9.134 `IBSET` — **Set bit**

Description:

IBSET returns the value of *I* with the bit at position *POS* set to one.

Standard: Fortran 95 and later

Class: Elemental function

Syntax: RESULT = IBSET(I, POS)

Arguments:

> I   The type shall be INTEGER.
>
> POS   The type shall be INTEGER.

Return value:

> The return value is of type INTEGER and of the same kind as *I*.

See also: Section 9.132 [IBCLR], page 169, Section 9.133 [IBITS], page 169, Section 9.129 [IAND], page 167, Section 9.144 [IOR], page 175, Section 9.137 [IEOR], page 171, Section 9.195 [MVBITS], page 202

9.135 ICHAR — Character-to-integer conversion function

Description:

> ICHAR(C) returns the code for the character in the first character position of C in the system's native character set. The correspondence between characters and their codes is not necessarily the same across different GNU Fortran implementations.

Standard: Fortran 95 and later, with *KIND* argument Fortran 2003 and later

Class: Elemental function

Syntax: RESULT = ICHAR(C [, KIND])

Arguments:

> C   Shall be a scalar CHARACTER, with INTENT(IN)
>
> KIND   (Optional) An INTEGER initialization expression indicating the kind parameter of the result.

Return value:

> The return value is of type INTEGER and of kind *KIND*. If *KIND* is absent, the return value is of default integer kind.

Example:

```
program test_ichar
  integer i
  i = ichar(' ')
end program test_ichar
```

Specific names:

Name	Argument	Return type	Standard
ICHAR(C)	CHARACTER C	INTEGER(4)	Fortran 77 and later

Note: No intrinsic exists to convert between a numeric value and a formatted character string representation – for instance, given the CHARACTER value '154', obtaining an INTEGER or REAL value with the value 154, or vice versa. Instead, this functionality is provided by internal-file I/O, as in the following example:

```
program read_val
  integer value
  character(len=10) string, string2
  string = '154'
```

```
! Convert a string to a numeric value
read (string,'(I10)') value
print *, value

! Convert a value to a formatted string
write (string2,'(I10)') value
print *, string2
end program read_val
```

See also: Section 9.5 [ACHAR], page 87, Section 9.55 [CHAR], page 119, Section 9.127 [IACHAR], page 165

9.136 `IDATE` — Get current local time subroutine (day/month/year)

Description:

`IDATE(VALUES)` Fills *VALUES* with the numerical values at the current local time. The day (in the range 1-31), month (in the range 1-12), and year appear in elements 1, 2, and 3 of *VALUES*, respectively. The year has four significant digits.

Standard: GNU extension

Class: Subroutine

Syntax: `CALL IDATE(VALUES)`

Arguments:

VALUES   The type shall be `INTEGER`, `DIMENSION(3)` and the kind shall be the default integer kind.

Return value:

Does not return anything.

Example:

```
program test_idate
  integer, dimension(3) :: tarray
  call idate(tarray)
  print *, tarray(1)
  print *, tarray(2)
  print *, tarray(3)
end program test_idate
```

9.137 `IEOR` — Bitwise logical exclusive or

Description:

`IEOR` returns the bitwise Boolean exclusive-OR of *I* and *J*.

Standard: Fortran 95 and later

Class: Elemental function

Syntax: `RESULT = IEOR(I, J)`

Arguments:

I   The type shall be `INTEGER`.

> *J*   The type shall be `INTEGER`, of the same kind as *I*. (As a GNU extension, different kinds are also permitted.)

Return value:

  The return type is `INTEGER`, of the same kind as the arguments. (If the argument kinds differ, it is of the same kind as the larger argument.)

See also: Section 9.144 [IOR], page 175, Section 9.129 [IAND], page 167, Section 9.133 [IBITS], page 169, Section 9.134 [IBSET], page 169, Section 9.132 [IBCLR], page 169, Section 9.200 [NOT], page 205

9.138 IERRNO — Get the last system error number

Description:

  Returns the last system error number, as given by the C `errno` variable.

Standard: GNU extension

Class: Function

Syntax: `RESULT = IERRNO()`

Arguments:

  None.

Return value:

  The return value is of type `INTEGER` and of the default integer kind.

See also: Section 9.206 [PERROR], page 209

9.139 IMAGE_INDEX — Function that converts a cosubscript to an image index

Description:

  Returns the image index belonging to a cosubscript.

Standard: Fortran 2008 and later

Class: Inquiry function.

Syntax: `RESULT = IMAGE_INDEX(COARRAY, SUB)`

Arguments: None.

  COARRAY Coarray of any type.
  SUB default integer rank-1 array of a size equal to the corank of *COARRAY*.

Return value:

  Scalar default integer with the value of the image index which corresponds to the cosubscripts. For invalid cosubscripts the result is zero.

Example:

```
INTEGER :: array[2,-1:4,8,*]
! Writes  28 (or 0 if there are fewer than 28 images)
WRITE (*,*) IMAGE_INDEX (array, [2,0,3,1])
```

See also: Section 9.257 [THIS_IMAGE], page 239, Section 9.202 [NUM_IMAGES], page 206

9.140 INDEX — Position of a substring within a string

Description:

Returns the position of the start of the first occurrence of string *SUBSTRING* as a substring in *STRING*, counting from one. If *SUBSTRING* is not present in *STRING*, zero is returned. If the *BACK* argument is present and true, the return value is the start of the last occurrence rather than the first.

Standard: Fortran 77 and later, with *KIND* argument Fortran 2003 and later

Class: Elemental function

Syntax: `RESULT = INDEX(STRING, SUBSTRING [, BACK [, KIND]])`

Arguments:

STRING	Shall be a scalar `CHARACTER`, with `INTENT(IN)`
SUBSTRING	Shall be a scalar `CHARACTER`, with `INTENT(IN)`
BACK	(Optional) Shall be a scalar `LOGICAL`, with `INTENT(IN)`
KIND	(Optional) An `INTEGER` initialization expression indicating the kind parameter of the result.

Return value:

The return value is of type `INTEGER` and of kind *KIND*. If *KIND* is absent, the return value is of default integer kind.

Specific names:

Name	Argument	Return type	Standard
`INDEX(STRING, SUBSTRING)`	`CHARACTER`	`INTEGER(4)`	Fortran 77 and later

See also: Section 9.227 [SCAN], page 220, Section 9.271 [VERIFY], page 246

9.141 INT — Convert to integer type

Description:

Convert to integer type

Standard: Fortran 77 and later

Class: Elemental function

Syntax: `RESULT = INT(A [, KIND))`

Arguments:

A	Shall be of type `INTEGER`, `REAL`, or `COMPLEX`.
KIND	(Optional) An `INTEGER` initialization expression indicating the kind parameter of the result.

Return value:

These functions return a `INTEGER` variable or array under the following rules:

(A)   If A is of type `INTEGER`, `INT(A) = A`

(B)   If A is of type `REAL` and $|A| < 1$, `INT(A)` equals 0. If $|A| \geq 1$, then `INT(A)` is the integer whose magnitude is the largest integer that does not exceed the magnitude of A and whose sign is the same as the sign of A.

(C)   If *A* is of type `COMPLEX`, rule B is applied to the real part of *A*.

Example:

```
program test_int
  integer :: i = 42
  complex :: z = (-3.7, 1.0)
  print *, int(i)
  print *, int(z), int(z,8)
end program
```

Specific names:

Name	Argument	Return type	Standard
INT(A)	REAL(4) A	INTEGER	Fortran 77 and later
IFIX(A)	REAL(4) A	INTEGER	Fortran 77 and later
IDINT(A)	REAL(8) A	INTEGER	Fortran 77 and later

9.142 INT2 — Convert to 16-bit integer type

Description:

Convert to a `KIND=2` integer type. This is equivalent to the standard `INT` intrinsic with an optional argument of `KIND=2`, and is only included for backwards compatibility.

The `SHORT` intrinsic is equivalent to `INT2`.

Standard: GNU extension

Class: Elemental function

Syntax: `RESULT = INT2(A)`

Arguments:

A   Shall be of type `INTEGER`, `REAL`, or `COMPLEX`.

Return value:

The return value is a `INTEGER(2)` variable.

See also: Section 9.141 [INT], page 173, Section 9.143 [INT8], page 174, Section 9.172 [LONG], page 190

9.143 INT8 — Convert to 64-bit integer type

Description:

Convert to a `KIND=8` integer type. This is equivalent to the standard `INT` intrinsic with an optional argument of `KIND=8`, and is only included for backwards compatibility.

Standard: GNU extension

Class: Elemental function

Syntax: `RESULT = INT8(A)`

Arguments:

A   Shall be of type `INTEGER`, `REAL`, or `COMPLEX`.

Return value:

> The return value is a INTEGER(8) variable.

See also: Section 9.141 [INT], page 173, Section 9.142 [INT2], page 174, Section 9.172 [LONG], page 190

9.144 IOR — Bitwise logical or

Description:

> IOR returns the bitwise Boolean inclusive-OR of *I* and *J*.

Standard: Fortran 95 and later

Class: Elemental function

Syntax: RESULT = IOR(I, J)

Arguments:

I	The type shall be INTEGER.
J	The type shall be INTEGER, of the same kind as *I*. (As a GNU extension, different kinds are also permitted.)

Return value:

> The return type is INTEGER, of the same kind as the arguments. (If the argument kinds differ, it is of the same kind as the larger argument.)

See also: Section 9.137 [IEOR], page 171, Section 9.129 [IAND], page 167, Section 9.133 [IBITS], page 169, Section 9.134 [IBSET], page 169, Section 9.132 [IBCLR], page 169, Section 9.200 [NOT], page 205

9.145 IPARITY — Bitwise XOR of array elements

Description:

> Reduces with bitwise XOR (exclusive or) the elements of *ARRAY* along dimension *DIM* if the corresponding element in *MASK* is TRUE.

Standard: Fortran 2008 and later

Class: Transformational function

Syntax:

```
RESULT = IPARITY(ARRAY[, MASK])
RESULT = IPARITY(ARRAY, DIM[, MASK])
```

Arguments:

ARRAY	Shall be an array of type INTEGER
DIM	(Optional) shall be a scalar of type INTEGER with a value in the range from 1 to n, where n equals the rank of *ARRAY*.
MASK	(Optional) shall be of type LOGICAL and either be a scalar or an array of the same shape as *ARRAY*.

Return value:

> The result is of the same type as *ARRAY*.

If *DIM* is absent, a scalar with the bitwise XOR of all elements in *ARRAY* is
returned. Otherwise, an array of rank n-1, where n equals the rank of *ARRAY*,
and a shape similar to that of *ARRAY* with dimension *DIM* dropped is returned.

Example:

```
PROGRAM test_iparity
  INTEGER(1) :: a(2)

  a(1) = b'00100100'
  a(2) = b'01101010'

  ! prints 01001110
  PRINT '(b8.8)', IPARITY(a)
END PROGRAM
```

See also: Section 9.130 [IANY], page 167, Section 9.128 [IALL], page 166, Section 9.137
[IEOR], page 171, Section 9.205 [PARITY], page 208

9.146 IRAND — Integer pseudo-random number

Description:

IRAND(FLAG) returns a pseudo-random number from a uniform distribution
between 0 and a system-dependent limit (which is in most cases 2147483647).
If *FLAG* is 0, the next number in the current sequence is returned; if *FLAG* is
1, the generator is restarted by CALL SRAND(0); if *FLAG* has any other value,
it is used as a new seed with SRAND.

This intrinsic routine is provided for backwards compatibility with GNU Fortran
77. It implements a simple modulo generator as provided by g77. For new code,
one should consider the use of Section 9.215 [RANDOM_NUMBER], page 213
as it implements a superior algorithm.

Standard: GNU extension

Class: Function

Syntax: RESULT = IRAND(I)

Arguments:

I   Shall be a scalar INTEGER of kind 4.

Return value:

The return value is of INTEGER(kind=4) type.

Example:

```
program test_irand
  integer,parameter :: seed = 86456

  call srand(seed)
  print *, irand(), irand(), irand(), irand()
  print *, irand(seed), irand(), irand(), irand()
end program test_irand
```

9.147 `IS_IOSTAT_END` — Test for end-of-file value

Description:

IS_IOSTAT_END tests whether an variable has the value of the I/O status "end of file". The function is equivalent to comparing the variable with the `IOSTAT_END` parameter of the intrinsic module `ISO_FORTRAN_ENV`.

Standard: Fortran 2003 and later

Class: Elemental function

Syntax: `RESULT = IS_IOSTAT_END(I)`

Arguments:

    I   Shall be of the type `INTEGER`.

Return value:

Returns a `LOGICAL` of the default kind, which `.TRUE.` if *I* has the value which indicates an end of file condition for `IOSTAT=` specifiers, and is `.FALSE.` otherwise.

Example:

```
PROGRAM iostat
  IMPLICIT NONE
  INTEGER :: stat, i
  OPEN(88, FILE='test.dat')
  READ(88, *, IOSTAT=stat) i
  IF(IS_IOSTAT_END(stat)) STOP 'END OF FILE'
END PROGRAM
```

9.148 `IS_IOSTAT_EOR` — Test for end-of-record value

Description:

IS_IOSTAT_EOR tests whether an variable has the value of the I/O status "end of record". The function is equivalent to comparing the variable with the `IOSTAT_EOR` parameter of the intrinsic module `ISO_FORTRAN_ENV`.

Standard: Fortran 2003 and later

Class: Elemental function

Syntax: `RESULT = IS_IOSTAT_EOR(I)`

Arguments:

    I   Shall be of the type `INTEGER`.

Return value:

Returns a `LOGICAL` of the default kind, which `.TRUE.` if *I* has the value which indicates an end of file condition for `IOSTAT=` specifiers, and is `.FALSE.` otherwise.

Example:

```
PROGRAM iostat
  IMPLICIT NONE
  INTEGER :: stat, i(50)
  OPEN(88, FILE='test.dat', FORM='UNFORMATTED')
```

```
        READ(88, IOSTAT=stat) i
        IF(IS_IOSTAT_EOR(stat)) STOP 'END OF RECORD'
      END PROGRAM
```

9.149 ISATTY — Whether a unit is a terminal device.

Description:

Determine whether a unit is connected to a terminal device.

Standard: GNU extension

Class: Function

Syntax: RESULT = ISATTY(UNIT)

Arguments:

    UNIT   Shall be a scalar INTEGER.

Return value:

Returns .TRUE. if the *UNIT* is connected to a terminal device, .FALSE. otherwise.

Example:

```
      PROGRAM test_isatty
        INTEGER(kind=1) :: unit
        DO unit = 1, 10
          write(*,*) isatty(unit=unit)
        END DO
      END PROGRAM
```

See also: Section 9.265 [TTYNAM], page 243

9.150 ISHFT — Shift bits

Description:

ISHFT returns a value corresponding to *I* with all of the bits shifted *SHIFT* places. A value of *SHIFT* greater than zero corresponds to a left shift, a value of zero corresponds to no shift, and a value less than zero corresponds to a right shift. If the absolute value of *SHIFT* is greater than BIT_SIZE(I), the value is undefined. Bits shifted out from the left end or right end are lost; zeros are shifted in from the opposite end.

Standard: Fortran 95 and later

Class: Elemental function

Syntax: RESULT = ISHFT(I, SHIFT)

Arguments:

    I   The type shall be INTEGER.

    SHIFT   The type shall be INTEGER.

Return value:

The return value is of type INTEGER and of the same kind as *I*.

See also: Section 9.151 [ISHFTC], page 179

9.151 ISHFTC — Shift bits circularly

Description:

ISHFTC returns a value corresponding to *I* with the rightmost *SIZE* bits shifted circularly *SHIFT* places; that is, bits shifted out one end are shifted into the opposite end. A value of *SHIFT* greater than zero corresponds to a left shift, a value of zero corresponds to no shift, and a value less than zero corresponds to a right shift. The absolute value of *SHIFT* must be less than *SIZE*. If the *SIZE* argument is omitted, it is taken to be equivalent to BIT_SIZE(I).

Standard: Fortran 95 and later

Class: Elemental function

Syntax: RESULT = ISHFTC(I, SHIFT [, SIZE])

Arguments:

I	The type shall be INTEGER.
SHIFT	The type shall be INTEGER.
SIZE	(Optional) The type shall be INTEGER; the value must be greater than zero and less than or equal to BIT_SIZE(I).

Return value:

The return value is of type INTEGER and of the same kind as *I*.

See also: Section 9.150 [ISHFT], page 178

9.152 ISNAN — Test for a NaN

Description:

ISNAN tests whether a floating-point value is an IEEE Not-a-Number (NaN).

Standard: GNU extension

Class: Elemental function

Syntax: ISNAN(X)

Arguments:

X	Variable of the type REAL.

Return value:

Returns a default-kind LOGICAL. The returned value is TRUE if *X* is a NaN and FALSE otherwise.

Example:

```
program test_nan
  implicit none
  real :: x
  x = -1.0
  x = sqrt(x)
  if (isnan(x)) stop '"x" is a NaN'
end program test_nan
```

9.153 ITIME — Get current local time subroutine (hour/minutes/seconds)

Description:

IDATE(VALUES) Fills *VALUES* with the numerical values at the current local time. The hour (in the range 1-24), minute (in the range 1-60), and seconds (in the range 1-60) appear in elements 1, 2, and 3 of *VALUES*, respectively.

Standard: GNU extension

Class: Subroutine

Syntax: CALL ITIME(VALUES)

Arguments:

VALUES   The type shall be INTEGER, DIMENSION(3) and the kind shall be the default integer kind.

Return value:

Does not return anything.

Example:

```
program test_itime
  integer, dimension(3) :: tarray
  call itime(tarray)
  print *, tarray(1)
  print *, tarray(2)
  print *, tarray(3)
end program test_itime
```

9.154 KILL — Send a signal to a process

Description:

Standard: Sends the signal specified by *SIGNAL* to the process *PID*. See kill(2).

This intrinsic is provided in both subroutine and function forms; however, only one form can be used in any given program unit.

Class: Subroutine, function

Syntax:

CALL KILL(C, VALUE [, STATUS])
STATUS = KILL(C, VALUE)

Arguments:

C   Shall be a scalar INTEGER, with INTENT(IN)
VALUE   Shall be a scalar INTEGER, with INTENT(IN)
STATUS   (Optional) status flag of type INTEGER(4) or INTEGER(8). Returns 0 on success, or a system-specific error code otherwise.

See also: Section 9.2 [ABORT], page 85, Section 9.94 [EXIT], page 145

9.155 KIND — Kind of an entity

Description:

KIND(X) returns the kind value of the entity X.

Standard: Fortran 95 and later

Class: Inquiry function

Syntax: K = KIND(X)

Arguments:

X   Shall be of type LOGICAL, INTEGER, REAL, COMPLEX or CHARACTER.

Return value:

The return value is a scalar of type INTEGER and of the default integer kind.

Example:

```
program test_kind
  integer,parameter :: kc = kind(' ')
  integer,parameter :: kl = kind(.true.)

  print *, "The default character kind is ", kc
  print *, "The default logical kind is ", kl
end program test_kind
```

9.156 LBOUND — Lower dimension bounds of an array

Description:

Returns the lower bounds of an array, or a single lower bound along the *DIM* dimension.

Standard: Fortran 95 and later, with *KIND* argument Fortran 2003 and later

Class: Inquiry function

Syntax: RESULT = LBOUND(ARRAY [, DIM [, KIND]])

Arguments:

ARRAY   Shall be an array, of any type.
DIM   (Optional) Shall be a scalar INTEGER.
KIND   (Optional) An INTEGER initialization expression indicating the kind parameter of the result.

Return value:

The return value is of type INTEGER and of kind *KIND*. If *KIND* is absent, the return value is of default integer kind. If *DIM* is absent, the result is an array of the lower bounds of *ARRAY*. If *DIM* is present, the result is a scalar corresponding to the lower bound of the array along that dimension. If *ARRAY* is an expression rather than a whole array or array structure component, or if it has a zero extent along the relevant dimension, the lower bound is taken to be 1.

See also: Section 9.266 [UBOUND], page 244, Section 9.157 [LCOBOUND], page 182

9.157 LCOBOUND — Lower codimension bounds of an array

Description:

Returns the lower bounds of a coarray, or a single lower cobound along the *DIM* codimension.

Standard: Fortran 2008 and later

Class: Inquiry function

Syntax: RESULT = LCOBOUND(COARRAY [, DIM [, KIND]])

Arguments:

ARRAY	Shall be an coarray, of any type.
DIM	(Optional) Shall be a scalar INTEGER.
KIND	(Optional) An INTEGER initialization expression indicating the kind parameter of the result.

Return value:

The return value is of type INTEGER and of kind *KIND*. If *KIND* is absent, the return value is of default integer kind. If *DIM* is absent, the result is an array of the lower cobounds of *COARRAY*. If *DIM* is present, the result is a scalar corresponding to the lower cobound of the array along that codimension.

See also: Section 9.267 [UCOBOUND], page 244, Section 9.156 [LBOUND], page 181

9.158 LEADZ — Number of leading zero bits of an integer

Description:

LEADZ returns the number of leading zero bits of an integer.

Standard: Fortran 2008 and later

Class: Elemental function

Syntax: RESULT = LEADZ(I)

Arguments:

I	Shall be of type INTEGER.

Return value:

The type of the return value is the default INTEGER. If all the bits of I are zero, the result value is BIT_SIZE(I).

Example:

```
PROGRAM test_leadz
  WRITE (*,*) BIT_SIZE(1)  ! prints 32
  WRITE (*,*) LEADZ(1)     ! prints 31
END PROGRAM
```

See also: Section 9.44 [BIT_SIZE], page 112, Section 9.261 [TRAILZ], page 241, Section 9.207 [POPCNT], page 209, Section 9.208 [POPPAR], page 210

9.159 LEN — Length of a character entity

Description:

Returns the length of a character string. If *STRING* is an array, the length of an element of *STRING* is returned. Note that *STRING* need not be defined when this intrinsic is invoked, since only the length, not the content, of *STRING* is needed.

Standard: Fortran 77 and later, with *KIND* argument Fortran 2003 and later

Class: Inquiry function

Syntax: L = LEN(STRING [, KIND])

Arguments:

STRING	Shall be a scalar or array of type **CHARACTER**, with **INTENT(IN)**
KIND	(Optional) An **INTEGER** initialization expression indicating the kind parameter of the result.

Return value:

The return value is of type **INTEGER** and of kind *KIND*. If *KIND* is absent, the return value is of default integer kind.

Specific names:

Name	Argument	Return type	Standard
LEN(STRING)	CHARACTER	INTEGER	Fortran 77 and later

See also: Section 9.160 [LEN_TRIM], page 183, Section 9.8 [ADJUSTL], page 89, Section 9.9 [ADJUSTR], page 89

9.160 LEN_TRIM — Length of a character entity without trailing blank characters

Description:

Returns the length of a character string, ignoring any trailing blanks.

Standard: Fortran 95 and later, with *KIND* argument Fortran 2003 and later

Class: Elemental function

Syntax: RESULT = LEN_TRIM(STRING [, KIND])

Arguments:

STRING	Shall be a scalar of type **CHARACTER**, with **INTENT(IN)**
KIND	(Optional) An **INTEGER** initialization expression indicating the kind parameter of the result.

Return value:

The return value is of type **INTEGER** and of kind *KIND*. If *KIND* is absent, the return value is of default integer kind.

See also: Section 9.159 [LEN], page 183, Section 9.8 [ADJUSTL], page 89, Section 9.9 [ADJUSTR], page 89

9.161 LGE — Lexical greater than or equal

Description:

Determines whether one string is lexically greater than or equal to another string, where the two strings are interpreted as containing ASCII character codes. If the String A and String B are not the same length, the shorter is compared as if spaces were appended to it to form a value that has the same length as the longer.

In general, the lexical comparison intrinsics LGE, LGT, LLE, and LLT differ from the corresponding intrinsic operators .GE., .GT., .LE., and .LT., in that the latter use the processor's character ordering (which is not ASCII on some targets), whereas the former always use the ASCII ordering.

Standard: Fortran 77 and later

Class: Elemental function

Syntax: RESULT = LGE(STRING_A, STRING_B)

Arguments:

STRING_A	Shall be of default CHARACTER type.
STRING_B	Shall be of default CHARACTER type.

Return value:

Returns .TRUE. if STRING_A >= STRING_B, and .FALSE. otherwise, based on the ASCII ordering.

Specific names:

Name	Argument	Return type	Standard
LGE(STRING_A, STRING_B)	CHARACTER	LOGICAL	Fortran 77 and later

See also: Section 9.162 [LGT], page 184, Section 9.164 [LLE], page 185, Section 9.165 [LLT], page 186

9.162 LGT — Lexical greater than

Description:

Determines whether one string is lexically greater than another string, where the two strings are interpreted as containing ASCII character codes. If the String A and String B are not the same length, the shorter is compared as if spaces were appended to it to form a value that has the same length as the longer.

In general, the lexical comparison intrinsics LGE, LGT, LLE, and LLT differ from the corresponding intrinsic operators .GE., .GT., .LE., and .LT., in that the latter use the processor's character ordering (which is not ASCII on some targets), whereas the former always use the ASCII ordering.

Standard: Fortran 77 and later

Class: Elemental function

Syntax: RESULT = LGT(STRING_A, STRING_B)

Arguments:

STRING_A	Shall be of default `CHARACTER` type.
STRING_B	Shall be of default `CHARACTER` type.

Return value:

Returns `.TRUE.` if `STRING_A > STRING_B`, and `.FALSE.` otherwise, based on the ASCII ordering.

Specific names:

Name	Argument	Return type	Standard
`LGT(STRING_A, STRING_B)`	`CHARACTER`	`LOGICAL`	Fortran 77 and later

See also: Section 9.161 [LGE], page 184, Section 9.164 [LLE], page 185, Section 9.165 [LLT], page 186

9.163 `LINK` — Create a hard link

Description:

Makes a (hard) link from file *PATH1* to *PATH2*. A null character (`CHAR(0)`) can be used to mark the end of the names in *PATH1* and *PATH2*; otherwise, trailing blanks in the file names are ignored. If the *STATUS* argument is supplied, it contains 0 on success or a nonzero error code upon return; see `link(2)`.

This intrinsic is provided in both subroutine and function forms; however, only one form can be used in any given program unit.

Standard: GNU extension

Class: Subroutine, function

Syntax:

```
CALL LINK(PATH1, PATH2 [, STATUS])
STATUS = LINK(PATH1, PATH2)
```

Arguments:

PATH1	Shall be of default `CHARACTER` type.
PATH2	Shall be of default `CHARACTER` type.
STATUS	(Optional) Shall be of default `INTEGER` type.

See also: Section 9.252 [SYMLNK], page 236, Section 9.269 [UNLINK], page 245

9.164 `LLE` — Lexical less than or equal

Description:

Determines whether one string is lexically less than or equal to another string, where the two strings are interpreted as containing ASCII character codes. If the String A and String B are not the same length, the shorter is compared as if spaces were appended to it to form a value that has the same length as the longer.

In general, the lexical comparison intrinsics LGE, LGT, LLE, and LLT differ from the corresponding intrinsic operators `.GE.`, `.GT.`, `.LE.`, and `.LT.`, in that the latter use the processor's character ordering (which is not ASCII on some targets), whereas the former always use the ASCII ordering.

Standard: Fortran 77 and later

Class: Elemental function

Syntax: RESULT = LLE(STRING_A, STRING_B)

Arguments:

STRING_A	Shall be of default **CHARACTER** type.
STRING_B	Shall be of default **CHARACTER** type.

Return value:

Returns .TRUE. if STRING_A <= STRING_B, and .FALSE. otherwise, based on the ASCII ordering.

Specific names:

Name	Argument	Return type	Standard
LLE(STRING_A, STRING_B)	CHARACTER	LOGICAL	Fortran 77 and later

See also: Section 9.161 [LGE], page 184, Section 9.162 [LGT], page 184, Section 9.165 [LLT], page 186

9.165 LLT — Lexical less than

Description:

Determines whether one string is lexically less than another string, where the two strings are interpreted as containing ASCII character codes. If the String A and String B are not the same length, the shorter is compared as if spaces were appended to it to form a value that has the same length as the longer.

In general, the lexical comparison intrinsics LGE, LGT, LLE, and LLT differ from the corresponding intrinsic operators .GE., .GT., .LE., and .LT., in that the latter use the processor's character ordering (which is not ASCII on some targets), whereas the former always use the ASCII ordering.

Standard: Fortran 77 and later

Class: Elemental function

Syntax: RESULT = LLT(STRING_A, STRING_B)

Arguments:

STRING_A	Shall be of default **CHARACTER** type.
STRING_B	Shall be of default **CHARACTER** type.

Return value:

Returns .TRUE. if STRING_A < STRING_B, and .FALSE. otherwise, based on the ASCII ordering.

Specific names:

Name	Argument	Return type	Standard
LLT(STRING_A, STRING_B)	CHARACTER	LOGICAL	Fortran 77 and later

See also: Section 9.161 [LGE], page 184, Section 9.162 [LGT], page 184, Section 9.164 [LLE], page 185

9.166 `LNBLNK` — Index of the last non-blank character in a string

Description:

Returns the length of a character string, ignoring any trailing blanks. This is identical to the standard `LEN_TRIM` intrinsic, and is only included for backwards compatibility.

Standard: GNU extension

Class: Elemental function

Syntax: `RESULT = LNBLNK(STRING)`

Arguments:

STRING   Shall be a scalar of type `CHARACTER`, with `INTENT(IN)`

Return value:

The return value is of `INTEGER(kind=4)` type.

See also: Section 9.140 [INDEX intrinsic], page 173, Section 9.160 [LEN_TRIM], page 183

9.167 `LOC` — Returns the address of a variable

Description:

`LOC(X)` returns the address of X as an integer.

Standard: GNU extension

Class: Inquiry function

Syntax: `RESULT = LOC(X)`

Arguments:

X   Variable of any type.

Return value:

The return value is of type `INTEGER`, with a `KIND` corresponding to the size (in bytes) of a memory address on the target machine.

Example:

```
program test_loc
  integer :: i
  real :: r
  i = loc(r)
  print *, i
end program test_loc
```

9.168 LOG — Natural logarithm function

Description:

LOG(X) computes the natural logarithm of X, i.e. the logarithm to the base e.

Standard: Fortran 77 and later

Class: Elemental function

Syntax: RESULT = LOG(X)

Arguments:

X   The type shall be REAL or COMPLEX.

Return value:

The return value is of type REAL or COMPLEX. The kind type parameter is the same as X. If X is COMPLEX, the imaginary part ω is in the range $-\pi < \omega \leq \pi$.

Example:

```
program test_log
  real(8) :: x = 2.7182818284590451_8
  complex :: z = (1.0, 2.0)
  x = log(x)     ! will yield (approximately) 1
  z = log(z)
end program test_log
```

Specific names:

Name	Argument	Return type	Standard
ALOG(X)	REAL(4) X	REAL(4)	f95, gnu
DLOG(X)	REAL(8) X	REAL(8)	f95, gnu
CLOG(X)	COMPLEX(4) X	COMPLEX(4)	f95, gnu
ZLOG(X)	COMPLEX(8) X	COMPLEX(8)	f95, gnu
CDLOG(X)	COMPLEX(8) X	COMPLEX(8)	f95, gnu

9.169 LOG10 — Base 10 logarithm function

Description:

LOG10(X) computes the base 10 logarithm of X.

Standard: Fortran 77 and later

Class: Elemental function

Syntax: RESULT = LOG10(X)

Arguments:

X   The type shall be REAL.

Return value:

The return value is of type REAL or COMPLEX. The kind type parameter is the same as X.

Example:

```
program test_log10
  real(8) :: x = 10.0_8
  x = log10(x)
end program test_log10
```

Specific names:

Name	Argument	Return type	Standard
ALOG10(X)	REAL(4) X	REAL(4)	Fortran 95 and later
DLOG10(X)	REAL(8) X	REAL(8)	Fortran 95 and later

9.170 LOG_GAMMA — Logarithm of the Gamma function

Description:

LOG_GAMMA(X) computes the natural logarithm of the absolute value of the Gamma (Γ) function.

Standard: Fortran 2008 and later

Class: Elemental function

Syntax: X = LOG_GAMMA(X)

Arguments:

X   Shall be of type REAL and neither zero nor a negative integer.

Return value:

The return value is of type REAL of the same kind as *X*.

Example:

```
program test_log_gamma
  real :: x = 1.0
  x = lgamma(x) ! returns 0.0
end program test_log_gamma
```

Specific names:

Name	Argument	Return type	Standard
LGAMMA(X)	REAL(4) X	REAL(4)	GNU Extension
ALGAMA(X)	REAL(4) X	REAL(4)	GNU Extension
DLGAMA(X)	REAL(8) X	REAL(8)	GNU Extension

See also: Gamma function: Section 9.111 [GAMMA], page 156

9.171 LOGICAL — Convert to logical type

Description:

Converts one kind of LOGICAL variable to another.

Standard: Fortran 95 and later

Class: Elemental function

Syntax: RESULT = LOGICAL(L [, KIND])

Arguments:

L   The type shall be LOGICAL.

KIND   (Optional) An INTEGER initialization expression indicating the kind parameter of the result.

Return value:

The return value is a LOGICAL value equal to *L*, with a kind corresponding to *KIND*, or of the default logical kind if *KIND* is not given.

See also: Section 9.141 [INT], page 173, Section 9.219 [REAL], page 216, Section 9.58 [CMPLX], page 121

9.172 LONG — Convert to integer type

Description:

Convert to a KIND=4 integer type, which is the same size as a C long integer. This is equivalent to the standard INT intrinsic with an optional argument of KIND=4, and is only included for backwards compatibility.

Standard: GNU extension

Class: Elemental function

Syntax: RESULT = LONG(A)

Arguments:

A   Shall be of type INTEGER, REAL, or COMPLEX.

Return value:

The return value is a INTEGER(4) variable.

See also: Section 9.141 [INT], page 173, Section 9.142 [INT2], page 174, Section 9.143 [INT8], page 174

9.173 LSHIFT — Left shift bits

Description:

LSHIFT returns a value corresponding to *I* with all of the bits shifted left by *SHIFT* places. If the absolute value of *SHIFT* is greater than BIT_SIZE(I), the value is undefined. Bits shifted out from the left end are lost; zeros are shifted in from the opposite end.

This function has been superseded by the ISHFT intrinsic, which is standard in Fortran 95 and later, and the SHIFTL intrinsic, which is standard in Fortran 2008 and later.

Standard: GNU extension

Class: Elemental function

Syntax: RESULT = LSHIFT(I, SHIFT)

Arguments:

I   The type shall be INTEGER.
SHIFT   The type shall be INTEGER.

Return value:

The return value is of type INTEGER and of the same kind as *I*.

See also: Section 9.150 [ISHFT], page 178, Section 9.151 [ISHFTC], page 179, Section 9.224 [RSHIFT], page 219, Section 9.235 [SHIFTA], page 225, Section 9.236 [SHIFTL], page 226, Section 9.237 [SHIFTR], page 226

9.174 LSTAT — Get file status

Description:

LSTAT is identical to Section 9.249 [STAT], page 233, except that if path is a symbolic link, then the link itself is statted, not the file that it refers to.

The elements in **VALUES** are the same as described by Section 9.249 [STAT], page 233.

This intrinsic is provided in both subroutine and function forms; however, only one form can be used in any given program unit.

Standard: GNU extension

Class: Subroutine, function

Syntax:

```
CALL LSTAT(NAME, VALUES [, STATUS])
STATUS = LSTAT(NAME, VALUES)
```

Arguments:

NAME	The type shall be **CHARACTER** of the default kind, a valid path within the file system.
VALUES	The type shall be **INTEGER(4)**, **DIMENSION(13)**.
STATUS	(Optional) status flag of type **INTEGER(4)**. Returns 0 on success and a system specific error code otherwise.

Example: See Section 9.249 [STAT], page 233 for an example.

See also: To stat an open file: Section 9.109 [FSTAT], page 155, to stat a file: Section 9.249 [STAT], page 233

9.175 LTIME — Convert time to local time info

Description:

Given a system time value *TIME* (as provided by the **TIME8** intrinsic), fills *VALUES* with values extracted from it appropriate to the local time zone using `localtime(3)`.

Standard: GNU extension

Class: Subroutine

Syntax: CALL LTIME(TIME, VALUES)

Arguments:

TIME	An **INTEGER** scalar expression corresponding to a system time, with **INTENT(IN)**.
VALUES	A default **INTEGER** array with 9 elements, with **INTENT(OUT)**.

Return value:

The elements of *VALUES* are assigned as follows:

1. Seconds after the minute, range 0–59 or 0–61 to allow for leap seconds

2. Minutes after the hour, range 0–59

3. Hours past midnight, range 0–23

4. Day of month, range 0–31

5. Number of months since January, range 0–12

6. Years since 1900

7. Number of days since Sunday, range 0–6

8. Days since January 1

9. Daylight savings indicator: positive if daylight savings is in effect, zero if not, and negative if the information is not available.

See also: Section 9.74 [CTIME], page 132, Section 9.123 [GMTIME], page 163, Section 9.258 [TIME], page 240, Section 9.259 [TIME8], page 240

9.176 `MALLOC` — **Allocate dynamic memory**

Description:

`MALLOC(SIZE)` allocates *SIZE* bytes of dynamic memory and returns the address of the allocated memory. The `MALLOC` intrinsic is an extension intended to be used with Cray pointers, and is provided in GNU Fortran to allow the user to compile legacy code. For new code using Fortran 95 pointers, the memory allocation intrinsic is `ALLOCATE`.

Standard: GNU extension

Class: Function

Syntax: PTR = MALLOC(SIZE)

Arguments:

SIZE   The type shall be `INTEGER`.

Return value:

The return value is of type `INTEGER(K)`, with K such that variables of type `INTEGER(K)` have the same size as C pointers (`sizeof(void *)`).

Example: The following example demonstrates the use of `MALLOC` and `FREE` with Cray pointers.

```
program test_malloc
  implicit none
  integer i
  real*8 x(*), z
  pointer(ptr_x,x)

  ptr_x = malloc(20*8)
  do i = 1, 20
    x(i) = sqrt(1.0d0 / i)
  end do
  z = 0
  do i = 1, 20
    z = z + x(i)
    print *, z
  end do
  call free(ptr_x)
end program test_malloc
```

See also: Section 9.107 [FREE], page 154

9.177 MASKL — Left justified mask

Description:

MASKL(I[, KIND]) has its leftmost *I* bits set to 1, and the remaining bits set to 0.

Standard: Fortran 2008 and later

Class: Elemental function

Syntax: RESULT = MASKL(I[, KIND])

Arguments:

I	Shall be of type INTEGER.
KIND	Shall be a scalar constant expression of type INTEGER.

Return value:

The return value is of type INTEGER. If *KIND* is present, it specifies the kind value of the return type; otherwise, it is of the default integer kind.

See also: Section 9.178 [MASKR], page 193

9.178 MASKR — Right justified mask

Description:

MASKL(I[, KIND]) has its rightmost *I* bits set to 1, and the remaining bits set to 0.

Standard: Fortran 2008 and later

Class: Elemental function

Syntax: RESULT = MASKR(I[, KIND])

Arguments:

I	Shall be of type INTEGER.
KIND	Shall be a scalar constant expression of type INTEGER.

Return value:

The return value is of type INTEGER. If *KIND* is present, it specifies the kind value of the return type; otherwise, it is of the default integer kind.

See also: Section 9.177 [MASKL], page 193

9.179 MATMUL — matrix multiplication

Description:

Performs a matrix multiplication on numeric or logical arguments.

Standard: Fortran 95 and later

Class: Transformational function

Syntax: RESULT = MATMUL(MATRIX_A, MATRIX_B)

Arguments:

MATRIX_A	An array of INTEGER, REAL, COMPLEX, or LOGICAL type, with a rank of one or two.
MATRIX_B	An array of INTEGER, REAL, or COMPLEX type if *MATRIX_A* is of a numeric type; otherwise, an array of LOGICAL type. The rank shall be one or two, and the first (or only) dimension of *MATRIX_B* shall be equal to the last (or only) dimension of *MATRIX_A*.

Return value:

The matrix product of *MATRIX_A* and *MATRIX_B*. The type and kind of the result follow the usual type and kind promotion rules, as for the * or .AND. operators.

See also:

9.180 MAX — Maximum value of an argument list

Description:

Returns the argument with the largest (most positive) value.

Standard: Fortran 77 and later

Class: Elemental function

Syntax: RESULT = MAX(A1, A2 [, A3 [, ...]])

Arguments:

A1	The type shall be INTEGER or REAL.
A2, A3, ...	An expression of the same type and kind as *A1*. (As a GNU extension, arguments of different kinds are permitted.)

Return value:

The return value corresponds to the maximum value among the arguments, and has the same type and kind as the first argument.

Specific names:

Name	Argument	Return type	Standard
MAX0(A1)	INTEGER(4) A1	INTEGER(4)	Fortran 77 and later
AMAX0(A1)	INTEGER(4) A1	REAL(MAX(X))	Fortran 77 and later
MAX1(A1)	REAL A1	INT(MAX(X))	Fortran 77 and later
AMAX1(A1)	REAL(4) A1	REAL(4)	Fortran 77 and later
DMAX1(A1)	REAL(8) A1	REAL(8)	Fortran 77 and later

See also: Section 9.182 [MAXLOC], page 195 Section 9.183 [MAXVAL], page 196, Section 9.188 [MIN], page 198

9.181 MAXEXPONENT — Maximum exponent of a real kind

Description:

MAXEXPONENT(X) returns the maximum exponent in the model of the type of X.

Standard: Fortran 95 and later

Class: Inquiry function

Syntax: `RESULT = MAXEXPONENT(X)`

Arguments:

X   Shall be of type `REAL`.

Return value:

The return value is of type `INTEGER` and of the default integer kind.

Example:

```
program exponents
  real(kind=4) :: x
  real(kind=8) :: y

  print *, minexponent(x), maxexponent(x)
  print *, minexponent(y), maxexponent(y)
end program exponents
```

9.182 `MAXLOC` — Location of the maximum value within an array

Description:

Determines the location of the element in the array with the maximum value, or, if the *DIM* argument is supplied, determines the locations of the maximum element along each row of the array in the *DIM* direction. If *MASK* is present, only the elements for which *MASK* is `.TRUE.` are considered. If more than one element in the array has the maximum value, the location returned is that of the first such element in array element order. If the array has zero size, or all of the elements of *MASK* are `.FALSE.`, then the result is an array of zeroes. Similarly, if *DIM* is supplied and all of the elements of *MASK* along a given row are zero, the result value for that row is zero.

Standard: Fortran 95 and later

Class: Transformational function

Syntax:

```
RESULT = MAXLOC(ARRAY, DIM [, MASK])
RESULT = MAXLOC(ARRAY [, MASK])
```

Arguments:

ARRAY   Shall be an array of type `INTEGER` or `REAL`.
DIM   (Optional) Shall be a scalar of type `INTEGER`, with a value between one and the rank of *ARRAY*, inclusive. It may not be an optional dummy argument.
MASK   Shall be an array of type `LOGICAL`, and conformable with *ARRAY*.

Return value:

If *DIM* is absent, the result is a rank-one array with a length equal to the rank of *ARRAY*. If *DIM* is present, the result is an array with a rank one less than the rank of *ARRAY*, and a size corresponding to the size of *ARRAY* with the

DIM dimension removed. If *DIM* is present and *ARRAY* has a rank of one, the result is a scalar. In all cases, the result is of default `INTEGER` type.

See also: Section 9.180 [MAX], page 194, Section 9.183 [MAXVAL], page 196

9.183 `MAXVAL` — Maximum value of an array

Description:

Determines the maximum value of the elements in an array value, or, if the *DIM* argument is supplied, determines the maximum value along each row of the array in the *DIM* direction. If *MASK* is present, only the elements for which *MASK* is `.TRUE.` are considered. If the array has zero size, or all of the elements of *MASK* are `.FALSE.`, then the result is `-HUGE(ARRAY)` if *ARRAY* is numeric, or a string of nulls if *ARRAY* is of character type.

Standard: Fortran 95 and later

Class: Transformational function

Syntax:

```
RESULT = MAXVAL(ARRAY, DIM [, MASK])
RESULT = MAXVAL(ARRAY [, MASK])
```

Arguments:

ARRAY	Shall be an array of type `INTEGER` or `REAL`.
DIM	(Optional) Shall be a scalar of type `INTEGER`, with a value between one and the rank of *ARRAY*, inclusive. It may not be an optional dummy argument.
MASK	Shall be an array of type `LOGICAL`, and conformable with *ARRAY*.

Return value:

If *DIM* is absent, or if *ARRAY* has a rank of one, the result is a scalar. If *DIM* is present, the result is an array with a rank one less than the rank of *ARRAY*, and a size corresponding to the size of *ARRAY* with the *DIM* dimension removed. In all cases, the result is of the same type and kind as *ARRAY*.

See also: Section 9.180 [MAX], page 194, Section 9.182 [MAXLOC], page 195

9.184 `MCLOCK` — Time function

Description:

Returns the number of clock ticks since the start of the process, based on the function `clock(3)` in the C standard library.

This intrinsic is not fully portable, such as to systems with 32-bit `INTEGER` types but supporting times wider than 32 bits. Therefore, the values returned by this intrinsic might be, or become, negative, or numerically less than previous values, during a single run of the compiled program.

Standard: GNU extension

Class: Function

Syntax: `RESULT = MCLOCK()`

Return value:

> The return value is a scalar of type `INTEGER(4)`, equal to the number of clock ticks since the start of the process, or `-1` if the system does not support `clock(3)`.

See also: Section 9.74 [CTIME], page 132, Section 9.123 [GMTIME], page 163, Section 9.175 [LTIME], page 191, Section 9.184 [MCLOCK], page 196, Section 9.258 [TIME], page 240

9.185 `MCLOCK8` — Time function (64-bit)

Description:

> Returns the number of clock ticks since the start of the process, based on the function `clock(3)` in the C standard library.
>
> *Warning:* this intrinsic does not increase the range of the timing values over that returned by `clock(3)`. On a system with a 32-bit `clock(3)`, `MCLOCK8` will return a 32-bit value, even though it is converted to a 64-bit `INTEGER(8)` value. That means overflows of the 32-bit value can still occur. Therefore, the values returned by this intrinsic might be or become negative or numerically less than previous values during a single run of the compiled program.

Standard: GNU extension

Class: Function

Syntax: `RESULT = MCLOCK8()`

Return value:

> The return value is a scalar of type `INTEGER(8)`, equal to the number of clock ticks since the start of the process, or `-1` if the system does not support `clock(3)`.

See also: Section 9.74 [CTIME], page 132, Section 9.123 [GMTIME], page 163, Section 9.175 [LTIME], page 191, Section 9.184 [MCLOCK], page 196, Section 9.259 [TIME8], page 240

9.186 `MERGE` — Merge variables

Description:

> Select values from two arrays according to a logical mask. The result is equal to *TSOURCE* if *MASK* is `.TRUE.`, or equal to *FSOURCE* if it is `.FALSE.`.

Standard: Fortran 95 and later

Class: Elemental function

Syntax: `RESULT = MERGE(TSOURCE, FSOURCE, MASK)`

Arguments:

TSOURCE	May be of any type.
FSOURCE	Shall be of the same type and type parameters as *TSOURCE*.
MASK	Shall be of type `LOGICAL`.

Return value:

> The result is of the same type and type parameters as *TSOURCE*.

9.187 MERGE_BITS — Merge of bits under mask

Description:

> MERGE_BITS(I, J, MASK) merges the bits of *I* and *J* as determined by the mask. The i-th bit of the result is equal to the i-th bit of *I* if the i-th bit of *MASK* is 1; it is equal to the i-th bit of *J* otherwise.

Standard: Fortran 2008 and later

Class: Elemental function

Syntax: RESULT = MERGE_BITS(I, J, MASK)

Arguments:

I	Shall be of type INTEGER.
J	Shall be of type INTEGER and of the same kind as *I*.
MASK	Shall be of type INTEGER and of the same kind as *I*.

Return value:

> The result is of the same type and kind as *I*.

9.188 MIN — Minimum value of an argument list

Description:

> Returns the argument with the smallest (most negative) value.

Standard: Fortran 77 and later

Class: Elemental function

Syntax: RESULT = MIN(A1, A2 [, A3, ...])

Arguments:

A1	The type shall be INTEGER or REAL.
A2, A3, ...	An expression of the same type and kind as *A1*. (As a GNU extension, arguments of different kinds are permitted.)

Return value:

> The return value corresponds to the maximum value among the arguments, and has the same type and kind as the first argument.

Specific names:

Name	Argument	Return type	Standard
MIN0(A1)	INTEGER(4) A1	INTEGER(4)	Fortran 77 and later
AMIN0(A1)	INTEGER(4) A1	REAL(4)	Fortran 77 and later
MIN1(A1)	REAL A1	INTEGER(4)	Fortran 77 and later
AMIN1(A1)	REAL(4) A1	REAL(4)	Fortran 77 and later
DMIN1(A1)	REAL(8) A1	REAL(8)	Fortran 77 and later

See also: Section 9.180 [MAX], page 194, Section 9.190 [MINLOC], page 199, Section 9.191 [MINVAL], page 200

9.189 MINEXPONENT — Minimum exponent of a real kind

Description:

MINEXPONENT(X) returns the minimum exponent in the model of the type of X.

Standard: Fortran 95 and later

Class: Inquiry function

Syntax: RESULT = MINEXPONENT(X)

Arguments:

              X   Shall be of type REAL.

Return value:

The return value is of type INTEGER and of the default integer kind.

Example: See MAXEXPONENT for an example.

9.190 MINLOC — Location of the minimum value within an array

Description:

Determines the location of the element in the array with the minimum value, or, if the *DIM* argument is supplied, determines the locations of the minimum element along each row of the array in the *DIM* direction. If *MASK* is present, only the elements for which *MASK* is .TRUE. are considered. If more than one element in the array has the minimum value, the location returned is that of the first such element in array element order. If the array has zero size, or all of the elements of *MASK* are .FALSE., then the result is an array of zeroes. Similarly, if *DIM* is supplied and all of the elements of *MASK* along a given row are zero, the result value for that row is zero.

Standard: Fortran 95 and later

Class: Transformational function

Syntax:

        RESULT = MINLOC(ARRAY, DIM [, MASK])
        RESULT = MINLOC(ARRAY [, MASK])

Arguments:

ARRAY	Shall be an array of type INTEGER or REAL.
DIM	(Optional) Shall be a scalar of type INTEGER, with a value between one and the rank of *ARRAY*, inclusive. It may not be an optional dummy argument.
MASK	Shall be an array of type LOGICAL, and conformable with *ARRAY*.

Return value:

If *DIM* is absent, the result is a rank-one array with a length equal to the rank of *ARRAY*. If *DIM* is present, the result is an array with a rank one less than the rank of *ARRAY*, and a size corresponding to the size of *ARRAY* with the

DIM dimension removed. If *DIM* is present and *ARRAY* has a rank of one, the result is a scalar. In all cases, the result is of default `INTEGER` type.

See also: Section 9.188 [MIN], page 198, Section 9.191 [MINVAL], page 200

9.191 `MINVAL` — Minimum value of an array

Description:

Determines the minimum value of the elements in an array value, or, if the *DIM* argument is supplied, determines the minimum value along each row of the array in the *DIM* direction. If *MASK* is present, only the elements for which *MASK* is `.TRUE.` are considered. If the array has zero size, or all of the elements of *MASK* are `.FALSE.`, then the result is `HUGE(ARRAY)` if *ARRAY* is numeric, or a string of `CHAR(255)` characters if *ARRAY* is of character type.

Standard: Fortran 95 and later

Class: Transformational function

Syntax:

```
RESULT = MINVAL(ARRAY, DIM [, MASK])
RESULT = MINVAL(ARRAY [, MASK])
```

Arguments:

ARRAY	Shall be an array of type `INTEGER` or `REAL`.
DIM	(Optional) Shall be a scalar of type `INTEGER`, with a value between one and the rank of *ARRAY*, inclusive. It may not be an optional dummy argument.
MASK	Shall be an array of type `LOGICAL`, and conformable with *ARRAY*.

Return value:

If *DIM* is absent, or if *ARRAY* has a rank of one, the result is a scalar. If *DIM* is present, the result is an array with a rank one less than the rank of *ARRAY*, and a size corresponding to the size of *ARRAY* with the *DIM* dimension removed. In all cases, the result is of the same type and kind as *ARRAY*.

See also: Section 9.188 [MIN], page 198, Section 9.190 [MINLOC], page 199

9.192 `MOD` — Remainder function

Description:

MOD(A,P) computes the remainder of the division of A by P.

Standard: Fortran 77 and later

Class: Elemental function

Syntax: `RESULT = MOD(A, P)`

Arguments:

A	Shall be a scalar of type `INTEGER` or `REAL`.
P	Shall be a scalar of the same type and kind as *A* and not equal to zero.

Return value:

> The return value is the result of `A - (INT(A/P) * P)`. The type and kind of the return value is the same as that of the arguments. The returned value has the same sign as A and a magnitude less than the magnitude of P.

Example:

```
program test_mod
  print *, mod(17,3)
  print *, mod(17.5,5.5)
  print *, mod(17.5d0,5.5)
  print *, mod(17.5,5.5d0)

  print *, mod(-17,3)
  print *, mod(-17.5,5.5)
  print *, mod(-17.5d0,5.5)
  print *, mod(-17.5,5.5d0)

  print *, mod(17,-3)
  print *, mod(17.5,-5.5)
  print *, mod(17.5d0,-5.5)
  print *, mod(17.5,-5.5d0)
end program test_mod
```

Specific names:

Name	Arguments	Return type	Standard
MOD(A,P)	INTEGER A,P	INTEGER	Fortran 95 and later
AMOD(A,P)	REAL(4) A,P	REAL(4)	Fortran 95 and later
DMOD(A,P)	REAL(8) A,P	REAL(8)	Fortran 95 and later

See also: Section 9.193 [MODULO], page 201

9.193 `MODULO` — **Modulo function**

Description:

> `MODULO(A,P)` computes the A modulo P.

Standard: Fortran 95 and later

Class: Elemental function

Syntax: `RESULT = MODULO(A, P)`

Arguments:

> A Shall be a scalar of type `INTEGER` or `REAL`.
>
> P Shall be a scalar of the same type and kind as A. It shall not be zero.

Return value:

> The type and kind of the result are those of the arguments.
>
> If A and P are of type `INTEGER`:
>> `MODULO(A,P)` has the value R such that `A=Q*P+R`, where Q is an integer and R is between 0 (inclusive) and P (exclusive).
>
> If A and P are of type `REAL`:
>> `MODULO(A,P)` has the value of `A - FLOOR (A / P) * P`.

The returned value has the same sign as P and a magnitude less than the magnitude of P.

Example:

```
program test_modulo
  print *, modulo(17,3)
  print *, modulo(17.5,5.5)

  print *, modulo(-17,3)
  print *, modulo(-17.5,5.5)

  print *, modulo(17,-3)
  print *, modulo(17.5,-5.5)
end program
```

See also: Section 9.192 [MOD], page 200

9.194 MOVE_ALLOC — Move allocation from one object to another

Description:

MOVE_ALLOC(FROM, TO) moves the allocation from *FROM* to *TO*. *FROM* will become deallocated in the process.

Standard: Fortran 2003 and later

Class: Pure subroutine

Syntax: CALL MOVE_ALLOC(FROM, TO)

Arguments:

FROM	ALLOCATABLE, INTENT(INOUT), may be of any type and kind.
TO	ALLOCATABLE, INTENT(OUT), shall be of the same type, kind and rank as *FROM*.

Return value:

None

Example:

```
program test_move_alloc
    integer, allocatable :: a(:), b(:)

    allocate(a(3))
    a = [ 1, 2, 3 ]
    call move_alloc(a, b)
    print *, allocated(a), allocated(b)
    print *, b
end program test_move_alloc
```

9.195 MVBITS — Move bits from one integer to another

Description:

Moves *LEN* bits from positions *FROMPOS* through FROMPOS+LEN-1 of *FROM* to positions *TOPOS* through TOPOS+LEN-1 of *TO*. The portion of argument *TO* not affected by the movement of bits is unchanged. The values of FROMPOS+LEN-1 and TOPOS+LEN-1 must be less than BIT_SIZE(FROM).

Standard: Fortran 95 and later

Class: Elemental subroutine

Syntax: `CALL MVBITS(FROM, FROMPOS, LEN, TO, TOPOS)`

Arguments:

FROM	The type shall be `INTEGER`.
FROMPOS	The type shall be `INTEGER`.
LEN	The type shall be `INTEGER`.
TO	The type shall be `INTEGER`, of the same kind as *FROM*.
TOPOS	The type shall be `INTEGER`.

See also: Section 9.132 [IBCLR], page 169, Section 9.134 [IBSET], page 169, Section 9.133 [IBITS], page 169, Section 9.129 [IAND], page 167, Section 9.144 [IOR], page 175, Section 9.137 [IEOR], page 171

9.196 NEAREST — Nearest representable number

Description:

NEAREST(X, S) returns the processor-representable number nearest to X in the direction indicated by the sign of S.

Standard: Fortran 95 and later

Class: Elemental function

Syntax: `RESULT = NEAREST(X, S)`

Arguments:

X	Shall be of type `REAL`.
S	Shall be of type `REAL` and not equal to zero.

Return value:

The return value is of the same type as X. If S is positive, NEAREST returns the processor-representable number greater than X and nearest to it. If S is negative, NEAREST returns the processor-representable number smaller than X and nearest to it.

Example:

```
program test_nearest
  real :: x, y
  x = nearest(42.0, 1.0)
  y = nearest(42.0, -1.0)
  write (*,"(3(G20.15))") x, y, x - y
end program test_nearest
```

9.197 NEW_LINE — New line character

Description:

NEW_LINE(C) returns the new-line character.

Standard: Fortran 2003 and later

Class: Inquiry function

Syntax: RESULT = NEW_LINE(C)

Arguments:

        C   The argument shall be a scalar or array of the type CHARACTER.

Return value:

        Returns a *CHARACTER* scalar of length one with the new-line character of the same kind as parameter *C*.

Example:

```
program newline
  implicit none
  write(*,'(A)') 'This is record 1.'//NEW_LINE('A')//'This is record 2.'
end program newline
```

9.198 `NINT` — **Nearest whole number**

Description:

        `NINT(A)` rounds its argument to the nearest whole number.

Standard: Fortran 77 and later, with *KIND* argument Fortran 90 and later

Class: Elemental function

Syntax: RESULT = NINT(A [, KIND])

Arguments:

        A   The type of the argument shall be **REAL**.

        KIND   (Optional) An **INTEGER** initialization expression indicating the kind parameter of the result.

Return value:

        Returns *A* with the fractional portion of its magnitude eliminated by rounding to the nearest whole number and with its sign preserved, converted to an **INTEGER** of the default kind.

Example:

```
program test_nint
  real(4) x4
  real(8) x8
  x4 = 1.234E0_4
  x8 = 4.321_8
  print *, nint(x4), idnint(x8)
end program test_nint
```

Specific names:

Name	Argument	Return Type	Standard
NINT(A)	REAL(4) A	INTEGER	Fortran 95 and later
IDNINT(A)	REAL(8) A	INTEGER	Fortran 95 and later

See also: Section 9.54 [CEILING], page 118, Section 9.101 [FLOOR], page 150

9.199 NORM2 — Euclidean vector norms

Description:

Calculates the Euclidean vector norm (L_2 norm) of of *ARRAY* along dimension *DIM*.

Standard: Fortran 2008 and later

Class: Transformational function

Syntax:

```
RESULT = NORM2(ARRAY[, DIM])
```

Arguments:

ARRAY	Shall be an array of type REAL
DIM	(Optional) shall be a scalar of type INTEGER with a value in the range from 1 to n, where n equals the rank of *ARRAY*.

Return value:

The result is of the same type as *ARRAY*.

If *DIM* is absent, a scalar with the square root of the sum of all elements in *ARRAY* squared is returned. Otherwise, an array of rank $n-1$, where n equals the rank of *ARRAY*, and a shape similar to that of *ARRAY* with dimension *DIM* dropped is returned.

Example:

```
PROGRAM test_sum
  REAL :: x(5) = [ real :: 1, 2, 3, 4, 5 ]
  print *, NORM2(x)  ! = sqrt(55.) ~ 7.416
END PROGRAM
```

9.200 NOT — Logical negation

Description:

NOT returns the bitwise Boolean inverse of *I*.

Standard: Fortran 95 and later

Class: Elemental function

Syntax: `RESULT = NOT(I)`

Arguments:

I	The type shall be INTEGER.

Return value:

The return type is INTEGER, of the same kind as the argument.

See also: Section 9.129 [IAND], page 167, Section 9.137 [IEOR], page 171, Section 9.144 [IOR], page 175, Section 9.133 [IBITS], page 169, Section 9.134 [IBSET], page 169, Section 9.132 [IBCLR], page 169

9.201 NULL — Function that returns an disassociated pointer

Description:

Returns a disassociated pointer.

If *MOLD* is present, a disassociated pointer of the same type is returned, otherwise the type is determined by context.

In Fortran 95, *MOLD* is optional. Please note that Fortran 2003 includes cases where it is required.

Standard: Fortran 95 and later

Class: Transformational function

Syntax: PTR => NULL([MOLD])

Arguments:

MOLD   (Optional) shall be a pointer of any association status and of any type.

Return value:

A disassociated pointer.

Example:

```
REAL, POINTER, DIMENSION(:) :: VEC => NULL ()
```

See also: Section 9.20 [ASSOCIATED], page 97

9.202 NUM_IMAGES — Function that returns the number of images

Description:

Returns the number of images.

Standard: Fortran 2008 and later. With *DISTANCE* or *FAILED* argument, Technical Specification (TS) 18508 or later

Class: Transformational function

Syntax: RESULT = NUM_IMAGES(DISTANCE, FAILED)

Arguments:

DISTANCE   (optional, intent(in)) Nonnegative scalar integer
FAILED   (optional, intent(in)) Scalar logical expression

Return value:

Scalar default-kind integer. If *DISTANCE* is not present or has value 0, the number of images in the current team is returned. For values smaller or equal distance to the initial team, it returns the number of images index on the ancestor team which has a distance of *DISTANCE* from the invoking team. If *DISTANCE* is larger than the distance to the initial team, the number of images of the initial team is returned. If *FAILED* is not present the total number of images is returned; if it has the value .TRUE., the number of failed images is returned, otherwise, the number of images which do have not the failed status.

Example:

```
INTEGER :: value[*]
INTEGER :: i
value = THIS_IMAGE()
SYNC ALL
IF (THIS_IMAGE() == 1) THEN
  DO i = 1, NUM_IMAGES()
    WRITE(*,'(2(a,i0))') 'value[', i, '] is ', value[i]
  END DO
END IF
```

See also: Section 9.257 [THIS_IMAGE], page 239, Section 9.139 [IMAGE_INDEX], page 172

9.203 OR — Bitwise logical OR

Description:

Bitwise logical OR.

This intrinsic routine is provided for backwards compatibility with GNU Fortran 77. For integer arguments, programmers should consider the use of the Section 9.144 [IOR], page 175 intrinsic defined by the Fortran standard.

Standard: GNU extension

Class: Function

Syntax: RESULT = OR(I, J)

Arguments:

I	The type shall be either a scalar INTEGER type or a scalar LOGICAL type.
J	The type shall be the same as the type of J.

Return value:

The return type is either a scalar INTEGER or a scalar LOGICAL. If the kind type parameters differ, then the smaller kind type is implicitly converted to larger kind, and the return has the larger kind.

Example:

```
PROGRAM test_or
  LOGICAL :: T = .TRUE., F = .FALSE.
  INTEGER :: a, b
  DATA a / Z'F' /, b / Z'3' /

  WRITE (*,*) OR(T, T), OR(T, F), OR(F, T), OR(F, F)
  WRITE (*,*) OR(a, b)
END PROGRAM
```

See also: Fortran 95 elemental function: Section 9.144 [IOR], page 175

9.204 PACK — Pack an array into an array of rank one

Description:

Stores the elements of *ARRAY* in an array of rank one.

The beginning of the resulting array is made up of elements whose *MASK* equals `TRUE`. Afterwards, positions are filled with elements taken from *VECTOR*.

Standard: Fortran 95 and later

Class: Transformational function

Syntax: `RESULT = PACK(ARRAY, MASK[,VECTOR])`

Arguments:

ARRAY	Shall be an array of any type.
MASK	Shall be an array of type `LOGICAL` and of the same size as *ARRAY*. Alternatively, it may be a `LOGICAL` scalar.
VECTOR	(Optional) shall be an array of the same type as *ARRAY* and of rank one. If present, the number of elements in *VECTOR* shall be equal to or greater than the number of true elements in *MASK*. If *MASK* is scalar, the number of elements in *VECTOR* shall be equal to or greater than the number of elements in *ARRAY*.

Return value:

The result is an array of rank one and the same type as that of *ARRAY*. If *VECTOR* is present, the result size is that of *VECTOR*, the number of `TRUE` values in *MASK* otherwise.

Example: Gathering nonzero elements from an array:

```
PROGRAM test_pack_1
  INTEGER :: m(6)
  m = (/ 1, 0, 0, 0, 5, 0 /)
  WRITE(*, FMT="(6(I0, ' '))") pack(m, m /= 0)   ! "1 5"
END PROGRAM
```

Gathering nonzero elements from an array and appending elements from *VECTOR*:

```
PROGRAM test_pack_2
  INTEGER :: m(4)
  m = (/ 1, 0, 0, 2 /)
  WRITE(*, FMT="(4(I0, ' '))") pack(m, m /= 0, (/ 0, 0, 3, 4 /))   ! "1 2 3 4"
END PROGRAM
```

See also: Section 9.270 [UNPACK], page 246

9.205 `PARITY` — Reduction with exclusive OR

Description:

Calculates the parity, i.e. the reduction using `.XOR.`, of *MASK* along dimension *DIM*.

Standard: Fortran 2008 and later

Class: Transformational function

Syntax:

`RESULT = PARITY(MASK[, DIM])`

Arguments:

LOGICAL	Shall be an array of type `LOGICAL`
DIM	(Optional) shall be a scalar of type `INTEGER` with a value in the range from 1 to n, where n equals the rank of *MASK*.

Return value:

The result is of the same type as *MASK*.

If *DIM* is absent, a scalar with the parity of all elements in *MASK* is returned, i.e. true if an odd number of elements is `.true.` and false otherwise. If *DIM* is present, an array of rank $n - 1$, where n equals the rank of *ARRAY*, and a shape similar to that of *MASK* with dimension *DIM* dropped is returned.

Example:

```
PROGRAM test_sum
   LOGICAL :: x(2) = [ .true., .false. ]
   print *, PARITY(x) ! prints "T" (true).
END PROGRAM
```

9.206 `PERROR` — Print system error message

Description:

Prints (on the C `stderr` stream) a newline-terminated error message corresponding to the last system error. This is prefixed by *STRING*, a colon and a space. See `perror(3)`.

Standard: GNU extension

Class: Subroutine

Syntax: `CALL PERROR(STRING)`

Arguments:

STRING	A scalar of type `CHARACTER` and of the default kind.

See also: Section 9.138 [IERRNO], page 172

9.207 `POPCNT` — Number of bits set

Description:

`POPCNT(I)` returns the number of bits set ('1' bits) in the binary representation of I.

Standard: Fortran 2008 and later

Class: Elemental function

Syntax: `RESULT = POPCNT(I)`

Arguments:

I	Shall be of type `INTEGER`.

Return value:

The return value is of type `INTEGER` and of the default integer kind.

See also: Section 9.208 [POPPAR], page 210, Section 9.158 [LEADZ], page 182, Section 9.261 [TRAILZ], page 241

Example:

```
program test_population
  print *, popcnt(127),        poppar(127)
  print *, popcnt(huge(0_4)), poppar(huge(0_4))
  print *, popcnt(huge(0_8)), poppar(huge(0_8))
end program test_population
```

9.208 POPPAR — Parity of the number of bits set

Description:

POPPAR(I) returns parity of the integer I, i.e. the parity of the number of bits set ('1' bits) in the binary representation of I. It is equal to 0 if I has an even number of bits set, and 1 for an odd number of '1' bits.

Standard: Fortran 2008 and later

Class: Elemental function

Syntax: RESULT = POPPAR(I)

Arguments:

I   Shall be of type INTEGER.

Return value:

The return value is of type INTEGER and of the default integer kind.

See also: Section 9.207 [POPCNT], page 209, Section 9.158 [LEADZ], page 182, Section 9.261 [TRAILZ], page 241

Example:

```
program test_population
  print *, popcnt(127),        poppar(127)
  print *, popcnt(huge(0_4)), poppar(huge(0_4))
  print *, popcnt(huge(0_8)), poppar(huge(0_8))
end program test_population
```

9.209 PRECISION — Decimal precision of a real kind

Description:

PRECISION(X) returns the decimal precision in the model of the type of X.

Standard: Fortran 95 and later

Class: Inquiry function

Syntax: RESULT = PRECISION(X)

Arguments:

X   Shall be of type REAL or COMPLEX.

Return value:

The return value is of type INTEGER and of the default integer kind.

See also: Section 9.232 [SELECTED_REAL_KIND], page 223, Section 9.217 [RANGE], page 215

Example:

```
program prec_and_range
  real(kind=4) :: x(2)
  complex(kind=8) :: y

  print *, precision(x), range(x)
  print *, precision(y), range(y)
end program prec_and_range
```

9.210 PRESENT — Determine whether an optional dummy argument is specified

Description:

Determines whether an optional dummy argument is present.

Standard: Fortran 95 and later

Class: Inquiry function

Syntax: RESULT = PRESENT(A)

Arguments:

A   May be of any type and may be a pointer, scalar or array
                  value, or a dummy procedure. It shall be the name of an
                  optional dummy argument accessible within the current sub-
                  routine or function.

Return value:

Returns either **TRUE** if the optional argument *A* is present, or **FALSE** otherwise.

Example:

```
PROGRAM test_present
  WRITE(*,*) f(), f(42)        ! "F T"
CONTAINS
  LOGICAL FUNCTION f(x)
    INTEGER, INTENT(IN), OPTIONAL :: x
    f = PRESENT(x)
  END FUNCTION
END PROGRAM
```

9.211 PRODUCT — Product of array elements

Description:

Multiplies the elements of *ARRAY* along dimension *DIM* if the corresponding
element in *MASK* is **TRUE**.

Standard: Fortran 95 and later

Class: Transformational function

Syntax:

```
RESULT = PRODUCT(ARRAY[, MASK])
RESULT = PRODUCT(ARRAY, DIM[, MASK])
```

Arguments:

ARRAY   Shall be an array of type **INTEGER**, **REAL** or **COMPLEX**.

DIM   (Optional) shall be a scalar of type `INTEGER` with a value in the range from 1 to n, where n equals the rank of *ARRAY*.

MASK   (Optional) shall be of type `LOGICAL` and either be a scalar or an array of the same shape as *ARRAY*.

Return value:

The result is of the same type as *ARRAY*.

If *DIM* is absent, a scalar with the product of all elements in *ARRAY* is returned. Otherwise, an array of rank n-1, where n equals the rank of *ARRAY*, and a shape similar to that of *ARRAY* with dimension *DIM* dropped is returned.

Example:

```
PROGRAM test_product
  INTEGER :: x(5) = (/ 1, 2, 3, 4 ,5 /)
  print *, PRODUCT(x)                    ! all elements, product = 120
  print *, PRODUCT(x, MASK=MOD(x, 2)==1) ! odd elements, product = 15
END PROGRAM
```

See also: Section 9.251 [SUM], page 235

9.212 `RADIX` — **Base of a model number**

Description:

`RADIX(X)` returns the base of the model representing the entity *X*.

Standard: Fortran 95 and later

Class: Inquiry function

Syntax: `RESULT = RADIX(X)`

Arguments:

X   Shall be of type `INTEGER` or `REAL`

Return value:

The return value is a scalar of type `INTEGER` and of the default integer kind.

See also: Section 9.232 [SELECTED_REAL_KIND], page 223

Example:

```
program test_radix
  print *, "The radix for the default integer kind is", radix(0)
  print *, "The radix for the default real kind is", radix(0.0)
end program test_radix
```

9.213 `RAN` — **Real pseudo-random number**

Description:

For compatibility with HP FORTRAN 77/iX, the `RAN` intrinsic is provided as an alias for `RAND`. See Section 9.214 [RAND], page 213 for complete documentation.

Standard: GNU extension

Class: Function

See also: Section 9.214 [RAND], page 213, Section 9.215 [RANDOM_NUMBER], page 213

9.214 RAND — Real pseudo-random number

Description:

RAND(FLAG) returns a pseudo-random number from a uniform distribution between 0 and 1. If *FLAG* is 0, the next number in the current sequence is returned; if *FLAG* is 1, the generator is restarted by CALL SRAND(0); if *FLAG* has any other value, it is used as a new seed with SRAND.

This intrinsic routine is provided for backwards compatibility with GNU Fortran 77. It implements a simple modulo generator as provided by g77. For new code, one should consider the use of Section 9.215 [RANDOM_NUMBER], page 213 as it implements a superior algorithm.

Standard: GNU extension

Class: Function

Syntax: RESULT = RAND(I)

Arguments:

I   Shall be a scalar INTEGER of kind 4.

Return value:

The return value is of REAL type and the default kind.

Example:

```
program test_rand
  integer,parameter :: seed = 86456

  call srand(seed)
  print *, rand(), rand(), rand(), rand()
  print *, rand(seed), rand(), rand(), rand()
end program test_rand
```

See also: Section 9.248 [SRAND], page 233, Section 9.215 [RANDOM_NUMBER], page 213

9.215 RANDOM_NUMBER — Pseudo-random number

Description:

Returns a single pseudorandom number or an array of pseudorandom numbers from the uniform distribution over the range $0 \leq x < 1$.

The runtime-library implements George Marsaglia's KISS (Keep It Simple Stupid) random number generator (RNG). This RNG combines:

1. The congruential generator $x(n) = 69069 \cdot x(n-1) + 1327217885$ with a period of 2^{32},

2. A 3-shift shift-register generator with a period of $2^{32} - 1$,

3. Two 16-bit multiply-with-carry generators with a period of $597273182964842497 > 2^{59}$.

The overall period exceeds 2^{123}.

Please note, this RNG is thread safe if used within OpenMP directives, i.e., its state will be consistent while called from multiple threads. However, the KISS generator does not create random numbers in parallel from multiple sources, but in sequence from a single source. If an OpenMP-enabled application heavily relies on random numbers, one should consider employing a dedicated parallel random number generator instead.

Standard: Fortran 95 and later

Class: Subroutine

Syntax: `RANDOM_NUMBER(HARVEST)`

Arguments:

    HARVEST   Shall be a scalar or an array of type `REAL`.

Example:

```
program test_random_number
  REAL :: r(5,5)
  CALL init_random_seed()            ! see example of RANDOM_SEED
  CALL RANDOM_NUMBER(r)
end program
```

See also: Section 9.216 [RANDOM_SEED], page 214

9.216 `RANDOM_SEED` — Initialize a pseudo-random number sequence

Description:

Restarts or queries the state of the pseudorandom number generator used by `RANDOM_NUMBER`.

If `RANDOM_SEED` is called without arguments, it is initialized to a default state. The example below shows how to initialize the random seed with a varying seed in order to ensure a different random number sequence for each invocation of the program. Note that setting any of the seed values to zero should be avoided as it can result in poor quality random numbers being generated.

Standard: Fortran 95 and later

Class: Subroutine

Syntax: `CALL RANDOM_SEED([SIZE, PUT, GET])`

Arguments:

    SIZE   (Optional) Shall be a scalar and of type default `INTEGER`, with `INTENT(OUT)`. It specifies the minimum size of the arrays used with the *PUT* and *GET* arguments.

    PUT   (Optional) Shall be an array of type default `INTEGER` and rank one. It is `INTENT(IN)` and the size of the array must be larger than or equal to the number returned by the *SIZE* argument.

    GET   (Optional) Shall be an array of type default `INTEGER` and rank one. It is `INTENT(OUT)` and the size of the array must be larger than or equal to the number returned by the *SIZE* argument.

Example:

```
subroutine init_random_seed()
  use iso_fortran_env, only: int64
  implicit none
  integer, allocatable :: seed(:)
  integer :: i, n, un, istat, dt(8), pid
  integer(int64) :: t

  call random_seed(size = n)
  allocate(seed(n))
  ! First try if the OS provides a random number generator
  open(newunit=un, file="/dev/urandom", access="stream", &
       form="unformatted", action="read", status="old", iostat=istat)
  if (istat == 0) then
     read(un) seed
     close(un)
  else
     ! Fallback to XOR:ing the current time and pid. The PID is
     ! useful in case one launches multiple instances of the same
     ! program in parallel.
     call system_clock(t)
     if (t == 0) then
        call date_and_time(values=dt)
        t = (dt(1) - 1970) * 365_int64 * 24 * 60 * 60 * 1000 &
             + dt(2) * 31_int64 * 24 * 60 * 60 * 1000 &
             + dt(3) * 24_int64 * 60 * 60 * 1000 &
             + dt(5) * 60 * 60 * 1000 &
             + dt(6) * 60 * 1000 + dt(7) * 1000 &
             + dt(8)
     end if
     pid = getpid()
     t = ieor(t, int(pid, kind(t)))
     do i = 1, n
        seed(i) = lcg(t)
     end do
  end if
  call random_seed(put=seed)
contains
  ! This simple PRNG might not be good enough for real work, but is
  ! sufficient for seeding a better PRNG.
  function lcg(s)
    integer :: lcg
    integer(int64) :: s
    if (s == 0) then
       s = 104729
    else
       s = mod(s, 4294967296_int64)
    end if
    s = mod(s * 279470273_int64, 4294967291_int64)
    lcg = int(mod(s, int(huge(0), int64)), kind(0))
  end function lcg
end subroutine init_random_seed
```

See also: Section 9.215 [RANDOM_NUMBER], page 213

9.217 RANGE — Decimal exponent range

Description:

RANGE(X) returns the decimal exponent range in the model of the type of X.

Standard: Fortran 95 and later

Class: Inquiry function

Syntax: `RESULT = RANGE(X)`

Arguments:

   X   Shall be of type `INTEGER`, `REAL` or `COMPLEX`.

Return value:

   The return value is of type `INTEGER` and of the default integer kind.

See also: Section 9.232 [SELECTED_REAL_KIND], page 223, Section 9.209 [PRECI-SION], page 210

Example: See `PRECISION` for an example.

9.218 `RANK` — Rank of a data object

Description:

   `RANK(A)` returns the rank of a scalar or array data object.

Standard: Technical Specification (TS) 29113

Class: Inquiry function

Syntax: `RESULT = RANK(A)`

Arguments:

   A   can be of any type

Return value:

   The return value is of type `INTEGER` and of the default integer kind. For arrays, their rank is returned; for scalars zero is returned.

Example:

```
program test_rank
  integer :: a
  real, allocatable :: b(:,:)

  print *, rank(a), rank(b) ! Prints:  0  2
end program test_rank
```

9.219 `REAL` — Convert to real type

Description:

   `REAL(A [, KIND])` converts its argument A to a real type. The `REALPART` function is provided for compatibility with **g77**, and its use is strongly discouraged.

Standard: Fortran 77 and later

Class: Elemental function

Syntax:

   `RESULT = REAL(A [, KIND])`
   `RESULT = REALPART(Z)`

Arguments:

A	Shall be `INTEGER`, `REAL`, or `COMPLEX`.
KIND	(Optional) An `INTEGER` initialization expression indicating the kind parameter of the result.

Return value:

These functions return a `REAL` variable or array under the following rules:

(A)   `REAL(A)` is converted to a default real type if *A* is an integer or real variable.

(B)   `REAL(A)` is converted to a real type with the kind type parameter of *A* if *A* is a complex variable.

(C)   `REAL(A, KIND)` is converted to a real type with kind type parameter *KIND* if *A* is a complex, integer, or real variable.

Example:

```
program test_real
  complex :: x = (1.0, 2.0)
  print *, real(x), real(x,8), realpart(x)
end program test_real
```

Specific names:

Name	Argument	Return type	Standard
`FLOAT(A)`	`INTEGER(4)`	`REAL(4)`	Fortran 77 and later
`DFLOAT(A)`	`INTEGER(4)`	`REAL(8)`	GNU extension
`SNGL(A)`	`INTEGER(8)`	`REAL(4)`	Fortran 77 and later

See also: Section 9.76 [DBLE], page 134

9.220 `RENAME` — **Rename a file**

Description:

Renames a file from file *PATH1* to *PATH2*. A null character (`CHAR(0)`) can be used to mark the end of the names in *PATH1* and *PATH2*; otherwise, trailing blanks in the file names are ignored. If the *STATUS* argument is supplied, it contains 0 on success or a nonzero error code upon return; see `rename(2)`.

This intrinsic is provided in both subroutine and function forms; however, only one form can be used in any given program unit.

Standard: GNU extension

Class: Subroutine, function

Syntax:

```
CALL RENAME(PATH1, PATH2 [, STATUS])
STATUS = RENAME(PATH1, PATH2)
```

Arguments:

PATH1	Shall be of default `CHARACTER` type.
PATH2	Shall be of default `CHARACTER` type.
STATUS	(Optional) Shall be of default `INTEGER` type.

See also: Section 9.163 [LINK], page 185

9.221 REPEAT — Repeated string concatenation

Description:

Concatenates *NCOPIES* copies of a string.

Standard: Fortran 95 and later

Class: Transformational function

Syntax: `RESULT = REPEAT(STRING, NCOPIES)`

Arguments:

STRING	Shall be scalar and of type `CHARACTER`.
NCOPIES	Shall be scalar and of type `INTEGER`.

Return value:

A new scalar of type `CHARACTER` built up from *NCOPIES* copies of *STRING*.

Example:

```
program test_repeat
  write(*,*) repeat("x", 5)   ! "xxxxx"
end program
```

9.222 RESHAPE — Function to reshape an array

Description:

Reshapes *SOURCE* to correspond to *SHAPE*. If necessary, the new array may be padded with elements from *PAD* or permuted as defined by *ORDER*.

Standard: Fortran 95 and later

Class: Transformational function

Syntax: `RESULT = RESHAPE(SOURCE, SHAPE[, PAD, ORDER])`

Arguments:

SOURCE	Shall be an array of any type.
SHAPE	Shall be of type `INTEGER` and an array of rank one. Its values must be positive or zero.
PAD	(Optional) shall be an array of the same type as *SOURCE*.
ORDER	(Optional) shall be of type `INTEGER` and an array of the same shape as *SHAPE*. Its values shall be a permutation of the numbers from 1 to n, where n is the size of *SHAPE*. If *ORDER* is absent, the natural ordering shall be assumed.

Return value:

The result is an array of shape *SHAPE* with the same type as *SOURCE*.

Example:

```
PROGRAM test_reshape
  INTEGER, DIMENSION(4) :: x
  WRITE(*,*) SHAPE(x)                        ! prints "4"
  WRITE(*,*) SHAPE(RESHAPE(x, (/2, 2/)))     ! prints "2 2"
END PROGRAM
```

See also: Section 9.234 [SHAPE], page 225

9.223 RRSPACING — Reciprocal of the relative spacing

Description:

RRSPACING(X) returns the reciprocal of the relative spacing of model numbers near *X*.

Standard: Fortran 95 and later

Class: Elemental function

Syntax: RESULT = RRSPACING(X)

Arguments:

    X   Shall be of type REAL.

Return value:

The return value is of the same type and kind as *X*. The value returned is equal to ABS(FRACTION(X)) * FLOAT(RADIX(X))**DIGITS(X).

See also: Section 9.245 [SPACING], page 231

9.224 RSHIFT — Right shift bits

Description:

RSHIFT returns a value corresponding to *I* with all of the bits shifted right by *SHIFT* places. If the absolute value of *SHIFT* is greater than BIT_SIZE(I), the value is undefined. Bits shifted out from the right end are lost. The fill is arithmetic: the bits shifted in from the left end are equal to the leftmost bit, which in two's complement representation is the sign bit.

This function has been superseded by the SHIFTA intrinsic, which is standard in Fortran 2008 and later.

Standard: GNU extension

Class: Elemental function

Syntax: RESULT = RSHIFT(I, SHIFT)

Arguments:

    I   The type shall be INTEGER.
    SHIFT   The type shall be INTEGER.

Return value:

The return value is of type INTEGER and of the same kind as *I*.

See also: Section 9.150 [ISHFT], page 178, Section 9.151 [ISHFTC], page 179, Section 9.173 [LSHIFT], page 190, Section 9.235 [SHIFTA], page 225, Section 9.237 [SHIFTR], page 226, Section 9.236 [SHIFTL], page 226

9.225 SAME_TYPE_AS — Query dynamic types for equality

Description:

Query dynamic types for equality.

Standard: Fortran 2003 and later

Class: Inquiry function

Syntax: RESULT = SAME_TYPE_AS(A, B)

Arguments:

      A   Shall be an object of extensible declared type or unlimited polymorphic.

      B   Shall be an object of extensible declared type or unlimited polymorphic.

Return value:

      The return value is a scalar of type default logical. It is true if and only if the dynamic type of A is the same as the dynamic type of B.

See also: Section 9.97 [EXTENDS_TYPE_OF], page 147

9.226 SCALE — Scale a real value

Description:

      SCALE(X,I) returns X * RADIX(X)**I.

Standard: Fortran 95 and later

Class: Elemental function

Syntax: RESULT = SCALE(X, I)

Arguments:

      X   The type of the argument shall be a REAL.

      I   The type of the argument shall be a INTEGER.

Return value:

      The return value is of the same type and kind as X. Its value is X * RADIX(X)**I.

Example:

```
program test_scale
  real :: x = 178.1387e-4
  integer :: i = 5
  print *, scale(x,i), x*radix(x)**i
end program test_scale
```

9.227 SCAN — Scan a string for the presence of a set of characters

Description:

      Scans a *STRING* for any of the characters in a *SET* of characters.

      If *BACK* is either absent or equals FALSE, this function returns the position of the leftmost character of *STRING* that is in *SET*. If *BACK* equals TRUE, the rightmost position is returned. If no character of *SET* is found in *STRING*, the result is zero.

Standard: Fortran 95 and later, with *KIND* argument Fortran 2003 and later

Class: Elemental function

Syntax: RESULT = SCAN(STRING, SET[, BACK [, KIND]])

Arguments:

STRING	Shall be of type CHARACTER.
SET	Shall be of type CHARACTER.
BACK	(Optional) shall be of type LOGICAL.
KIND	(Optional) An INTEGER initialization expression indicating the kind parameter of the result.

Return value:

The return value is of type INTEGER and of kind *KIND*. If *KIND* is absent, the return value is of default integer kind.

Example:

```
PROGRAM test_scan
  WRITE(*,*) SCAN("FORTRAN", "AO")          ! 2, found 'O'
  WRITE(*,*) SCAN("FORTRAN", "AO", .TRUE.)  ! 6, found 'A'
  WRITE(*,*) SCAN("FORTRAN", "C++")         ! 0, found none
END PROGRAM
```

See also: Section 9.140 [INDEX intrinsic], page 173, Section 9.271 [VERIFY], page 246

9.228 SECNDS — Time function

Description:

SECNDS(X) gets the time in seconds from the real-time system clock. *X* is a reference time, also in seconds. If this is zero, the time in seconds from midnight is returned. This function is non-standard and its use is discouraged.

Standard: GNU extension

Class: Function

Syntax: RESULT = SECNDS (X)

Arguments:

T	Shall be of type REAL(4).
X	Shall be of type REAL(4).

Return value:

None

Example:

```
program test_secnds
    integer :: i
    real(4) :: t1, t2
    print *, secnds (0.0)    ! seconds since midnight
    t1 = secnds (0.0)        ! reference time
    do i = 1, 10000000       ! do something
    end do
    t2 = secnds (t1)         ! elapsed time
    print *, "Something took ", t2, " seconds."
end program test_secnds
```

9.229 SECOND — CPU time function

Description:

Returns a `REAL(4)` value representing the elapsed CPU time in seconds. This provides the same functionality as the standard `CPU_TIME` intrinsic, and is only included for backwards compatibility.

This intrinsic is provided in both subroutine and function forms; however, only one form can be used in any given program unit.

Standard: GNU extension

Class: Subroutine, function

Syntax:

```
CALL SECOND(TIME)
TIME = SECOND()
```

Arguments:

TIME   Shall be of type `REAL(4)`.

Return value:

In either syntax, *TIME* is set to the process's current runtime in seconds.

See also: Section 9.72 [CPU_TIME], page 130

9.230 SELECTED_CHAR_KIND — Choose character kind

Description:

`SELECTED_CHAR_KIND(NAME)` returns the kind value for the character set named *NAME*, if a character set with such a name is supported, or −1 otherwise. Currently, supported character sets include "ASCII" and "DEFAULT", which are equivalent, and "ISO_10646" (Universal Character Set, UCS-4) which is commonly known as Unicode.

Standard: Fortran 2003 and later

Class: Transformational function

Syntax: RESULT = SELECTED_CHAR_KIND(NAME)

Arguments:

NAME   Shall be a scalar and of the default character type.

Example:

```
program character_kind
  use iso_fortran_env
  implicit none
  integer, parameter :: ascii = selected_char_kind ("ascii")
  integer, parameter :: ucs4  = selected_char_kind ('ISO_10646')

  character(kind=ascii, len=26) :: alphabet
  character(kind=ucs4,  len=30) :: hello_world

  alphabet = ascii_"abcdefghijklmnopqrstuvwxyz"
  hello_world = ucs4_'Hello World and Ni Hao -- ' &
```

```
                    // char (int (z'4F60'), ucs4)      &
                    // char (int (z'597D'), ucs4)

            write (*,*) alphabet

            open (output_unit, encoding='UTF-8')
            write (*,*) trim (hello_world)
        end program character_kind
```

9.231 SELECTED_INT_KIND — Choose integer kind

Description:

SELECTED_INT_KIND(R) return the kind value of the smallest integer type that can represent all values ranging from -10^R (exclusive) to 10^R (exclusive). If there is no integer kind that accommodates this range, SELECTED_INT_KIND returns -1.

Standard: Fortran 95 and later

Class: Transformational function

Syntax: RESULT = SELECTED_INT_KIND(R)

Arguments:

R   Shall be a scalar and of type INTEGER.

Example:

```
        program large_integers
          integer,parameter :: k5 = selected_int_kind(5)
          integer,parameter :: k15 = selected_int_kind(15)
          integer(kind=k5) :: i5
          integer(kind=k15) :: i15

          print *, huge(i5), huge(i15)

          ! The following inequalities are always true
          print *, huge(i5) >= 10_k5**5-1
          print *, huge(i15) >= 10_k15**15-1
        end program large_integers
```

9.232 SELECTED_REAL_KIND — Choose real kind

Description:

SELECTED_REAL_KIND(P,R) returns the kind value of a real data type with decimal precision of at least P digits, exponent range of at least R, and with a radix of RADIX.

Standard: Fortran 95 and later, with RADIX Fortran 2008 or later

Class: Transformational function

Syntax: RESULT = SELECTED_REAL_KIND([P, R, RADIX])

Arguments:

P   (Optional) shall be a scalar and of type INTEGER.
R   (Optional) shall be a scalar and of type INTEGER.

RADIX   (Optional) shall be a scalar and of type `INTEGER`.

Before Fortran 2008, at least one of the arguments R or P shall be present; since Fortran 2008, they are assumed to be zero if absent.

Return value:

      `SELECTED_REAL_KIND` returns the value of the kind type parameter of a real data type with decimal precision of at least `P` digits, a decimal exponent range of at least `R`, and with the requested `RADIX`. If the `RADIX` parameter is absent, real kinds with any radix can be returned. If more than one real data type meet the criteria, the kind of the data type with the smallest decimal precision is returned. If no real data type matches the criteria, the result is

-1 if the processor does not support a real data type with a
        precision greater than or equal to `P`, but the `R` and `RADIX` requirements can be fulfilled

-2 if the processor does not support a real type with an exponent
        range greater than or equal to `R`, but `P` and `RADIX` are fulfillable

-3 if `RADIX` but not `P` and `R` requirements
        are fulfillable

-4 if `RADIX` and either `P` or `R` requirements
        are fulfillable

-5 if there is no real type with the given `RADIX`

See also: Section 9.209 [PRECISION], page 210, Section 9.217 [RANGE], page 215, Section 9.212 [RADIX], page 212

Example:

```
program real_kinds
  integer,parameter :: p6 = selected_real_kind(6)
  integer,parameter :: p10r100 = selected_real_kind(10,100)
  integer,parameter :: r400 = selected_real_kind(r=400)
  real(kind=p6) :: x
  real(kind=p10r100) :: y
  real(kind=r400) :: z

  print *, precision(x), range(x)
  print *, precision(y), range(y)
  print *, precision(z), range(z)
end program real_kinds
```

9.233 SET_EXPONENT — Set the exponent of the model

Description:

      `SET_EXPONENT(X, I)` returns the real number whose fractional part is that that of X and whose exponent part is I.

Standard: Fortran 95 and later

Class: Elemental function

Syntax: `RESULT = SET_EXPONENT(X, I)`

Arguments:

X	Shall be of type REAL.
I	Shall be of type INTEGER.

Return value:

The return value is of the same type and kind as X. The real number whose fractional part is that that of X and whose exponent part if I is returned; it is FRACTION(X) * RADIX(X)**I.

Example:

```
PROGRAM test_setexp
  REAL :: x = 178.1387e-4
  INTEGER :: i = 17
  PRINT *, SET_EXPONENT(x, i), FRACTION(x) * RADIX(x)**i
END PROGRAM
```

9.234 SHAPE — Determine the shape of an array

Description:

Determines the shape of an array.

Standard: Fortran 95 and later, with *KIND* argument Fortran 2003 and later

Class: Inquiry function

Syntax: RESULT = SHAPE(SOURCE [, KIND])

Arguments:

SOURCE	Shall be an array or scalar of any type. If *SOURCE* is a pointer it must be associated and allocatable arrays must be allocated.
KIND	(Optional) An INTEGER initialization expression indicating the kind parameter of the result.

Return value:

An INTEGER array of rank one with as many elements as *SOURCE* has dimensions. The elements of the resulting array correspond to the extend of *SOURCE* along the respective dimensions. If *SOURCE* is a scalar, the result is the rank one array of size zero. If *KIND* is absent, the return value has the default integer kind otherwise the specified kind.

Example:

```
PROGRAM test_shape
  INTEGER, DIMENSION(-1:1, -1:2) :: A
  WRITE(*,*) SHAPE(A)            ! (/ 3, 4 /)
  WRITE(*,*) SIZE(SHAPE(42))     ! (/ /)
END PROGRAM
```

See also: Section 9.222 [RESHAPE], page 218, Section 9.242 [SIZE], page 229

9.235 SHIFTA — Right shift with fill

Description:

SHIFTA returns a value corresponding to I with all of the bits shifted right by *SHIFT* places. If the absolute value of *SHIFT* is greater than BIT_SIZE(I), the value is undefined. Bits shifted out from the right end are lost. The fill is arithmetic: the bits shifted in from the left end are equal to the leftmost bit, which in two's complement representation is the sign bit.

Standard: Fortran 2008 and later

Class: Elemental function

Syntax: RESULT = SHIFTA(I, SHIFT)

Arguments:

I	The type shall be INTEGER.
SHIFT	The type shall be INTEGER.

Return value:

The return value is of type INTEGER and of the same kind as *I*.

See also: Section 9.236 [SHIFTL], page 226, Section 9.237 [SHIFTR], page 226

9.236 SHIFTL — Left shift

Description:

SHIFTL returns a value corresponding to *I* with all of the bits shifted left by *SHIFT* places. If the absolute value of *SHIFT* is greater than BIT_SIZE(I), the value is undefined. Bits shifted out from the left end are lost, and bits shifted in from the right end are set to 0.

Standard: Fortran 2008 and later

Class: Elemental function

Syntax: RESULT = SHIFTL(I, SHIFT)

Arguments:

I	The type shall be INTEGER.
SHIFT	The type shall be INTEGER.

Return value:

The return value is of type INTEGER and of the same kind as *I*.

See also: Section 9.235 [SHIFTA], page 225, Section 9.237 [SHIFTR], page 226

9.237 SHIFTR — Right shift

Description:

SHIFTR returns a value corresponding to *I* with all of the bits shifted right by *SHIFT* places. If the absolute value of *SHIFT* is greater than BIT_SIZE(I), the value is undefined. Bits shifted out from the right end are lost, and bits shifted in from the left end are set to 0.

Standard: Fortran 2008 and later

Class: Elemental function

Syntax: RESULT = SHIFTR(I, SHIFT)

Arguments:

I	The type shall be `INTEGER`.
SHIFT	The type shall be `INTEGER`.

Return value:

The return value is of type `INTEGER` and of the same kind as *I*.

See also: Section 9.235 [SHIFTA], page 225, Section 9.236 [SHIFTL], page 226

9.238 `SIGN` — Sign copying function

Description:

SIGN(A,B) returns the value of *A* with the sign of *B*.

Standard: Fortran 77 and later

Class: Elemental function

Syntax: `RESULT = SIGN(A, B)`

Arguments:

A	Shall be of type `INTEGER` or `REAL`
B	Shall be of the same type and kind as *A*

Return value:

The kind of the return value is that of *A* and *B*. If $B \geq 0$ then the result is `ABS(A)`, else it is `-ABS(A)`.

Example:

```
program test_sign
  print *, sign(-12,1)
  print *, sign(-12,0)
  print *, sign(-12,-1)

  print *, sign(-12.,1.)
  print *, sign(-12.,0.)
  print *, sign(-12.,-1.)
end program test_sign
```

Specific names:

Name	Arguments	Return type	Standard
SIGN(A,B)	REAL(4) A, B	REAL(4)	f77, gnu
ISIGN(A,B)	INTEGER(4) A, B	INTEGER(4)	f77, gnu
DSIGN(A,B)	REAL(8) A, B	REAL(8)	f77, gnu

9.239 `SIGNAL` — Signal handling subroutine (or function)

Description:

SIGNAL(NUMBER, HANDLER [, STATUS]) causes external subroutine *HANDLER* to be executed with a single integer argument when signal *NUMBER* occurs. If *HANDLER* is an integer, it can be used to turn off handling of signal *NUMBER* or revert to its default action. See `signal(2)`.

If `SIGNAL` is called as a subroutine and the *STATUS* argument is supplied, it is set to the value returned by `signal(2)`.

Standard: GNU extension

Class: Subroutine, function

Syntax:

```
CALL SIGNAL(NUMBER, HANDLER [, STATUS])
STATUS = SIGNAL(NUMBER, HANDLER)
```

Arguments:

NUMBER	Shall be a scalar integer, with `INTENT(IN)`
HANDLER	Signal handler (`INTEGER FUNCTION` or `SUBROUTINE`) or dummy/global `INTEGER` scalar. `INTEGER`. It is `INTENT(IN)`.
STATUS	(Optional) *STATUS* shall be a scalar integer. It has `INTENT(OUT)`.

Return value:

The `SIGNAL` function returns the value returned by `signal(2)`.

Example:

```
program test_signal
  intrinsic signal
  external handler_print

  call signal (12, handler_print)
  call signal (10, 1)

  call sleep (30)
end program test_signal
```

9.240 `SIN` — Sine function

Description:

`SIN(X)` computes the sine of *X*.

Standard: Fortran 77 and later

Class: Elemental function

Syntax: `RESULT = SIN(X)`

Arguments:

X	The type shall be `REAL` or `COMPLEX`.

Return value:

The return value has same type and kind as *X*.

Example:

```
program test_sin
  real :: x = 0.0
  x = sin(x)
end program test_sin
```

Specific names:

Name	Argument	Return type	Standard
`SIN(X)`	`REAL(4) X`	`REAL(4)`	f77, gnu
`DSIN(X)`	`REAL(8) X`	`REAL(8)`	f95, gnu

CSIN(X)	COMPLEX(4) X	COMPLEX(4)	f95, gnu
ZSIN(X)	COMPLEX(8) X	COMPLEX(8)	f95, gnu
CDSIN(X)	COMPLEX(8) X	COMPLEX(8)	f95, gnu

See also: Section 9.18 [ASIN], page 96

9.241 SINH — Hyperbolic sine function

Description:

SINH(X) computes the hyperbolic sine of *X*.

Standard: Fortran 95 and later, for a complex argument Fortran 2008 or later

Class: Elemental function

Syntax: RESULT = SINH(X)

Arguments:

X	The type shall be REAL or COMPLEX.

Return value:

The return value has same type and kind as *X*.

Example:

```
program test_sinh
  real(8) :: x = - 1.0_8
  x = sinh(x)
end program test_sinh
```

Specific names:

Name	Argument	Return type	Standard
SINH(X)	REAL(4) X	REAL(4)	Fortran 95 and later
DSINH(X)	REAL(8) X	REAL(8)	Fortran 95 and later

See also: Section 9.19 [ASINH], page 96

9.242 SIZE — Determine the size of an array

Description:

Determine the extent of *ARRAY* along a specified dimension *DIM*, or the total number of elements in *ARRAY* if *DIM* is absent.

Standard: Fortran 95 and later, with *KIND* argument Fortran 2003 and later

Class: Inquiry function

Syntax: RESULT = SIZE(ARRAY[, DIM [, KIND]])

Arguments:

ARRAY	Shall be an array of any type. If *ARRAY* is a pointer it must be associated and allocatable arrays must be allocated.
DIM	(Optional) shall be a scalar of type INTEGER and its value shall be in the range from 1 to n, where n equals the rank of *ARRAY*.
KIND	(Optional) An INTEGER initialization expression indicating the kind parameter of the result.

Return value:

>   The return value is of type INTEGER and of kind *KIND*. If *KIND* is absent, the
>   return value is of default integer kind.

Example:

```
PROGRAM test_size
  WRITE(*,*) SIZE((/ 1, 2 /))     ! 2
END PROGRAM
```

See also: Section 9.234 [SHAPE], page 225, Section 9.222 [RESHAPE], page 218

9.243 SIZEOF — Size in bytes of an expression

Description:

>   SIZEOF(X) calculates the number of bytes of storage the expression X occupies.

Standard: GNU extension

Class: Inquiry function

Syntax: N = SIZEOF(X)

Arguments:

>   *X*   The argument shall be of any type, rank or shape.

Return value:

>   The return value is of type integer and of the system-dependent kind *C_SIZE_T*
>   (from the *ISO_C_BINDING* module). Its value is the number of bytes occupied
>   by the argument. If the argument has the POINTER attribute, the number
>   of bytes of the storage area pointed to is returned. If the argument is of a
>   derived type with POINTER or ALLOCATABLE components, the return value does
>   not account for the sizes of the data pointed to by these components. If the
>   argument is polymorphic, the size according to the dynamic type is returned.
>   The argument may not be a procedure or procedure pointer. Note that the code
>   assumes for arrays that those are contiguous; for contiguous arrays, it returns
>   the storage or an array element multiplied by the size of the array.

Example:

```
integer :: i
real :: r, s(5)
print *, (sizeof(s)/sizeof(r) == 5)
end
```

>   The example will print .TRUE. unless you are using a platform where default
>   REAL variables are unusually padded.

See also: Section 9.53 [C_SIZEOF], page 117, Section 9.250 [STORAGE_SIZE], page 234

9.244 SLEEP — Sleep for the specified number of seconds

Description:

>   Calling this subroutine causes the process to pause for *SECONDS* seconds.

Standard: GNU extension

Class: Subroutine

Syntax: `CALL SLEEP(SECONDS)`

Arguments:

      SECONDS   The type shall be of default `INTEGER`.

Example:

```
program test_sleep
  call sleep(5)
end
```

9.245 SPACING — Smallest distance between two numbers of a given type

Description:

      Determines the distance between the argument X and the nearest adjacent number of the same type.

Standard: Fortran 95 and later

Class: Elemental function

Syntax: `RESULT = SPACING(X)`

Arguments:

      X Shall be of type `REAL`.

Return value:

      The result is of the same type as the input argument X.

Example:

```
PROGRAM test_spacing
   INTEGER, PARAMETER :: SGL = SELECTED_REAL_KIND(p=6, r=37)
   INTEGER, PARAMETER :: DBL = SELECTED_REAL_KIND(p=13, r=200)

   WRITE(*,*) spacing(1.0_SGL)     ! "1.1920929E-07"          on i686
   WRITE(*,*) spacing(1.0_DBL)     ! "2.220446049250313E-016" on i686
END PROGRAM
```

See also: Section 9.223 [RRSPACING], page 219

9.246 SPREAD — Add a dimension to an array

Description:

      Replicates a *SOURCE* array *NCOPIES* times along a specified dimension *DIM*.

Standard: Fortran 95 and later

Class: Transformational function

Syntax: `RESULT = SPREAD(SOURCE, DIM, NCOPIES)`

Arguments:

      SOURCE   Shall be a scalar or an array of any type and a rank less than seven.

DIM	Shall be a scalar of type INTEGER with a value in the range from 1 to n+1, where n equals the rank of *SOURCE*.
NCOPIES	Shall be a scalar of type INTEGER.

Return value:

The result is an array of the same type as *SOURCE* and has rank n+1 where n equals the rank of *SOURCE*.

Example:

```
PROGRAM test_spread
  INTEGER :: a = 1, b(2) = (/ 1, 2 /)
  WRITE(*,*) SPREAD(A, 1, 2)            ! "1 1"
  WRITE(*,*) SPREAD(B, 1, 2)            ! "1 1 2 2"
END PROGRAM
```

See also: Section 9.270 [UNPACK], page 246

9.247 SQRT — Square-root function

Description:

SQRT(X) computes the square root of *X*.

Standard: Fortran 77 and later

Class: Elemental function

Syntax: RESULT = SQRT(X)

Arguments:

X	The type shall be REAL or COMPLEX.

Return value:

The return value is of type REAL or COMPLEX. The kind type parameter is the same as *X*.

Example:

```
program test_sqrt
  real(8) :: x = 2.0_8
  complex :: z = (1.0, 2.0)
  x = sqrt(x)
  z = sqrt(z)
end program test_sqrt
```

Specific names:

Name	Argument	Return type	Standard
SQRT(X)	REAL(4) X	REAL(4)	Fortran 95 and later
DSQRT(X)	REAL(8) X	REAL(8)	Fortran 95 and later
CSQRT(X)	COMPLEX(4) X	COMPLEX(4)	Fortran 95 and later
ZSQRT(X)	COMPLEX(8) X	COMPLEX(8)	GNU extension
CDSQRT(X)	COMPLEX(8) X	COMPLEX(8)	GNU extension

9.248 SRAND — Reinitialize the random number generator

Description:

SRAND reinitializes the pseudo-random number generator called by RAND and IRAND. The new seed used by the generator is specified by the required argument *SEED*.

Standard: GNU extension

Class: Subroutine

Syntax: CALL SRAND(SEED)

Arguments:

SEED   Shall be a scalar INTEGER(kind=4).

Return value:

Does not return anything.

Example: See RAND and IRAND for examples.

Notes: The Fortran standard specifies the intrinsic subroutines RANDOM_SEED to initialize the pseudo-random number generator and RANDOM_NUMBER to generate pseudo-random numbers. These subroutines should be used in new codes.

Please note that in GNU Fortran, these two sets of intrinsics (RAND, IRAND and SRAND on the one hand, RANDOM_NUMBER and RANDOM_SEED on the other hand) access two independent pseudo-random number generators.

See also: Section 9.214 [RAND], page 213, Section 9.216 [RANDOM_SEED], page 214, Section 9.215 [RANDOM_NUMBER], page 213

9.249 STAT — Get file status

Description:

This function returns information about a file. No permissions are required on the file itself, but execute (search) permission is required on all of the directories in path that lead to the file.

The elements that are obtained and stored in the array VALUES:

VALUES(1)	Device ID
VALUES(2)	Inode number
VALUES(3)	File mode
VALUES(4)	Number of links
VALUES(5)	Owner's uid
VALUES(6)	Owner's gid
VALUES(7)	ID of device containing directory entry for file (0 if not available)
VALUES(8)	File size (bytes)
VALUES(9)	Last access time
VALUES(10)	Last modification time
VALUES(11)	Last file status change time
VALUES(12)	Preferred I/O block size (-1 if not available)

VALUES(13)   Number of blocks allocated (-1 if not available)

Not all these elements are relevant on all systems. If an element is not relevant, it is returned as 0.

This intrinsic is provided in both subroutine and function forms; however, only one form can be used in any given program unit.

Standard: GNU extension

Class: Subroutine, function

Syntax:

```
CALL STAT(NAME, VALUES [, STATUS])
STATUS = STAT(NAME, VALUES)
```

Arguments:

NAME	The type shall be CHARACTER, of the default kind and a valid path within the file system.
VALUES	The type shall be INTEGER(4), DIMENSION(13).
STATUS	(Optional) status flag of type INTEGER(4). Returns 0 on success and a system specific error code otherwise.

Example:

```
PROGRAM test_stat
  INTEGER, DIMENSION(13) :: buff
  INTEGER :: status

  CALL STAT("/etc/passwd", buff, status)

  IF (status == 0) THEN
    WRITE (*, FMT="('Device ID:',              T30, I19)") buff(1)
    WRITE (*, FMT="('Inode number:',           T30, I19)") buff(2)
    WRITE (*, FMT="('File mode (octal):',      T30, O19)") buff(3)
    WRITE (*, FMT="('Number of links:',        T30, I19)") buff(4)
    WRITE (*, FMT="('Owner''s uid:',           T30, I19)") buff(5)
    WRITE (*, FMT="('Owner''s gid:',           T30, I19)") buff(6)
    WRITE (*, FMT="('Device where located:',   T30, I19)") buff(7)
    WRITE (*, FMT="('File size:',              T30, I19)") buff(8)
    WRITE (*, FMT="('Last access time:',       T30, A19)") CTIME(buff(9))
    WRITE (*, FMT="('Last modification time',  T30, A19)") CTIME(buff(10))
    WRITE (*, FMT="('Last status change time:', T30, A19)") CTIME(buff(11))
    WRITE (*, FMT="('Preferred block size:',   T30, I19)") buff(12)
    WRITE (*, FMT="('No. of blocks allocated:', T30, I19)") buff(13)
  END IF
END PROGRAM
```

See also: To stat an open file: Section 9.109 [FSTAT], page 155, to stat a link: Section 9.174 [LSTAT], page 191

9.250 STORAGE_SIZE — Storage size in bits

Description:

Returns the storage size of argument *A* in bits.

Standard: Fortran 2008 and later

Class: Inquiry function

Syntax: RESULT = STORAGE_SIZE(A [, KIND])

Arguments:

      A   Shall be a scalar or array of any type.

      KIND   (Optional) shall be a scalar integer constant expression.

Return Value:

The result is a scalar integer with the kind type parameter specified by KIND (or default integer type if KIND is missing). The result value is the size expressed in bits for an element of an array that has the dynamic type and type parameters of A.

See also: Section 9.53 [C_SIZEOF], page 117, Section 9.243 [SIZEOF], page 230

9.251 SUM — Sum of array elements

Description:

Adds the elements of *ARRAY* along dimension *DIM* if the corresponding element in *MASK* is TRUE.

Standard: Fortran 95 and later

Class: Transformational function

Syntax:

```
RESULT = SUM(ARRAY[, MASK])
RESULT = SUM(ARRAY, DIM[, MASK])
```

Arguments:

      ARRAY   Shall be an array of type INTEGER, REAL or COMPLEX.

      DIM   (Optional) shall be a scalar of type INTEGER with a value in the range from 1 to n, where n equals the rank of *ARRAY*.

      MASK   (Optional) shall be of type LOGICAL and either be a scalar or an array of the same shape as *ARRAY*.

Return value:

The result is of the same type as *ARRAY*.

If *DIM* is absent, a scalar with the sum of all elements in *ARRAY* is returned. Otherwise, an array of rank n-1, where n equals the rank of *ARRAY*, and a shape similar to that of *ARRAY* with dimension *DIM* dropped is returned.

Example:

```
PROGRAM test_sum
  INTEGER :: x(5) = (/ 1, 2, 3, 4 ,5 /)
  print *, SUM(x)                    ! all elements, sum = 15
  print *, SUM(x, MASK=MOD(x, 2)==1) ! odd elements, sum = 9
END PROGRAM
```

See also: Section 9.211 [PRODUCT], page 211

9.252 SYMLNK — Create a symbolic link

Description:

Makes a symbolic link from file *PATH1* to *PATH2*. A null character (CHAR(0)) can be used to mark the end of the names in *PATH1* and *PATH2*; otherwise, trailing blanks in the file names are ignored. If the *STATUS* argument is supplied, it contains 0 on success or a nonzero error code upon return; see symlink(2). If the system does not supply symlink(2), ENOSYS is returned.

This intrinsic is provided in both subroutine and function forms; however, only one form can be used in any given program unit.

Standard: GNU extension

Class: Subroutine, function

Syntax:

```
CALL SYMLNK(PATH1, PATH2 [, STATUS])
STATUS = SYMLNK(PATH1, PATH2)
```

Arguments:

PATH1	Shall be of default CHARACTER type.
PATH2	Shall be of default CHARACTER type.
STATUS	(Optional) Shall be of default INTEGER type.

See also: Section 9.163 [LINK], page 185, Section 9.269 [UNLINK], page 245

9.253 SYSTEM — Execute a shell command

Description:

Passes the command *COMMAND* to a shell (see system(3)). If argument *STATUS* is present, it contains the value returned by system(3), which is presumably 0 if the shell command succeeded. Note that which shell is used to invoke the command is system-dependent and environment-dependent.

This intrinsic is provided in both subroutine and function forms; however, only one form can be used in any given program unit.

Note that the system function need not be thread-safe. It is the responsibility of the user to ensure that system is not called concurrently.

Standard: GNU extension

Class: Subroutine, function

Syntax:

```
CALL SYSTEM(COMMAND [, STATUS])
STATUS = SYSTEM(COMMAND)
```

Arguments:

COMMAND	Shall be of default CHARACTER type.
STATUS	(Optional) Shall be of default INTEGER type.

See also: Section 9.93 [EXECUTE_COMMAND_LINE], page 144, which is part of the Fortran 2008 standard and should considered in new code for future portability.

9.254 SYSTEM_CLOCK — Time function

Description:

Determines the *COUNT* of a processor clock since an unspecified time in the past modulo *COUNT_MAX*, *COUNT_RATE* determines the number of clock ticks per second. If the platform supports a monotonic clock, that clock is used and can, depending on the platform clock implementation, provide up to nanosecond resolution. If a monotonic clock is not available, the implementation falls back to a realtime clock.

COUNT_RATE is system dependent and can vary depending on the kind of the arguments. For *kind=4* arguments (and smaller integer kinds), *COUNT* represents milliseconds, while for *kind=8* arguments (and larger integer kinds), *COUNT* typically represents micro- or nanoseconds depending on resolution of the underlying platform clock. *COUNT_MAX* usually equals `HUGE(COUNT_MAX)`. Note that the millisecond resolution of the *kind=4* version implies that the *COUNT* will wrap around in roughly 25 days. In order to avoid issues with the wrap around and for more precise timing, please use the *kind=8* version.

If there is no clock, or querying the clock fails, *COUNT* is set to `-HUGE(COUNT)`, and *COUNT_RATE* and *COUNT_MAX* are set to zero.

When running on a platform using the GNU C library (glibc) version 2.16 or older, or a derivative thereof, the high resolution monotonic clock is available only when linking with the *rt* library. This can be done explicitly by adding the `-lrt` flag when linking the application, but is also done implicitly when using OpenMP.

On the Windows platform, the version with *kind=4* arguments uses the `GetTickCount` function, whereas the *kind=8* version uses `QueryPerformanceCounter` and `QueryPerformanceCounterFrequency`. For more information, and potential caveats, please see the platform documentation.

Standard: Fortran 95 and later

Class: Subroutine

Syntax: `CALL SYSTEM_CLOCK([COUNT, COUNT_RATE, COUNT_MAX])`

Arguments:

COUNT (Optional) shall be a scalar of type `INTEGER` with `INTENT(OUT)`.

COUNT_RATE (Optional) shall be a scalar of type `INTEGER` or `REAL`, with `INTENT(OUT)`.

COUNT_MAX (Optional) shall be a scalar of type `INTEGER` with `INTENT(OUT)`.

Example:

```
PROGRAM test_system_clock
  INTEGER :: count, count_rate, count_max
  CALL SYSTEM_CLOCK(count, count_rate, count_max)
  WRITE(*,*) count, count_rate, count_max
END PROGRAM
```

See also: Section 9.75 [DATE_AND_TIME], page 133, Section 9.72 [CPU_TIME], page 130

9.255 `TAN` — Tangent function

Description:
>   `TAN(X)` computes the tangent of X.

Standard: Fortran 77 and later, for a complex argument Fortran 2008 or later

Class: Elemental function

Syntax: `RESULT = TAN(X)`

Arguments:
> X The type shall be `REAL` or `COMPLEX`.

Return value:
>   The return value has same type and kind as X.

Example:

```
program test_tan
  real(8) :: x = 0.165_8
  x = tan(x)
end program test_tan
```

Specific names:

Name	Argument	Return type	Standard
`TAN(X)`	`REAL(4) X`	`REAL(4)`	Fortran 95 and later
`DTAN(X)`	`REAL(8) X`	`REAL(8)`	Fortran 95 and later

See also: Section 9.21 [ATAN], page 98

9.256 `TANH` — Hyperbolic tangent function

Description:
>   `TANH(X)` computes the hyperbolic tangent of X.

Standard: Fortran 77 and later, for a complex argument Fortran 2008 or later

Class: Elemental function

Syntax: `X = TANH(X)`

Arguments:
> X The type shall be `REAL` or `COMPLEX`.

Return value:
>   The return value has same type and kind as X. If X is complex, the imaginary part of the result is in radians. If X is `REAL`, the return value lies in the range $-1 \leq tanh(x) \leq 1$.

Example:

```
program test_tanh
  real(8) :: x = 2.1_8
  x = tanh(x)
end program test_tanh
```

Specific names:

Name	Argument	Return type	Standard
TANH(X)	REAL(4) X	REAL(4)	Fortran 95 and later
DTANH(X)	REAL(8) X	REAL(8)	Fortran 95 and later

See also: Section 9.23 [ATANH], page 99

9.257 `THIS_IMAGE` — Function that returns the cosubscript index of this image

Description:

Returns the cosubscript for this image.

Standard: Fortran 2008 and later. With *DISTANCE* argument, Technical Specification (TS) 18508 or later

Class: Transformational function

Syntax:

```
RESULT = THIS_IMAGE()
RESULT = THIS_IMAGE(DISTANCE)
RESULT = THIS_IMAGE(COARRAY [, DIM])
```

Arguments:

DISTANCE	(optional, intent(in)) Nonnegative scalar integer (not permitted together with *COARRAY*).
COARRAY	Coarray of any type (optional; if *DIM* present, required).
DIM	default integer scalar (optional). If present, *DIM* shall be between one and the corank of *COARRAY*.

Return value:

Default integer. If *COARRAY* is not present, it is scalar; if *DISTANCE* is not present or has value 0, its value is the image index on the invoking image for the current team, for values smaller or equal distance to the initial team, it returns the image index on the ancestor team which has a distance of *DISTANCE* from the invoking team. If *DISTANCE* is larger than the distance to the initial team, the image index of the initial team is returned. Otherwise when the *COARRAY* is present, if *DIM* is not present, a rank-1 array with corank elements is returned, containing the cosubscripts for *COARRAY* specifying the invoking image. If *DIM* is present, a scalar is returned, with the value of the *DIM* element of `THIS_IMAGE(COARRAY)`.

Example:

```
INTEGER :: value[*]
INTEGER :: i
value = THIS_IMAGE()
SYNC ALL
IF (THIS_IMAGE() == 1) THEN
  DO i = 1, NUM_IMAGES()
    WRITE(*,'(2(a,i0))') 'value[', i, '] is ', value[i]
  END DO
END IF
```

```
! Check whether the current image is the initial image
IF (THIS_IMAGE(HUGE(1)) /= THIS_IMAGE())
  error stop "something is rotten here"
```

See also: Section 9.202 [NUM_IMAGES], page 206, Section 9.139 [IMAGE_INDEX], page 172

9.258 TIME — Time function

Description:

Returns the current time encoded as an integer (in the manner of the function `time(3)` in the C standard library). This value is suitable for passing to `CTIME`, `GMTIME`, and `LTIME`.

This intrinsic is not fully portable, such as to systems with 32-bit `INTEGER` types but supporting times wider than 32 bits. Therefore, the values returned by this intrinsic might be, or become, negative, or numerically less than previous values, during a single run of the compiled program.

See Section 9.259 [TIME8], page 240, for information on a similar intrinsic that might be portable to more GNU Fortran implementations, though to fewer Fortran compilers.

Standard: GNU extension

Class: Function

Syntax: `RESULT = TIME()`

Return value:

The return value is a scalar of type `INTEGER(4)`.

See also: Section 9.74 [CTIME], page 132, Section 9.123 [GMTIME], page 163, Section 9.175 [LTIME], page 191, Section 9.184 [MCLOCK], page 196, Section 9.259 [TIME8], page 240

9.259 TIME8 — Time function (64-bit)

Description:

Returns the current time encoded as an integer (in the manner of the function `time(3)` in the C standard library). This value is suitable for passing to `CTIME`, `GMTIME`, and `LTIME`.

Warning: this intrinsic does not increase the range of the timing values over that returned by `time(3)`. On a system with a 32-bit `time(3)`, TIME8 will return a 32-bit value, even though it is converted to a 64-bit `INTEGER(8)` value. That means overflows of the 32-bit value can still occur. Therefore, the values returned by this intrinsic might be or become negative or numerically less than previous values during a single run of the compiled program.

Standard: GNU extension

Class: Function

Syntax: `RESULT = TIME8()`

Return value:

The return value is a scalar of type `INTEGER(8)`.

See also: Section 9.74 [CTIME], page 132, Section 9.123 [GMTIME], page 163,
Section 9.175 [LTIME], page 191, Section 9.185 [MCLOCK8], page 197,
Section 9.258 [TIME], page 240

9.260 `TINY` — Smallest positive number of a real kind

Description:

`TINY(X)` returns the smallest positive (non zero) number in the model of the
type of `X`.

Standard: Fortran 95 and later

Class: Inquiry function

Syntax: `RESULT = TINY(X)`

Arguments:

X   Shall be of type `REAL`.

Return value:

The return value is of the same type and kind as X

Example: See `HUGE` for an example.

9.261 `TRAILZ` — Number of trailing zero bits of an integer

Description:

`TRAILZ` returns the number of trailing zero bits of an integer.

Standard: Fortran 2008 and later

Class: Elemental function

Syntax: `RESULT = TRAILZ(I)`

Arguments:

I   Shall be of type `INTEGER`.

Return value:

The type of the return value is the default `INTEGER`. If all the bits of `I` are zero,
the result value is `BIT_SIZE(I)`.

Example:

```
PROGRAM test_trailz
  WRITE (*,*) TRAILZ(8)   ! prints 3
END PROGRAM
```

See also: Section 9.44 [BIT_SIZE], page 112, Section 9.158 [LEADZ], page 182,
Section 9.208 [POPPAR], page 210, Section 9.207 [POPCNT], page 209

9.262 TRANSFER — Transfer bit patterns

Description:

Interprets the bitwise representation of *SOURCE* in memory as if it is the representation of a variable or array of the same type and type parameters as *MOLD*.

This is approximately equivalent to the C concept of *casting* one type to another.

Standard: Fortran 95 and later

Class: Transformational function

Syntax: RESULT = TRANSFER(SOURCE, MOLD[, SIZE])

Arguments:

SOURCE	Shall be a scalar or an array of any type.
MOLD	Shall be a scalar or an array of any type.
SIZE	(Optional) shall be a scalar of type INTEGER.

Return value:

The result has the same type as *MOLD*, with the bit level representation of *SOURCE*. If *SIZE* is present, the result is a one-dimensional array of length *SIZE*. If *SIZE* is absent but *MOLD* is an array (of any size or shape), the result is a one- dimensional array of the minimum length needed to contain the entirety of the bitwise representation of *SOURCE*. If *SIZE* is absent and *MOLD* is a scalar, the result is a scalar.

If the bitwise representation of the result is longer than that of *SOURCE*, then the leading bits of the result correspond to those of *SOURCE* and any trailing bits are filled arbitrarily.

When the resulting bit representation does not correspond to a valid representation of a variable of the same type as *MOLD*, the results are undefined, and subsequent operations on the result cannot be guaranteed to produce sensible behavior. For example, it is possible to create LOGICAL variables for which VAR and .NOT.VAR both appear to be true.

Example:

```
PROGRAM test_transfer
  integer :: x = 2143289344
  print *, transfer(x, 1.0)    ! prints "NaN" on i686
END PROGRAM
```

9.263 TRANSPOSE — Transpose an array of rank two

Description:

Transpose an array of rank two. Element (i, j) of the result has the value MATRIX(j, i), for all i, j.

Standard: Fortran 95 and later

Class: Transformational function

Syntax: RESULT = TRANSPOSE(MATRIX)

Arguments:

      MATRIX   Shall be an array of any type and have a rank of two.

Return value:

      The result has the same type as *MATRIX*, and has shape (/ m, n /) if *MA-TRIX* has shape (/ n, m /).

9.264 TRIM — Remove trailing blank characters of a string

Description:

      Removes trailing blank characters of a string.

Standard: Fortran 95 and later

Class: Transformational function

Syntax: RESULT = TRIM(STRING)

Arguments:

      STRING   Shall be a scalar of type CHARACTER.

Return value:

      A scalar of type CHARACTER which length is that of *STRING* less the number of trailing blanks.

Example:

```
PROGRAM test_trim
  CHARACTER(len=10), PARAMETER :: s = "GFORTRAN  "
  WRITE(*,*) LEN(s), LEN(TRIM(s))  ! "10 8", with/without trailing blanks
END PROGRAM
```

See also: Section 9.8 [ADJUSTL], page 89, Section 9.9 [ADJUSTR], page 89

9.265 TTYNAM — Get the name of a terminal device.

Description:

      Get the name of a terminal device. For more information, see ttyname(3).

      This intrinsic is provided in both subroutine and function forms; however, only one form can be used in any given program unit.

Standard: GNU extension

Class: Subroutine, function

Syntax:

      CALL TTYNAM(UNIT, NAME)
      NAME = TTYNAM(UNIT)

Arguments:

      UNIT   Shall be a scalar INTEGER.
      NAME   Shall be of type CHARACTER.

Example:

```
PROGRAM test_ttynam
  INTEGER :: unit
  DO unit = 1, 10
    IF (isatty(unit=unit)) write(*,*) ttynam(unit)
  END DO
END PROGRAM
```

See also: Section 9.149 [ISATTY], page 178

9.266 UBOUND — Upper dimension bounds of an array

Description:

Returns the upper bounds of an array, or a single upper bound along the *DIM* dimension.

Standard: Fortran 95 and later, with *KIND* argument Fortran 2003 and later

Class: Inquiry function

Syntax: RESULT = UBOUND(ARRAY [, DIM [, KIND]])

Arguments:

ARRAY	Shall be an array, of any type.
DIM	(Optional) Shall be a scalar INTEGER.
KIND	(Optional) An INTEGER initialization expression indicating the kind parameter of the result.

Return value:

The return value is of type INTEGER and of kind *KIND*. If *KIND* is absent, the return value is of default integer kind. If *DIM* is absent, the result is an array of the upper bounds of *ARRAY*. If *DIM* is present, the result is a scalar corresponding to the upper bound of the array along that dimension. If *ARRAY* is an expression rather than a whole array or array structure component, or if it has a zero extent along the relevant dimension, the upper bound is taken to be the number of elements along the relevant dimension.

See also: Section 9.156 [LBOUND], page 181, Section 9.157 [LCOBOUND], page 182

9.267 UCOBOUND — Upper codimension bounds of an array

Description:

Returns the upper cobounds of a coarray, or a single upper cobound along the *DIM* codimension.

Standard: Fortran 2008 and later

Class: Inquiry function

Syntax: RESULT = UCOBOUND(COARRAY [, DIM [, KIND]])

Arguments:

ARRAY	Shall be an coarray, of any type.
DIM	(Optional) Shall be a scalar INTEGER.
KIND	(Optional) An INTEGER initialization expression indicating the kind parameter of the result.

Return value:

> The return value is of type INTEGER and of kind *KIND*. If *KIND* is absent, the return value is of default integer kind. If *DIM* is absent, the result is an array of the lower cobounds of *COARRAY*. If *DIM* is present, the result is a scalar corresponding to the lower cobound of the array along that codimension.

See also: Section 9.157 [LCOBOUND], page 182, Section 9.156 [LBOUND], page 181

9.268 UMASK — Set the file creation mask

Description:

> Sets the file creation mask to *MASK*. If called as a function, it returns the old value. If called as a subroutine and argument *OLD* if it is supplied, it is set to the old value. See umask(2).

Standard: GNU extension

Class: Subroutine, function

Syntax:

```
CALL UMASK(MASK [, OLD])
OLD = UMASK(MASK)
```

Arguments:

MASK	Shall be a scalar of type INTEGER.
OLD	(Optional) Shall be a scalar of type INTEGER.

9.269 UNLINK — Remove a file from the file system

Description:

> Unlinks the file *PATH*. A null character (CHAR(0)) can be used to mark the end of the name in *PATH*; otherwise, trailing blanks in the file name are ignored. If the *STATUS* argument is supplied, it contains 0 on success or a nonzero error code upon return; see unlink(2).

> This intrinsic is provided in both subroutine and function forms; however, only one form can be used in any given program unit.

Standard: GNU extension

Class: Subroutine, function

Syntax:

```
CALL UNLINK(PATH [, STATUS])
STATUS = UNLINK(PATH)
```

Arguments:

PATH	Shall be of default CHARACTER type.
STATUS	(Optional) Shall be of default INTEGER type.

See also: Section 9.163 [LINK], page 185, Section 9.252 [SYMLNK], page 236

9.270 UNPACK — Unpack an array of rank one into an array

Description:

Store the elements of *VECTOR* in an array of higher rank.

Standard: Fortran 95 and later

Class: Transformational function

Syntax: `RESULT = UNPACK(VECTOR, MASK, FIELD)`

Arguments:

VECTOR	Shall be an array of any type and rank one. It shall have at least as many elements as *MASK* has `TRUE` values.
MASK	Shall be an array of type `LOGICAL`.
FIELD	Shall be of the same type as *VECTOR* and have the same shape as *MASK*.

Return value:

The resulting array corresponds to *FIELD* with `TRUE` elements of *MASK* replaced by values from *VECTOR* in array element order.

Example:

```
PROGRAM test_unpack
  integer :: vector(2)  = (/1,1/)
  logical :: mask(4)  = (/ .TRUE., .FALSE., .FALSE., .TRUE. /)
  integer :: field(2,2) = 0, unity(2,2)

  ! result: unity matrix
  unity = unpack(vector, reshape(mask, (/2,2/)), field)
END PROGRAM
```

See also: Section 9.204 [PACK], page 207, Section 9.246 [SPREAD], page 231

9.271 VERIFY — Scan a string for characters not a given set

Description:

Verifies that all the characters in *STRING* belong to the set of characters in *SET*.

If *BACK* is either absent or equals `FALSE`, this function returns the position of the leftmost character of *STRING* that is not in *SET*. If *BACK* equals `TRUE`, the rightmost position is returned. If all characters of *STRING* are found in *SET*, the result is zero.

Standard: Fortran 95 and later, with *KIND* argument Fortran 2003 and later

Class: Elemental function

Syntax: `RESULT = VERIFY(STRING, SET[, BACK [, KIND]])`

Arguments:

STRING	Shall be of type `CHARACTER`.
SET	Shall be of type `CHARACTER`.
BACK	(Optional) shall be of type `LOGICAL`.
KIND	(Optional) An `INTEGER` initialization expression indicating the kind parameter of the result.

Return value:

The return value is of type `INTEGER` and of kind *KIND*. If *KIND* is absent, the return value is of default integer kind.

Example:

```
PROGRAM test_verify
  WRITE(*,*) VERIFY("FORTRAN", "AO")          ! 1, found 'F'
  WRITE(*,*) VERIFY("FORTRAN", "FOO")         ! 3, found 'R'
  WRITE(*,*) VERIFY("FORTRAN", "C++")         ! 1, found 'F'
  WRITE(*,*) VERIFY("FORTRAN", "C++", .TRUE.) ! 7, found 'N'
  WRITE(*,*) VERIFY("FORTRAN", "FORTRAN")     ! 0' found none
END PROGRAM
```

See also: Section 9.227 [SCAN], page 220, Section 9.140 [INDEX intrinsic], page 173

9.272 XOR — Bitwise logical exclusive OR

Description:

Bitwise logical exclusive or.

This intrinsic routine is provided for backwards compatibility with GNU Fortran 77. For integer arguments, programmers should consider the use of the Section 9.137 [IEOR], page 171 intrinsic and for logical arguments the `.NEQV.` operator, which are both defined by the Fortran standard.

Standard: GNU extension

Class: Function

Syntax: `RESULT = XOR(I, J)`

Arguments:

I	The type shall be either a scalar `INTEGER` type or a scalar `LOGICAL` type.
J	The type shall be the same as the type of *I*.

Return value:

The return type is either a scalar `INTEGER` or a scalar `LOGICAL`. If the kind type parameters differ, then the smaller kind type is implicitly converted to larger kind, and the return has the larger kind.

Example:

```
PROGRAM test_xor
  LOGICAL :: T = .TRUE., F = .FALSE.
  INTEGER :: a, b
  DATA a / Z'F' /, b / Z'3' /

  WRITE (*,*) XOR(T, T), XOR(T, F), XOR(F, T), XOR(F, F)
  WRITE (*,*) XOR(a, b)
END PROGRAM
```

See also: Fortran 95 elemental function: Section 9.137 [IEOR], page 171

10 Intrinsic Modules

10.1 ISO_FORTRAN_ENV

Standard: Fortran 2003 and later, except when otherwise noted

The `ISO_FORTRAN_ENV` module provides the following scalar default-integer named constants:

ATOMIC_INT_KIND:
>   Default-kind integer constant to be used as kind parameter when defining integer variables used in atomic operations. (Fortran 2008 or later.)

ATOMIC_LOGICAL_KIND:
>   Default-kind integer constant to be used as kind parameter when defining logical variables used in atomic operations. (Fortran 2008 or later.)

CHARACTER_KINDS:
>   Default-kind integer constant array of rank one containing the supported kind parameters of the `CHARACTER` type. (Fortran 2008 or later.)

CHARACTER_STORAGE_SIZE:
>   Size in bits of the character storage unit.

ERROR_UNIT:
>   Identifies the preconnected unit used for error reporting.

FILE_STORAGE_SIZE:
>   Size in bits of the file-storage unit.

INPUT_UNIT:
>   Identifies the preconnected unit identified by the asterisk (*) in `READ` statement.

INT8, INT16, INT32, INT64:
>   Kind type parameters to specify an INTEGER type with a storage size of 16, 32, and 64 bits. It is negative if a target platform does not support the particular kind. (Fortran 2008 or later.)

INTEGER_KINDS:
>   Default-kind integer constant array of rank one containing the supported kind parameters of the `INTEGER` type. (Fortran 2008 or later.)

IOSTAT_END:
>   The value assigned to the variable passed to the `IOSTAT=` specifier of an input/output statement if an end-of-file condition occurred.

IOSTAT_EOR:
>   The value assigned to the variable passed to the `IOSTAT=` specifier of an input/output statement if an end-of-record condition occurred.

IOSTAT_INQUIRE_INTERNAL_UNIT:
>   Scalar default-integer constant, used by `INQUIRE` for the `IOSTAT=` specifier to denote an that a unit number identifies an internal unit. (Fortran 2008 or later.)

NUMERIC_STORAGE_SIZE:
  The size in bits of the numeric storage unit.

LOGICAL_KINDS:
  Default-kind integer constant array of rank one containing the supported kind
  parameters of the LOGICAL type. (Fortran 2008 or later.)

OUTPUT_UNIT:
  Identifies the preconnected unit identified by the asterisk (∗) in WRITE statement.

REAL32, REAL64, REAL128:
  Kind type parameters to specify a REAL type with a storage size of 32, 64,
  and 128 bits. It is negative if a target platform does not support the particular
  kind. (Fortran 2008 or later.)

REAL_KINDS:
  Default-kind integer constant array of rank one containing the supported kind
  parameters of the REAL type. (Fortran 2008 or later.)

STAT_LOCKED:
  Scalar default-integer constant used as STAT= return value by LOCK to denote
  that the lock variable is locked by the executing image. (Fortran 2008 or later.)

STAT_LOCKED_OTHER_IMAGE:
  Scalar default-integer constant used as STAT= return value by UNLOCK to denote
  that the lock variable is locked by another image. (Fortran 2008 or later.)

STAT_STOPPED_IMAGE:
  Positive, scalar default-integer constant used as STAT= return value if the
  argument in the statement requires synchronisation with an image, which has
  initiated the termination of the execution. (Fortran 2008 or later.)

STAT_FAILED_IMAGE:
  Positive, scalar default-integer constant used as STAT= return value if the
  argument in the statement requires communication with an image, which has
  is in the failed state. (TS 18508 or later.)

STAT_UNLOCKED:
  Scalar default-integer constant used as STAT= return value by UNLOCK to denote
  that the lock variable is unlocked. (Fortran 2008 or later.)

The module provides the following derived type:

LOCK_TYPE:
  Derived type with private components to be use with the LOCK and UNLOCK
  statement. A variable of its type has to be always declared as coarray and may
  not appear in a variable-definition context. (Fortran 2008 or later.)

The module also provides the following intrinsic procedures: Section 9.65
[COMPILER_OPTIONS], page 126 and Section 9.66 [COMPILER_VERSION], page 127.

10.2 `ISO_C_BINDING`

Standard: Fortran 2003 and later, GNU extensions

The following intrinsic procedures are provided by the module; their definition can be found in the section Intrinsic Procedures of this manual.

`C_ASSOCIATED`
`C_F_POINTER`
`C_F_PROCPOINTER`
`C_FUNLOC`

`C_LOC`

`C_SIZEOF`

The `ISO_C_BINDING` module provides the following named constants of type default integer, which can be used as KIND type parameters.

In addition to the integer named constants required by the Fortran 2003 standard and `C_PTRDIFF_T` of TS 29113, GNU Fortran provides as an extension named constants for the 128-bit integer types supported by the C compiler: `C_INT128_T`, `C_INT_LEAST128_T`, `C_INT_FAST128_T`. Furthermore, if `__float128` is supported in C, the named constants `C_FLOAT128`, `C_FLOAT128_COMPLEX` are defined.

Fortran Type	Named constant	C type	Extension
INTEGER	C_INT	int	
INTEGER	C_SHORT	short int	
INTEGER	C_LONG	long int	
INTEGER	C_LONG_LONG	long long int	
INTEGER	C_SIGNED_CHAR	signed char/unsigned char	
INTEGER	C_SIZE_T	size_t	
INTEGER	C_INT8_T	int8_t	
INTEGER	C_INT16_T	int16_t	
INTEGER	C_INT32_T	int32_t	
INTEGER	C_INT64_T	int64_t	
INTEGER	C_INT128_T	int128_t	Ext.
INTEGER	C_INT_LEAST8_T	int_least8_t	
INTEGER	C_INT_LEAST16_T	int_least16_t	
INTEGER	C_INT_LEAST32_T	int_least32_t	
INTEGER	C_INT_LEAST64_T	int_least64_t	
INTEGER	C_INT_LEAST128_T	int_least128_t	Ext.
INTEGER	C_INT_FAST8_T	int_fast8_t	
INTEGER	C_INT_FAST16_T	int_fast16_t	
INTEGER	C_INT_FAST32_T	int_fast32_t	
INTEGER	C_INT_FAST64_T	int_fast64_t	
INTEGER	C_INT_FAST128_T	int_fast128_t	Ext.
INTEGER	C_INTMAX_T	intmax_t	
INTEGER	C_INTPTR_T	intptr_t	
INTEGER	C_PTRDIFF_T	intptr_t	TS 29113
REAL	C_FLOAT	float	
REAL	C_DOUBLE	double	

REAL	C_LONG_DOUBLE	long double	
REAL	C_FLOAT128	__float128	Ext.
COMPLEX	C_FLOAT_COMPLEX	float _Complex	
COMPLEX	C_DOUBLE_COMPLEX	double _Complex	
COMPLEX	C_LONG_DOUBLE_COMPLEX	long double _Complex	
REAL	C_FLOAT128_COMPLEX	__float128 _Complex	Ext.
LOGICAL	C_BOOL	_Bool	
CHARACTER	C_CHAR	char	

Additionally, the following parameters of type `CHARACTER(KIND=C_CHAR)` are defined.

Name	C definition	Value
C_NULL_CHAR	null character	'\0'
C_ALERT	alert	'\a'
C_BACKSPACE	backspace	'\b'
C_FORM_FEED	form feed	'\f'
C_NEW_LINE	new line	'\n'
C_CARRIAGE_RETURN	carriage return	'\r'
C_HORIZONTAL_TAB	horizontal tab	'\t'
C_VERTICAL_TAB	vertical tab	'\v'

Moreover, the following two named constants are defined:

Name	Type
C_NULL_PTR	C_PTR
C_NULL_FUNPTR	C_FUNPTR

Both are equivalent to the value `NULL` in C.

10.3 IEEE modules: `IEEE_EXCEPTIONS`, `IEEE_ARITHMETIC`, and `IEEE_FEATURES`

Standard: Fortran 2003 and later

The `IEEE_EXCEPTIONS`, `IEEE_ARITHMETIC`, and `IEEE_FEATURES` intrinsic modules provide support for exceptions and IEEE arithmetic, as defined in Fortran 2003 and later standards, and the IEC 60559:1989 standard (*Binary floating-point arithmetic for microprocessor systems*). These modules are only provided on the following supported platforms:

- i386 and x86_64 processors
- platforms which use the GNU C Library (glibc)
- platforms with support for SysV/386 routines for floating point interface (including Solaris and BSDs)
- platforms with the AIX OS

For full compliance with the Fortran standards, code using the `IEEE_EXCEPTIONS` or `IEEE_ARITHMETIC` modules should be compiled with the following options: `-fno-unsafe-math-optimizations -frounding-math -fsignaling-nans`.

10.4 OpenMP Modules `OMP_LIB` and `OMP_LIB_KINDS`

Standard: OpenMP Application Program Interface v4.0

The OpenMP Fortran runtime library routines are provided both in a form of two Fortran 90 modules, named `OMP_LIB` and `OMP_LIB_KINDS`, and in a form of a Fortran `include` file named 'omp_lib.h'. The procedures provided by `OMP_LIB` can be found in the Section "Introduction" in *GNU Offloading and Multi Processing Runtime Library* manual, the named constants defined in the modules are listed below.

For details refer to the actual OpenMP Application Program Interface v4.0.

`OMP_LIB_KINDS` provides the following scalar default-integer named constants:

```
omp_lock_kind
omp_nest_lock_kind
omp_proc_bind_kind
omp_sched_kind
```

`OMP_LIB` provides the scalar default-integer named constant `openmp_version` with a value of the form *yyyymm*, where `yyyy` is the year and *mm* the month of the OpenMP version; for OpenMP v4.0 the value is 201307.

The following scalar integer named constants of the kind `omp_sched_kind`:

```
omp_sched_static
omp_sched_dynamic
omp_sched_guided
omp_sched_auto
```

And the following scalar integer named constants of the kind `omp_proc_bind_kind`:

```
omp_proc_bind_false
omp_proc_bind_true
omp_proc_bind_master
omp_proc_bind_close
omp_proc_bind_spread
```

10.5 OpenACC Module `OPENACC`

Standard: OpenACC Application Programming Interface v2.0

The OpenACC Fortran runtime library routines are provided both in a form of a Fortran 90 module, named `OPENACC`, and in form of a Fortran `include` file named 'openacc_lib.h'. The procedures provided by `OPENACC` can be found in the Section "Introduction" in *GNU Offloading and Multi Processing Runtime Library* manual, the named constants defined in the modules are listed below.

For details refer to the actual OpenACC Application Programming Interface v2.0.

`OPENACC` provides the scalar default-integer named constant `openacc_version` with a value of the form *yyyymm*, where `yyyy` is the year and *mm* the month of the OpenACC version; for OpenACC v2.0 the value is 201306.

Contributing

Free software is only possible if people contribute to efforts to create it. We're always in need of more people helping out with ideas and comments, writing documentation and contributing code.

If you want to contribute to GNU Fortran, have a look at the long lists of projects you can take on. Some of these projects are small, some of them are large; some are completely orthogonal to the rest of what is happening on GNU Fortran, but others are "mainstream" projects in need of enthusiastic hackers. All of these projects are important! We will eventually get around to the things here, but they are also things doable by someone who is willing and able.

Contributors to GNU Fortran

Most of the parser was hand-crafted by *Andy Vaught*, who is also the initiator of the whole project. Thanks Andy! Most of the interface with GCC was written by *Paul Brook*.

The following individuals have contributed code and/or ideas and significant help to the GNU Fortran project (in alphabetical order):

- Janne Blomqvist
- Steven Bosscher
- Paul Brook
- Tobias Burnus
- François-Xavier Coudert
- Bud Davis
- Jerry DeLisle
- Erik Edelmann
- Bernhard Fischer
- Daniel Franke
- Richard Guenther
- Richard Henderson
- Katherine Holcomb
- Jakub Jelinek
- Niels Kristian Bech Jensen
- Steven Johnson
- Steven G. Kargl
- Thomas Koenig
- Asher Langton
- H. J. Lu
- Toon Moene
- Brooks Moses
- Andrew Pinski
- Tim Prince

- Christopher D. Rickett
- Richard Sandiford
- Tobias Schlüter
- Roger Sayle
- Paul Thomas
- Andy Vaught
- Feng Wang
- Janus Weil
- Daniel Kraft

The following people have contributed bug reports, smaller or larger patches, and much needed feedback and encouragement for the GNU Fortran project:

- Bill Clodius
- Dominique d'Humières
- Kate Hedstrom
- Erik Schnetter
- Joost VandeVondele

Many other individuals have helped debug, test and improve the GNU Fortran compiler over the past few years, and we welcome you to do the same! If you already have done so, and you would like to see your name listed in the list above, please contact us.

Projects

Help build the test suite

> Solicit more code for donation to the test suite: the more extensive the testsuite, the smaller the risk of breaking things in the future! We can keep code private on request.

Bug hunting/squishing

> Find bugs and write more test cases! Test cases are especially very welcome, because it allows us to concentrate on fixing bugs instead of isolating them. Going through the bugzilla database at `https://gcc.gnu.org/bugzilla/` to reduce testcases posted there and add more information (for example, for which version does the testcase work, for which versions does it fail?) is also very helpful.

Proposed Extensions

Here's a list of proposed extensions for the GNU Fortran compiler, in no particular order. Most of these are necessary to be fully compatible with existing Fortran compilers, but they are not part of the official J3 Fortran 95 standard.

Compiler extensions:

- User-specified alignment rules for structures.
- Automatically extend single precision constants to double.

- Compile code that conserves memory by dynamically allocating common and module storage either on stack or heap.
- Compile flag to generate code for array conformance checking (suggest -CC).
- User control of symbol names (underscores, etc).
- Compile setting for maximum size of stack frame size before spilling parts to static or heap.
- Flag to force local variables into static space.
- Flag to force local variables onto stack.

Environment Options

- Pluggable library modules for random numbers, linear algebra. LA should use BLAS calling conventions.
- Environment variables controlling actions on arithmetic exceptions like overflow, underflow, precision loss—Generate NaN, abort, default. action.
- Set precision for fp units that support it (i387).
- Variable for setting fp rounding mode.
- Variable to fill uninitialized variables with a user-defined bit pattern.
- Environment variable controlling filename that is opened for that unit number.
- Environment variable to clear/trash memory being freed.
- Environment variable to control tracing of allocations and frees.
- Environment variable to display allocated memory at normal program end.
- Environment variable for filename for * IO-unit.
- Environment variable for temporary file directory.
- Environment variable forcing standard output to be line buffered (Unix).

GNU General Public License

Version 3, 29 June 2007

Copyright © 2007 Free Software Foundation, Inc. http://fsf.org/

Preamble

The GNU General Public License is a free, copyleft license for software and other kinds of works.

The licenses for most software and other practical works are designed to take away your freedom to share and change the works. By contrast, the GNU General Public License is intended to guarantee your freedom to share and change all versions of a program–to make sure it remains free software for all its users. We, the Free Software Foundation, use the GNU General Public License for most of our software; it applies also to any other work released this way by its authors. You can apply it to your programs, too.

When we speak of free software, we are referring to freedom, not price. Our General Public Licenses are designed to make sure that you have the freedom to distribute copies of free software (and charge for them if you wish), that you receive source code or can get it if you want it, that you can change the software or use pieces of it in new free programs, and that you know you can do these things.

To protect your rights, we need to prevent others from denying you these rights or asking you to surrender the rights. Therefore, you have certain responsibilities if you distribute copies of the software, or if you modify it: responsibilities to respect the freedom of others.

For example, if you distribute copies of such a program, whether gratis or for a fee, you must pass on to the recipients the same freedoms that you received. You must make sure that they, too, receive or can get the source code. And you must show them these terms so they know their rights.

Developers that use the GNU GPL protect your rights with two steps: (1) assert copyright on the software, and (2) offer you this License giving you legal permission to copy, distribute and/or modify it.

For the developers' and authors' protection, the GPL clearly explains that there is no warranty for this free software. For both users' and authors' sake, the GPL requires that modified versions be marked as changed, so that their problems will not be attributed erroneously to authors of previous versions.

Some devices are designed to deny users access to install or run modified versions of the software inside them, although the manufacturer can do so. This is fundamentally incompatible with the aim of protecting users' freedom to change the software. The systematic pattern of such abuse occurs in the area of products for individuals to use, which is precisely where it is most unacceptable. Therefore, we have designed this version of the GPL to prohibit the practice for those products. If such problems arise substantially in other domains, we stand ready to extend this provision to those domains in future versions of the GPL, as needed to protect the freedom of users.

Finally, every program is threatened constantly by software patents. States should not allow patents to restrict development and use of software on general-purpose computers, but in those that do, we wish to avoid the special danger that patents applied to a free program could make it effectively proprietary. To prevent this, the GPL assures that patents cannot be used to render the program non-free.

The precise terms and conditions for copying, distribution and modification follow.

TERMS AND CONDITIONS

0. Definitions.

   "This License" refers to version 3 of the GNU General Public License.

   "Copyright" also means copyright-like laws that apply to other kinds of works, such as semiconductor masks.

   "The Program" refers to any copyrightable work licensed under this License. Each licensee is addressed as "you". "Licensees" and "recipients" may be individuals or organizations.

   To "modify" a work means to copy from or adapt all or part of the work in a fashion requiring copyright permission, other than the making of an exact copy. The resulting work is called a "modified version" of the earlier work or a work "based on" the earlier work.

   A "covered work" means either the unmodified Program or a work based on the Program.

   To "propagate" a work means to do anything with it that, without permission, would make you directly or secondarily liable for infringement under applicable copyright law, except executing it on a computer or modifying a private copy. Propagation includes copying, distribution (with or without modification), making available to the public, and in some countries other activities as well.

   To "convey" a work means any kind of propagation that enables other parties to make or receive copies. Mere interaction with a user through a computer network, with no transfer of a copy, is not conveying.

   An interactive user interface displays "Appropriate Legal Notices" to the extent that it includes a convenient and prominently visible feature that (1) displays an appropriate copyright notice, and (2) tells the user that there is no warranty for the work (except to the extent that warranties are provided), that licensees may convey the work under this License, and how to view a copy of this License. If the interface presents a list of user commands or options, such as a menu, a prominent item in the list meets this criterion.

1. Source Code.

   The "source code" for a work means the preferred form of the work for making modifications to it. "Object code" means any non-source form of a work.

   A "Standard Interface" means an interface that either is an official standard defined by a recognized standards body, or, in the case of interfaces specified for a particular programming language, one that is widely used among developers working in that language.

The "System Libraries" of an executable work include anything, other than the work as a whole, that (a) is included in the normal form of packaging a Major Component, but which is not part of that Major Component, and (b) serves only to enable use of the work with that Major Component, or to implement a Standard Interface for which an implementation is available to the public in source code form. A "Major Component", in this context, means a major essential component (kernel, window system, and so on) of the specific operating system (if any) on which the executable work runs, or a compiler used to produce the work, or an object code interpreter used to run it.

The "Corresponding Source" for a work in object code form means all the source code needed to generate, install, and (for an executable work) run the object code and to modify the work, including scripts to control those activities. However, it does not include the work's System Libraries, or general-purpose tools or generally available free programs which are used unmodified in performing those activities but which are not part of the work. For example, Corresponding Source includes interface definition files associated with source files for the work, and the source code for shared libraries and dynamically linked subprograms that the work is specifically designed to require, such as by intimate data communication or control flow between those subprograms and other parts of the work.

The Corresponding Source need not include anything that users can regenerate automatically from other parts of the Corresponding Source.

The Corresponding Source for a work in source code form is that same work.

2. Basic Permissions.

All rights granted under this License are granted for the term of copyright on the Program, and are irrevocable provided the stated conditions are met. This License explicitly affirms your unlimited permission to run the unmodified Program. The output from running a covered work is covered by this License only if the output, given its content, constitutes a covered work. This License acknowledges your rights of fair use or other equivalent, as provided by copyright law.

You may make, run and propagate covered works that you do not convey, without conditions so long as your license otherwise remains in force. You may convey covered works to others for the sole purpose of having them make modifications exclusively for you, or provide you with facilities for running those works, provided that you comply with the terms of this License in conveying all material for which you do not control copyright. Those thus making or running the covered works for you must do so exclusively on your behalf, under your direction and control, on terms that prohibit them from making any copies of your copyrighted material outside their relationship with you.

Conveying under any other circumstances is permitted solely under the conditions stated below. Sublicensing is not allowed; section 10 makes it unnecessary.

3. Protecting Users' Legal Rights From Anti-Circumvention Law.

No covered work shall be deemed part of an effective technological measure under any applicable law fulfilling obligations under article 11 of the WIPO copyright treaty adopted on 20 December 1996, or similar laws prohibiting or restricting circumvention of such measures.

When you convey a covered work, you waive any legal power to forbid circumvention of technological measures to the extent such circumvention is effected by exercising rights under this License with respect to the covered work, and you disclaim any intention to limit operation or modification of the work as a means of enforcing, against the work's users, your or third parties' legal rights to forbid circumvention of technological measures.

4. Conveying Verbatim Copies.

You may convey verbatim copies of the Program's source code as you receive it, in any medium, provided that you conspicuously and appropriately publish on each copy an appropriate copyright notice; keep intact all notices stating that this License and any non-permissive terms added in accord with section 7 apply to the code; keep intact all notices of the absence of any warranty; and give all recipients a copy of this License along with the Program.

You may charge any price or no price for each copy that you convey, and you may offer support or warranty protection for a fee.

5. Conveying Modified Source Versions.

You may convey a work based on the Program, or the modifications to produce it from the Program, in the form of source code under the terms of section 4, provided that you also meet all of these conditions:

a. The work must carry prominent notices stating that you modified it, and giving a relevant date.

b. The work must carry prominent notices stating that it is released under this License and any conditions added under section 7. This requirement modifies the requirement in section 4 to "keep intact all notices".

c. You must license the entire work, as a whole, under this License to anyone who comes into possession of a copy. This License will therefore apply, along with any applicable section 7 additional terms, to the whole of the work, and all its parts, regardless of how they are packaged. This License gives no permission to license the work in any other way, but it does not invalidate such permission if you have separately received it.

d. If the work has interactive user interfaces, each must display Appropriate Legal Notices; however, if the Program has interactive interfaces that do not display Appropriate Legal Notices, your work need not make them do so.

A compilation of a covered work with other separate and independent works, which are not by their nature extensions of the covered work, and which are not combined with it such as to form a larger program, in or on a volume of a storage or distribution medium, is called an "aggregate" if the compilation and its resulting copyright are not used to limit the access or legal rights of the compilation's users beyond what the individual works permit. Inclusion of a covered work in an aggregate does not cause this License to apply to the other parts of the aggregate.

6. Conveying Non-Source Forms.

You may convey a covered work in object code form under the terms of sections 4 and 5, provided that you also convey the machine-readable Corresponding Source under the terms of this License, in one of these ways:

a. Convey the object code in, or embodied in, a physical product (including a physical distribution medium), accompanied by the Corresponding Source fixed on a durable physical medium customarily used for software interchange.

b. Convey the object code in, or embodied in, a physical product (including a physical distribution medium), accompanied by a written offer, valid for at least three years and valid for as long as you offer spare parts or customer support for that product model, to give anyone who possesses the object code either (1) a copy of the Corresponding Source for all the software in the product that is covered by this License, on a durable physical medium customarily used for software interchange, for a price no more than your reasonable cost of physically performing this conveying of source, or (2) access to copy the Corresponding Source from a network server at no charge.

c. Convey individual copies of the object code with a copy of the written offer to provide the Corresponding Source. This alternative is allowed only occasionally and noncommercially, and only if you received the object code with such an offer, in accord with subsection 6b.

d. Convey the object code by offering access from a designated place (gratis or for a charge), and offer equivalent access to the Corresponding Source in the same way through the same place at no further charge. You need not require recipients to copy the Corresponding Source along with the object code. If the place to copy the object code is a network server, the Corresponding Source may be on a different server (operated by you or a third party) that supports equivalent copying facilities, provided you maintain clear directions next to the object code saying where to find the Corresponding Source. Regardless of what server hosts the Corresponding Source, you remain obligated to ensure that it is available for as long as needed to satisfy these requirements.

e. Convey the object code using peer-to-peer transmission, provided you inform other peers where the object code and Corresponding Source of the work are being offered to the general public at no charge under subsection 6d.

A separable portion of the object code, whose source code is excluded from the Corresponding Source as a System Library, need not be included in conveying the object code work.

A "User Product" is either (1) a "consumer product", which means any tangible personal property which is normally used for personal, family, or household purposes, or (2) anything designed or sold for incorporation into a dwelling. In determining whether a product is a consumer product, doubtful cases shall be resolved in favor of coverage. For a particular product received by a particular user, "normally used" refers to a typical or common use of that class of product, regardless of the status of the particular user or of the way in which the particular user actually uses, or expects or is expected to use, the product. A product is a consumer product regardless of whether the product has substantial commercial, industrial or non-consumer uses, unless such uses represent the only significant mode of use of the product.

"Installation Information" for a User Product means any methods, procedures, authorization keys, or other information required to install and execute modified versions of a covered work in that User Product from a modified version of its Corresponding Source.

The information must suffice to ensure that the continued functioning of the modified object code is in no case prevented or interfered with solely because modification has been made.

If you convey an object code work under this section in, or with, or specifically for use in, a User Product, and the conveying occurs as part of a transaction in which the right of possession and use of the User Product is transferred to the recipient in perpetuity or for a fixed term (regardless of how the transaction is characterized), the Corresponding Source conveyed under this section must be accompanied by the Installation Information. But this requirement does not apply if neither you nor any third party retains the ability to install modified object code on the User Product (for example, the work has been installed in ROM).

The requirement to provide Installation Information does not include a requirement to continue to provide support service, warranty, or updates for a work that has been modified or installed by the recipient, or for the User Product in which it has been modified or installed. Access to a network may be denied when the modification itself materially and adversely affects the operation of the network or violates the rules and protocols for communication across the network.

Corresponding Source conveyed, and Installation Information provided, in accord with this section must be in a format that is publicly documented (and with an implementation available to the public in source code form), and must require no special password or key for unpacking, reading or copying.

7. Additional Terms.

"Additional permissions" are terms that supplement the terms of this License by making exceptions from one or more of its conditions. Additional permissions that are applicable to the entire Program shall be treated as though they were included in this License, to the extent that they are valid under applicable law. If additional permissions apply only to part of the Program, that part may be used separately under those permissions, but the entire Program remains governed by this License without regard to the additional permissions.

When you convey a copy of a covered work, you may at your option remove any additional permissions from that copy, or from any part of it. (Additional permissions may be written to require their own removal in certain cases when you modify the work.) You may place additional permissions on material, added by you to a covered work, for which you have or can give appropriate copyright permission.

Notwithstanding any other provision of this License, for material you add to a covered work, you may (if authorized by the copyright holders of that material) supplement the terms of this License with terms:

a. Disclaiming warranty or limiting liability differently from the terms of sections 15 and 16 of this License; or

b. Requiring preservation of specified reasonable legal notices or author attributions in that material or in the Appropriate Legal Notices displayed by works containing it; or

c. Prohibiting misrepresentation of the origin of that material, or requiring that modified versions of such material be marked in reasonable ways as different from the original version; or

    d. Limiting the use for publicity purposes of names of licensors or authors of the material; or

    e. Declining to grant rights under trademark law for use of some trade names, trademarks, or service marks; or

    f. Requiring indemnification of licensors and authors of that material by anyone who conveys the material (or modified versions of it) with contractual assumptions of liability to the recipient, for any liability that these contractual assumptions directly impose on those licensors and authors.

All other non-permissive additional terms are considered "further restrictions" within the meaning of section 10. If the Program as you received it, or any part of it, contains a notice stating that it is governed by this License along with a term that is a further restriction, you may remove that term. If a license document contains a further restriction but permits relicensing or conveying under this License, you may add to a covered work material governed by the terms of that license document, provided that the further restriction does not survive such relicensing or conveying.

If you add terms to a covered work in accord with this section, you must place, in the relevant source files, a statement of the additional terms that apply to those files, or a notice indicating where to find the applicable terms.

Additional terms, permissive or non-permissive, may be stated in the form of a separately written license, or stated as exceptions; the above requirements apply either way.

8. Termination.

You may not propagate or modify a covered work except as expressly provided under this License. Any attempt otherwise to propagate or modify it is void, and will automatically terminate your rights under this License (including any patent licenses granted under the third paragraph of section 11).

However, if you cease all violation of this License, then your license from a particular copyright holder is reinstated (a) provisionally, unless and until the copyright holder explicitly and finally terminates your license, and (b) permanently, if the copyright holder fails to notify you of the violation by some reasonable means prior to 60 days after the cessation.

Moreover, your license from a particular copyright holder is reinstated permanently if the copyright holder notifies you of the violation by some reasonable means, this is the first time you have received notice of violation of this License (for any work) from that copyright holder, and you cure the violation prior to 30 days after your receipt of the notice.

Termination of your rights under this section does not terminate the licenses of parties who have received copies or rights from you under this License. If your rights have been terminated and not permanently reinstated, you do not qualify to receive new licenses for the same material under section 10.

9. Acceptance Not Required for Having Copies.

You are not required to accept this License in order to receive or run a copy of the Program. Ancillary propagation of a covered work occurring solely as a consequence of using peer-to-peer transmission to receive a copy likewise does not require acceptance.

However, nothing other than this License grants you permission to propagate or modify any covered work. These actions infringe copyright if you do not accept this License. Therefore, by modifying or propagating a covered work, you indicate your acceptance of this License to do so.

10. Automatic Licensing of Downstream Recipients.

Each time you convey a covered work, the recipient automatically receives a license from the original licensors, to run, modify and propagate that work, subject to this License. You are not responsible for enforcing compliance by third parties with this License.

An "entity transaction" is a transaction transferring control of an organization, or substantially all assets of one, or subdividing an organization, or merging organizations. If propagation of a covered work results from an entity transaction, each party to that transaction who receives a copy of the work also receives whatever licenses to the work the party's predecessor in interest had or could give under the previous paragraph, plus a right to possession of the Corresponding Source of the work from the predecessor in interest, if the predecessor has it or can get it with reasonable efforts.

You may not impose any further restrictions on the exercise of the rights granted or affirmed under this License. For example, you may not impose a license fee, royalty, or other charge for exercise of rights granted under this License, and you may not initiate litigation (including a cross-claim or counterclaim in a lawsuit) alleging that any patent claim is infringed by making, using, selling, offering for sale, or importing the Program or any portion of it.

11. Patents.

A "contributor" is a copyright holder who authorizes use under this License of the Program or a work on which the Program is based. The work thus licensed is called the contributor's "contributor version".

A contributor's "essential patent claims" are all patent claims owned or controlled by the contributor, whether already acquired or hereafter acquired, that would be infringed by some manner, permitted by this License, of making, using, or selling its contributor version, but do not include claims that would be infringed only as a consequence of further modification of the contributor version. For purposes of this definition, "control" includes the right to grant patent sublicenses in a manner consistent with the requirements of this License.

Each contributor grants you a non-exclusive, worldwide, royalty-free patent license under the contributor's essential patent claims, to make, use, sell, offer for sale, import and otherwise run, modify and propagate the contents of its contributor version.

In the following three paragraphs, a "patent license" is any express agreement or commitment, however denominated, not to enforce a patent (such as an express permission to practice a patent or covenant not to sue for patent infringement). To "grant" such a patent license to a party means to make such an agreement or commitment not to enforce a patent against the party.

If you convey a covered work, knowingly relying on a patent license, and the Corresponding Source of the work is not available for anyone to copy, free of charge and under the terms of this License, through a publicly available network server or other readily accessible means, then you must either (1) cause the Corresponding Source to be so available, or (2) arrange to deprive yourself of the benefit of the patent license for this particular work, or (3) arrange, in a manner consistent with the requirements of this License, to extend the patent license to downstream recipients. "Knowingly relying" means you have actual knowledge that, but for the patent license, your conveying the covered work in a country, or your recipient's use of the covered work in a country, would infringe one or more identifiable patents in that country that you have reason to believe are valid.

If, pursuant to or in connection with a single transaction or arrangement, you convey, or propagate by procuring conveyance of, a covered work, and grant a patent license to some of the parties receiving the covered work authorizing them to use, propagate, modify or convey a specific copy of the covered work, then the patent license you grant is automatically extended to all recipients of the covered work and works based on it.

A patent license is "discriminatory" if it does not include within the scope of its coverage, prohibits the exercise of, or is conditioned on the non-exercise of one or more of the rights that are specifically granted under this License. You may not convey a covered work if you are a party to an arrangement with a third party that is in the business of distributing software, under which you make payment to the third party based on the extent of your activity of conveying the work, and under which the third party grants, to any of the parties who would receive the covered work from you, a discriminatory patent license (a) in connection with copies of the covered work conveyed by you (or copies made from those copies), or (b) primarily for and in connection with specific products or compilations that contain the covered work, unless you entered into that arrangement, or that patent license was granted, prior to 28 March 2007.

Nothing in this License shall be construed as excluding or limiting any implied license or other defenses to infringement that may otherwise be available to you under applicable patent law.

12. No Surrender of Others' Freedom.

If conditions are imposed on you (whether by court order, agreement or otherwise) that contradict the conditions of this License, they do not excuse you from the conditions of this License. If you cannot convey a covered work so as to satisfy simultaneously your obligations under this License and any other pertinent obligations, then as a consequence you may not convey it at all. For example, if you agree to terms that obligate you to collect a royalty for further conveying from those to whom you convey the Program, the only way you could satisfy both those terms and this License would be to refrain entirely from conveying the Program.

13. Use with the GNU Affero General Public License.

Notwithstanding any other provision of this License, you have permission to link or combine any covered work with a work licensed under version 3 of the GNU Affero General Public License into a single combined work, and to convey the resulting work. The terms of this License will continue to apply to the part which is the covered work, but the special requirements of the GNU Affero General Public License, section 13, concerning interaction through a network will apply to the combination as such.

14. Revised Versions of this License.

The Free Software Foundation may publish revised and/or new versions of the GNU General Public License from time to time. Such new versions will be similar in spirit to the present version, but may differ in detail to address new problems or concerns.

Each version is given a distinguishing version number. If the Program specifies that a certain numbered version of the GNU General Public License "or any later version" applies to it, you have the option of following the terms and conditions either of that numbered version or of any later version published by the Free Software Foundation. If the Program does not specify a version number of the GNU General Public License, you may choose any version ever published by the Free Software Foundation.

If the Program specifies that a proxy can decide which future versions of the GNU General Public License can be used, that proxy's public statement of acceptance of a version permanently authorizes you to choose that version for the Program.

Later license versions may give you additional or different permissions. However, no additional obligations are imposed on any author or copyright holder as a result of your choosing to follow a later version.

15. Disclaimer of Warranty.

THERE IS NO WARRANTY FOR THE PROGRAM, TO THE EXTENT PERMITTED BY APPLICABLE LAW. EXCEPT WHEN OTHERWISE STATED IN WRITING THE COPYRIGHT HOLDERS AND/OR OTHER PARTIES PROVIDE THE PROGRAM "AS IS" WITHOUT WARRANTY OF ANY KIND, EITHER EXPRESSED OR IMPLIED, INCLUDING, BUT NOT LIMITED TO, THE IMPLIED WARRANTIES OF MERCHANTABILITY AND FITNESS FOR A PARTICULAR PURPOSE. THE ENTIRE RISK AS TO THE QUALITY AND PERFORMANCE OF THE PROGRAM IS WITH YOU. SHOULD THE PROGRAM PROVE DEFECTIVE, YOU ASSUME THE COST OF ALL NECESSARY SERVICING, REPAIR OR CORRECTION.

16. Limitation of Liability.

IN NO EVENT UNLESS REQUIRED BY APPLICABLE LAW OR AGREED TO IN WRITING WILL ANY COPYRIGHT HOLDER, OR ANY OTHER PARTY WHO MODIFIES AND/OR CONVEYS THE PROGRAM AS PERMITTED ABOVE, BE LIABLE TO YOU FOR DAMAGES, INCLUDING ANY GENERAL, SPECIAL, INCIDENTAL OR CONSEQUENTIAL DAMAGES ARISING OUT OF THE USE OR INABILITY TO USE THE PROGRAM (INCLUDING BUT NOT LIMITED TO LOSS OF DATA OR DATA BEING RENDERED INACCURATE OR LOSSES SUSTAINED BY YOU OR THIRD PARTIES OR A FAILURE OF THE PROGRAM TO OPERATE WITH ANY OTHER PROGRAMS), EVEN IF SUCH HOLDER OR OTHER PARTY HAS BEEN ADVISED OF THE POSSIBILITY OF SUCH DAMAGES.

17. Interpretation of Sections 15 and 16.

If the disclaimer of warranty and limitation of liability provided above cannot be given local legal effect according to their terms, reviewing courts shall apply local law that most closely approximates an absolute waiver of all civil liability in connection with the Program, unless a warranty or assumption of liability accompanies a copy of the Program in return for a fee.

END OF TERMS AND CONDITIONS

How to Apply These Terms to Your New Programs

If you develop a new program, and you want it to be of the greatest possible use to the public, the best way to achieve this is to make it free software which everyone can redistribute and change under these terms.

To do so, attach the following notices to the program. It is safest to attach them to the start of each source file to most effectively state the exclusion of warranty; and each file should have at least the "copyright" line and a pointer to where the full notice is found.

```
one line to give the program's name and a brief idea of what it does.
Copyright (C) year name of author

This program is free software: you can redistribute it and/or modify
it under the terms of the GNU General Public License as published by
the Free Software Foundation, either version 3 of the License, or (at
your option) any later version.

This program is distributed in the hope that it will be useful, but
WITHOUT ANY WARRANTY; without even the implied warranty of
MERCHANTABILITY or FITNESS FOR A PARTICULAR PURPOSE.  See the GNU
General Public License for more details.

You should have received a copy of the GNU General Public License
along with this program.  If not, see http://www.gnu.org/licenses/.
```

Also add information on how to contact you by electronic and paper mail.

If the program does terminal interaction, make it output a short notice like this when it starts in an interactive mode:

```
program Copyright (C) year name of author
This program comes with ABSOLUTELY NO WARRANTY; for details type 'show w'.
This is free software, and you are welcome to redistribute it
under certain conditions; type 'show c' for details.
```

The hypothetical commands 'show w' and 'show c' should show the appropriate parts of the General Public License. Of course, your program's commands might be different; for a GUI interface, you would use an "about box".

You should also get your employer (if you work as a programmer) or school, if any, to sign a "copyright disclaimer" for the program, if necessary. For more information on this, and how to apply and follow the GNU GPL, see http://www.gnu.org/licenses/.

The GNU General Public License does not permit incorporating your program into proprietary programs. If your program is a subroutine library, you may consider it more useful to permit linking proprietary applications with the library. If this is what you want to do, use the GNU Lesser General Public License instead of this License. But first, please read http://www.gnu.org/philosophy/why-not-lgpl.html.

GNU Free Documentation License

Version 1.3, 3 November 2008

Copyright © 2000, 2001, 2002, 2007, 2008 Free Software Foundation, Inc.
`http://fsf.org/`

0. PREAMBLE

The purpose of this License is to make a manual, textbook, or other functional and useful document *free* in the sense of freedom: to assure everyone the effective freedom to copy and redistribute it, with or without modifying it, either commercially or non-commercially. Secondarily, this License preserves for the author and publisher a way to get credit for their work, while not being considered responsible for modifications made by others.

This License is a kind of "copyleft", which means that derivative works of the document must themselves be free in the same sense. It complements the GNU General Public License, which is a copyleft license designed for free software.

We have designed this License in order to use it for manuals for free software, because free software needs free documentation: a free program should come with manuals providing the same freedoms that the software does. But this License is not limited to software manuals; it can be used for any textual work, regardless of subject matter or whether it is published as a printed book. We recommend this License principally for works whose purpose is instruction or reference.

1. APPLICABILITY AND DEFINITIONS

This License applies to any manual or other work, in any medium, that contains a notice placed by the copyright holder saying it can be distributed under the terms of this License. Such a notice grants a world-wide, royalty-free license, unlimited in duration, to use that work under the conditions stated herein. The "Document", below, refers to any such manual or work. Any member of the public is a licensee, and is addressed as "you". You accept the license if you copy, modify or distribute the work in a way requiring permission under copyright law.

A "Modified Version" of the Document means any work containing the Document or a portion of it, either copied verbatim, or with modifications and/or translated into another language.

A "Secondary Section" is a named appendix or a front-matter section of the Document that deals exclusively with the relationship of the publishers or authors of the Document to the Document's overall subject (or to related matters) and contains nothing that could fall directly within that overall subject. (Thus, if the Document is in part a textbook of mathematics, a Secondary Section may not explain any mathematics.) The relationship could be a matter of historical connection with the subject or with related matters, or of legal, commercial, philosophical, ethical or political position regarding them.

The "Invariant Sections" are certain Secondary Sections whose titles are designated, as being those of Invariant Sections, in the notice that says that the Document is released under this License. If a section does not fit the above definition of Secondary then it is not allowed to be designated as Invariant. The Document may contain zero Invariant Sections. If the Document does not identify any Invariant Sections then there are none.

The "Cover Texts" are certain short passages of text that are listed, as Front-Cover Texts or Back-Cover Texts, in the notice that says that the Document is released under this License. A Front-Cover Text may be at most 5 words, and a Back-Cover Text may be at most 25 words.

A "Transparent" copy of the Document means a machine-readable copy, represented in a format whose specification is available to the general public, that is suitable for revising the document straightforwardly with generic text editors or (for images composed of pixels) generic paint programs or (for drawings) some widely available drawing editor, and that is suitable for input to text formatters or for automatic translation to a variety of formats suitable for input to text formatters. A copy made in an otherwise Transparent file format whose markup, or absence of markup, has been arranged to thwart or discourage subsequent modification by readers is not Transparent. An image format is not Transparent if used for any substantial amount of text. A copy that is not "Transparent" is called "Opaque".

Examples of suitable formats for Transparent copies include plain ASCII without markup, Texinfo input format, LaTeX input format, SGML or XML using a publicly available DTD, and standard-conforming simple HTML, PostScript or PDF designed for human modification. Examples of transparent image formats include PNG, XCF and JPG. Opaque formats include proprietary formats that can be read and edited only by proprietary word processors, SGML or XML for which the DTD and/or processing tools are not generally available, and the machine-generated HTML, PostScript or PDF produced by some word processors for output purposes only.

The "Title Page" means, for a printed book, the title page itself, plus such following pages as are needed to hold, legibly, the material this License requires to appear in the title page. For works in formats which do not have any title page as such, "Title Page" means the text near the most prominent appearance of the work's title, preceding the beginning of the body of the text.

The "publisher" means any person or entity that distributes copies of the Document to the public.

A section "Entitled XYZ" means a named subunit of the Document whose title either is precisely XYZ or contains XYZ in parentheses following text that translates XYZ in another language. (Here XYZ stands for a specific section name mentioned below, such as "Acknowledgements", "Dedications", "Endorsements", or "History".) To "Preserve the Title" of such a section when you modify the Document means that it remains a section "Entitled XYZ" according to this definition.

The Document may include Warranty Disclaimers next to the notice which states that this License applies to the Document. These Warranty Disclaimers are considered to be included by reference in this License, but only as regards disclaiming warranties: any other implication that these Warranty Disclaimers may have is void and has no effect on the meaning of this License.

2. VERBATIM COPYING

You may copy and distribute the Document in any medium, either commercially or noncommercially, provided that this License, the copyright notices, and the license notice saying this License applies to the Document are reproduced in all copies, and that you add no other conditions whatsoever to those of this License. You may not use technical measures to obstruct or control the reading or further copying of the copies you make or distribute. However, you may accept compensation in exchange for copies. If you distribute a large enough number of copies you must also follow the conditions in section 3.

You may also lend copies, under the same conditions stated above, and you may publicly display copies.

3. COPYING IN QUANTITY

If you publish printed copies (or copies in media that commonly have printed covers) of the Document, numbering more than 100, and the Document's license notice requires Cover Texts, you must enclose the copies in covers that carry, clearly and legibly, all these Cover Texts: Front-Cover Texts on the front cover, and Back-Cover Texts on the back cover. Both covers must also clearly and legibly identify you as the publisher of these copies. The front cover must present the full title with all words of the title equally prominent and visible. You may add other material on the covers in addition. Copying with changes limited to the covers, as long as they preserve the title of the Document and satisfy these conditions, can be treated as verbatim copying in other respects.

If the required texts for either cover are too voluminous to fit legibly, you should put the first ones listed (as many as fit reasonably) on the actual cover, and continue the rest onto adjacent pages.

If you publish or distribute Opaque copies of the Document numbering more than 100, you must either include a machine-readable Transparent copy along with each Opaque copy, or state in or with each Opaque copy a computer-network location from which the general network-using public has access to download using public-standard network protocols a complete Transparent copy of the Document, free of added material. If you use the latter option, you must take reasonably prudent steps, when you begin distribution of Opaque copies in quantity, to ensure that this Transparent copy will remain thus accessible at the stated location until at least one year after the last time you distribute an Opaque copy (directly or through your agents or retailers) of that edition to the public.

It is requested, but not required, that you contact the authors of the Document well before redistributing any large number of copies, to give them a chance to provide you with an updated version of the Document.

4. MODIFICATIONS

You may copy and distribute a Modified Version of the Document under the conditions of sections 2 and 3 above, provided that you release the Modified Version under precisely this License, with the Modified Version filling the role of the Document, thus licensing distribution and modification of the Modified Version to whoever possesses a copy of it. In addition, you must do these things in the Modified Version:

A. Use in the Title Page (and on the covers, if any) a title distinct from that of the Document, and from those of previous versions (which should, if there were any, be listed in the History section of the Document). You may use the same title as a previous version if the original publisher of that version gives permission.

B. List on the Title Page, as authors, one or more persons or entities responsible for authorship of the modifications in the Modified Version, together with at least five of the principal authors of the Document (all of its principal authors, if it has fewer than five), unless they release you from this requirement.

C. State on the Title page the name of the publisher of the Modified Version, as the publisher.

D. Preserve all the copyright notices of the Document.

E. Add an appropriate copyright notice for your modifications adjacent to the other copyright notices.

F. Include, immediately after the copyright notices, a license notice giving the public permission to use the Modified Version under the terms of this License, in the form shown in the Addendum below.

G. Preserve in that license notice the full lists of Invariant Sections and required Cover Texts given in the Document's license notice.

H. Include an unaltered copy of this License.

I. Preserve the section Entitled "History", Preserve its Title, and add to it an item stating at least the title, year, new authors, and publisher of the Modified Version as given on the Title Page. If there is no section Entitled "History" in the Document, create one stating the title, year, authors, and publisher of the Document as given on its Title Page, then add an item describing the Modified Version as stated in the previous sentence.

J. Preserve the network location, if any, given in the Document for public access to a Transparent copy of the Document, and likewise the network locations given in the Document for previous versions it was based on. These may be placed in the "History" section. You may omit a network location for a work that was published at least four years before the Document itself, or if the original publisher of the version it refers to gives permission.

K. For any section Entitled "Acknowledgements" or "Dedications", Preserve the Title of the section, and preserve in the section all the substance and tone of each of the contributor acknowledgements and/or dedications given therein.

L. Preserve all the Invariant Sections of the Document, unaltered in their text and in their titles. Section numbers or the equivalent are not considered part of the section titles.

M. Delete any section Entitled "Endorsements". Such a section may not be included in the Modified Version.

N. Do not retitle any existing section to be Entitled "Endorsements" or to conflict in title with any Invariant Section.

O. Preserve any Warranty Disclaimers.

If the Modified Version includes new front-matter sections or appendices that qualify as Secondary Sections and contain no material copied from the Document, you may at your option designate some or all of these sections as invariant. To do this, add their titles to the list of Invariant Sections in the Modified Version's license notice. These titles must be distinct from any other section titles.

You may add a section Entitled "Endorsements", provided it contains nothing but endorsements of your Modified Version by various parties—for example, statements of peer review or that the text has been approved by an organization as the authoritative definition of a standard.

You may add a passage of up to five words as a Front-Cover Text, and a passage of up to 25 words as a Back-Cover Text, to the end of the list of Cover Texts in the Modified Version. Only one passage of Front-Cover Text and one of Back-Cover Text may be added by (or through arrangements made by) any one entity. If the Document already includes a cover text for the same cover, previously added by you or by arrangement made by the same entity you are acting on behalf of, you may not add another; but you may replace the old one, on explicit permission from the previous publisher that added the old one.

The author(s) and publisher(s) of the Document do not by this License give permission to use their names for publicity for or to assert or imply endorsement of any Modified Version.

5. COMBINING DOCUMENTS

You may combine the Document with other documents released under this License, under the terms defined in section 4 above for modified versions, provided that you include in the combination all of the Invariant Sections of all of the original documents, unmodified, and list them all as Invariant Sections of your combined work in its license notice, and that you preserve all their Warranty Disclaimers.

The combined work need only contain one copy of this License, and multiple identical Invariant Sections may be replaced with a single copy. If there are multiple Invariant Sections with the same name but different contents, make the title of each such section unique by adding at the end of it, in parentheses, the name of the original author or publisher of that section if known, or else a unique number. Make the same adjustment to the section titles in the list of Invariant Sections in the license notice of the combined work.

In the combination, you must combine any sections Entitled "History" in the various original documents, forming one section Entitled "History"; likewise combine any sections Entitled "Acknowledgements", and any sections Entitled "Dedications". You must delete all sections Entitled "Endorsements."

6. COLLECTIONS OF DOCUMENTS

You may make a collection consisting of the Document and other documents released under this License, and replace the individual copies of this License in the various documents with a single copy that is included in the collection, provided that you follow the rules of this License for verbatim copying of each of the documents in all other respects.

You may extract a single document from such a collection, and distribute it individually under this License, provided you insert a copy of this License into the extracted document, and follow this License in all other respects regarding verbatim copying of that document.

7. AGGREGATION WITH INDEPENDENT WORKS

A compilation of the Document or its derivatives with other separate and independent documents or works, in or on a volume of a storage or distribution medium, is called an "aggregate" if the copyright resulting from the compilation is not used to limit the legal rights of the compilation's users beyond what the individual works permit. When the Document is included in an aggregate, this License does not apply to the other works in the aggregate which are not themselves derivative works of the Document.

If the Cover Text requirement of section 3 is applicable to these copies of the Document, then if the Document is less than one half of the entire aggregate, the Document's Cover Texts may be placed on covers that bracket the Document within the aggregate, or the electronic equivalent of covers if the Document is in electronic form. Otherwise they must appear on printed covers that bracket the whole aggregate.

8. TRANSLATION

Translation is considered a kind of modification, so you may distribute translations of the Document under the terms of section 4. Replacing Invariant Sections with translations requires special permission from their copyright holders, but you may include translations of some or all Invariant Sections in addition to the original versions of these Invariant Sections. You may include a translation of this License, and all the license notices in the Document, and any Warranty Disclaimers, provided that you also include the original English version of this License and the original versions of those notices and disclaimers. In case of a disagreement between the translation and the original version of this License or a notice or disclaimer, the original version will prevail.

If a section in the Document is Entitled "Acknowledgements", "Dedications", or "History", the requirement (section 4) to Preserve its Title (section 1) will typically require changing the actual title.

9. TERMINATION

You may not copy, modify, sublicense, or distribute the Document except as expressly provided under this License. Any attempt otherwise to copy, modify, sublicense, or distribute it is void, and will automatically terminate your rights under this License.

However, if you cease all violation of this License, then your license from a particular copyright holder is reinstated (a) provisionally, unless and until the copyright holder explicitly and finally terminates your license, and (b) permanently, if the copyright holder fails to notify you of the violation by some reasonable means prior to 60 days after the cessation.

Moreover, your license from a particular copyright holder is reinstated permanently if the copyright holder notifies you of the violation by some reasonable means, this is the first time you have received notice of violation of this License (for any work) from that copyright holder, and you cure the violation prior to 30 days after your receipt of the notice.

Termination of your rights under this section does not terminate the licenses of parties who have received copies or rights from you under this License. If your rights have been terminated and not permanently reinstated, receipt of a copy of some or all of the same material does not give you any rights to use it.

10. FUTURE REVISIONS OF THIS LICENSE

The Free Software Foundation may publish new, revised versions of the GNU Free Documentation License from time to time. Such new versions will be similar in spirit to the present version, but may differ in detail to address new problems or concerns. See `http://www.gnu.org/copyleft/`.

Each version of the License is given a distinguishing version number. If the Document specifies that a particular numbered version of this License "or any later version" applies to it, you have the option of following the terms and conditions either of that specified version or of any later version that has been published (not as a draft) by the Free Software Foundation. If the Document does not specify a version number of this License, you may choose any version ever published (not as a draft) by the Free Software Foundation. If the Document specifies that a proxy can decide which future versions of this License can be used, that proxy's public statement of acceptance of a version permanently authorizes you to choose that version for the Document.

11. RELICENSING

"Massive Multiauthor Collaboration Site" (or "MMC Site") means any World Wide Web server that publishes copyrightable works and also provides prominent facilities for anybody to edit those works. A public wiki that anybody can edit is an example of such a server. A "Massive Multiauthor Collaboration" (or "MMC") contained in the site means any set of copyrightable works thus published on the MMC site.

"CC-BY-SA" means the Creative Commons Attribution-Share Alike 3.0 license published by Creative Commons Corporation, a not-for-profit corporation with a principal place of business in San Francisco, California, as well as future copyleft versions of that license published by that same organization.

"Incorporate" means to publish or republish a Document, in whole or in part, as part of another Document.

An MMC is "eligible for relicensing" if it is licensed under this License, and if all works that were first published under this License somewhere other than this MMC, and subsequently incorporated in whole or in part into the MMC, (1) had no cover texts or invariant sections, and (2) were thus incorporated prior to November 1, 2008.

The operator of an MMC Site may republish an MMC contained in the site under CC-BY-SA on the same site at any time before August 1, 2009, provided the MMC is eligible for relicensing.

ADDENDUM: How to use this License for your documents

To use this License in a document you have written, include a copy of the License in the document and put the following copyright and license notices just after the title page:

```
Copyright (C)  year  your name.
Permission is granted to copy, distribute and/or modify this document
under the terms of the GNU Free Documentation License, Version 1.3
or any later version published by the Free Software Foundation;
with no Invariant Sections, no Front-Cover Texts, and no Back-Cover
Texts.  A copy of the license is included in the section entitled ''GNU
Free Documentation License''.
```

If you have Invariant Sections, Front-Cover Texts and Back-Cover Texts, replace the "with...Texts." line with this:

```
with the Invariant Sections being list their titles, with
the Front-Cover Texts being list, and with the Back-Cover Texts
being list.
```

If you have Invariant Sections without Cover Texts, or some other combination of the three, merge those two alternatives to suit the situation.

If your document contains nontrivial examples of program code, we recommend releasing these examples in parallel under your choice of free software license, such as the GNU General Public License, to permit their use in free software.

Funding Free Software

If you want to have more free software a few years from now, it makes sense for you to help encourage people to contribute funds for its development. The most effective approach known is to encourage commercial redistributors to donate.

Users of free software systems can boost the pace of development by encouraging for-a-fee distributors to donate part of their selling price to free software developers—the Free Software Foundation, and others.

The way to convince distributors to do this is to demand it and expect it from them. So when you compare distributors, judge them partly by how much they give to free software development. Show distributors they must compete to be the one who gives the most.

To make this approach work, you must insist on numbers that you can compare, such as, "We will donate ten dollars to the Frobnitz project for each disk sold." Don't be satisfied with a vague promise, such as "A portion of the profits are donated," since it doesn't give a basis for comparison.

Even a precise fraction "of the profits from this disk" is not very meaningful, since creative accounting and unrelated business decisions can greatly alter what fraction of the sales price counts as profit. If the price you pay is $50, ten percent of the profit is probably less than a dollar; it might be a few cents, or nothing at all.

Some redistributors do development work themselves. This is useful too; but to keep everyone honest, you need to inquire how much they do, and what kind. Some kinds of development make much more long-term difference than others. For example, maintaining a separate version of a program contributes very little; maintaining the standard version of a program for the whole community contributes much. Easy new ports contribute little, since someone else would surely do them; difficult ports such as adding a new CPU to the GNU Compiler Collection contribute more; major new features or packages contribute the most.

By establishing the idea that supporting further development is "the proper thing to do" when distributing free software for a fee, we can assure a steady flow of resources into making more free software.

Option Index

gfortran's command line options are indexed here without any initial '-' or '--'. Where an option has both positive and negative forms (such as -foption and -fno-option), relevant entries in the manual are indexed under the most appropriate form; it may sometimes be useful to look up both forms.

Keyword Index

D